Voices
in the
Kitchen

Number Nine:
Rio Grande/Río Bravo
Borderlands Culture and Traditions
Norma E. Cantú, General Editor

Voices
in the
Kitchen

....

*Views of Food and the World
from Working-Class Mexican
and Mexican American Women*

....

Meredith E. Abarca

Texas A&M University Press
College Station

The paper used in this book meets the minimum requirements
of the American National Standard for Permanence
of Paper for Printed Library Materials, Z39.48–1984.
Binding materials have been chosen for durability.

Library of Congress Cataloging-in-Publication Data

Abarca, Meredith E., 1967–
Voices in the kitchen : views of food and the world from working-class
Mexican and Mexican American women / Meredith E. Abarca.—1st ed.
p. cm. — (Rio Grande/Río Bravo : Borderlands Culture and Traditions ; no. 9)
Includes bibliographical references and index.
ISBN 1-58544-477-4 (cloth : alk. paper)
ISBN 1-58544-531-2 (pbk. : alk. paper)
1. Cookery, Mexican. 2. Cookery, American. 3. Food habits. I. Title.
II. Series
TX716.M4A33 2006
641.5972—dc22
2005025255

Para mi 'amá,
el lucero de mi andar

Contents

Acknowledgments   ix

Introduction
What's for Breakfast? *Los chilaquiles de mi 'amá,*
of course!   3

Chapter 1
A *Place* of Their Own: Appropriating the Kitchen *Space*   18

Chapter 2
Sazón: The Flavors of Culinary Epistemology   50

Chapter 3
Homemade Culinary Art (*El arte culinario casero*):
Cooks-as-Artists   78

Chapter 4
Kitchen Talk: Cooks-as-Writers   109

Chapter 5
The Literary Kitchen: Writers-as-Cooks   135

Conclusion
Maybe Dessert First? *Charlas Culinarias*   164

Notes   171
Bibliography   211
Index   231

Acknowledgments

Any project involves community effort, and when it is years in the making, such a community goes through significant changes and new people enter its development at different stages. With this said, I first extend my apologies to those I might forget to mention.

Voices in the Kitchen owes its foundation, most of all, to women of the *charlas culinarias*. I take this opportunity to say *estoy muy agradecida por sus palabras:* Liduvina Vélez, Alma Contreras, Esperanza Vélez, Guadalupe Flores, Aurora Larios Cárdenas, María Luisa Villicaña, Irma Vásquez, Hilaria Cortés, Imelda Silva, Susana García viuda de Melo, Alma Welty, Erika Morales, Alicia Villanueva, Verónica Abarca, Ángeles Herrera, Raquel Merlo, María Abarca, Norma Salazar, Ana María Ruvalcaba, María Díaz, Lucy Fischer-West. Not all these women are quoted in the book, but their ideas have influenced my thinking about food.

Adalijiza Sosa-Riddell I thank for her dedication to supporting "younger" generations of Chicana scholars. Her support let me present the initial stages of this study in Mujeres en Letras y Cambio Social. Norma Cantú presented on the same panel. Years later, in another conference, National Association for Chicana and Chicano Studies, I casually mentioned my search for a publisher. Once again, Norma Cantú, who was sitting next to me, leaned over my shoulder and said, "Let's talk. I might have a suggestion." She led me to my editor, Mary Lenn Dixon, whom I thank for her belief in the project and for her encouraging laughter during our phone conversations. I also thank Rosa Linda Fregoso, Angie Chabram-Dernessesian, Brenda Schilgen, Seth Schein, and Smadar Lavie. To Barbara Gunn, a special thanks for her years of friendship and her willingness to read endless early drafts. I am also grateful for the supportive advice and guidance of my graduate advisor and dissertation director, David Van Leer. Erica Johnson, Teresa Herrera, and Virginia Gutiérrez, your friendship made graduate school meaningful and memorable.

To Evelyn Posey and Howard Daudistel, *mil gracias* for your support. I give a special thanks to my writing group, Yolanda Leyva and Shirley A. Thomas, for their critical commentary and gentle forgiveness for the creative spelling of a dyslexic. To all of my students in the folklore class I inherited from John O. West and the course Women Philosophers in the Kitchen, I give my thanks for their knowledge and their family's cooking stories. As we learned to value ordinary home cooking, we grew intellectually, personally, and spiritually. Skip Clark, whose commitment to make me part of the El Paso, Texas, community, flourished in a collaboration with Howard Campbell, El Paso Museum of Archaeology, and a group of my students in creating the exhibition: *Mamá's Molcajete: The Mestizaje of Mexican Cuisines.* I also thank Skip for his quiet and continuous presence.

Thanks to Patricia Flynn and Jacqueline Powell for their unwavering faith in a sixteen-year-old girl who dreamed in broken English of one day going to college. I thank my godparents, Margie Whalen and Scott Paterson, for taking me into their home and making me part of their family, and for countless years of academic support and personal love. Much love to you both, from Miff. In the midst of revisions, attending conferences, meetings, teaching, keeping house, and balancing a checkbook, when I have felt most utterly overwhelmed, jokingly I have said, "I need a good wife." Yet, in the most fragile and vulnerable moments, I realize that El Paso gave me something better, an honorary mom, Lucy Fischer-West, who nourishes me with her meals and helps me maintain a sense of peace with her love. Only an honorary mom would deprive herself of sleep to edit her honorary child's manuscript. Love you lots and lots, Miffy. Finally, to my siblings and our *'amá.* Felix, in silence we speak of our mutual pride for each other; Chava, for the integrity I have learned from you. To Alma, for her willingness to say "yes" every time the phone rings and I say, "I need . . ." Panqui, may our journeys reconnect. Hugo, thank you for living in my heart; your spirit gives me faith. To Nitssia, for the gift of a profound experience, witnessing the birth of a life. To *mi 'amá,* for the voice that gives me courage.

Voices
in the
Kitchen

What's for Breakfast?
Los chilaquiles de mi 'amá,
of course!

We have all heard from nutritionists that breakfast is the most important meal of the day. While I have ignored it on many occasions, this time I will follow the experts' advice and begin with the breakfast that gives this book its basic yet essential nourishment: *los chilaquiles de mi 'amá.* This dish flavors the premise of *Voices in the Kitchen,* that everyday cooking is a language. Literally, *chilaquiles* are a breakfast I grew up eating: fried corn tortillas with tomato-chile sauce. Symbolically, they are the culinary metaphor for how working-class women speak with the seasoning of their food. *Los chilaquiles* also blur the distinction between theory and action, between the field of knowledge in the library or laboratory and the field of knowledge in an ordinary home kitchen.

This book is a research project where the personal *is* political on at least two counts: the reason for embarking on it and the core of women whose culinary philosophies give substance to it. When I graduated from college in the early 1990s, I knew I needed to get away from the academic institution. I needed to leave that world, at least for a while, before going to graduate school since I was becoming rather cynical and skeptical about most of the textual knowledge I encountered. I am particularly referring to feminist theories of female subjectivity and agency. All these theories were meant to raise my consciousness and help me liberate myself from the patriarchal, socially constructed, restricted, and oppressive places assigned to women due to gender, class, and ethnicity. The source of my cynicism and skepticism was a vivid understanding that textual knowledge is not accessible to a large group of women, like the ones in my family—working-class women. Most women I know are not part of an academic world; they belong, as part of me will always belong, to a nonacademic world where textual knowledge does not directly influence their everyday life. I am not saying that working-class women are devoid of knowledge, subjectivity, and acts of agency. What I am saying is that these women rarely read feminists' books or express themselves in a written textual form. Sometimes their claims of self-agency are not even verbal.

My frustrations, therefore, were a product of my personal life. A strong, smart, and independent woman, who did not passively accept her role within the domestic sphere, raised me. My mother, Liduvina Vélez, clearly understands the double-gender implications and limitations embedded in the patriarchal, capitalist, and Catholic world in which she had been raised. Yet she has not accepted at face value the rules of her social milieu. When she felt suffocated by societal demands, she became an active agent in changing her life and creating new paths. Why, then, I wondered, did I not see my mother's story or stories like it in the feminist works I was reading in college?

Kitchens and cooking, a place and activity that most women engage in regardless of educational level, ethnicity, or class status, form the praxis to bridge the gap between academic theoretical discourses about female subjectivity and quotidian working-class practices of female agency. A study of the social and philosophical dimensions of cooking illustrates how female subjectivity and acts of agency take place in both the academic and nonacademic world. Everyday cooking, food as voice, reveals the existence of a different field of epistemology. Food as voice comes "forth as a powerful, highly charged, and personalized voice." For Annie Hauck-Lawson, professor of health and nutrition, food voice "emerges as a term that crystallizes the dynamic, creative, symbolic, and highly individualized ways that food serves as a channel of communication."[1]

In my desire to understand the discourses of quotidian cooking and how a woman seasons her sense of self through such practice, the theoretical foundation for this research is a series of *charlas culinarias* (culinary chats) I have had with Mexican and Chicana working-class women. With the *charlas culinarias,* the personal *becomes* political. This book began to take root in graduate school with a feminist course on the importance of creative expression for women. While I agreed with every theoretical argument we read, my frustrations with academia remained. Only three artistic expressions were presented in this course: painting, writing, and composing. If creative expression forms a vital part of what makes us human, what then happens to women whose life circumstances do not permit them the time, space, and money for these three creative outlets? During the semester, images of my mother and her kitchen often emerged. Thus, I began to explore the kitchen site as a form of studio and cooking as an artistic expression. I also began this academic exploration with my mother, Liduvina Vélez. I had firsthand knowledge of her culinary creative expression, and she is a Mexican working-class woman. As the project developed, my mother has been the tie that holds together all the *charlas culinarias.* Guided by her request to have *charlas culinarias* with women who, according to her, "han pasado por etapas muy difíciles en la vida y tienen una historia que contar" (have experienced difficult phases in their lives and have a story to tell), she often set up the logistics of the *charlas.* In the words of cultural anthropologists, Liduvina Vélez has defined what they call the "notion of field" of the ethnographic and theoretical aspect of this book, hereafter referred to as *Voices.*

• •
Recipe: Methodology from the Ground Up

Significance

Methodology from the ground up gives a unique flavor to domestic space, particularly the kitchen as a site of knowledge and empowerment. It provides a general set of instructions for preparing decolonizing methodologies, which Linda Tuhiwai Smith defines as approaching "cultural protocols, values, and behaviors as . . . integral 'factors' to be built in to research explicitly, to be thought about reflectively, to be declared openly as part of the research design."[2] The kitchen and cooking as decolonizing methodologies create a type of thirdspace feminism where the activity of cooking yields forms of epistemologies that go beyond just knowing how to cook. "The maneuvering of paradigms," as Emma Pérez defines thirdspace feminism, is in the hands of those actually doing the cooking. These women mark their subjectivity oftentimes "neglected and ignored" by those of us outside the kitchen.[3] Domestic space as a field of epistemology validates the social, cultural, and economic significance of women's household work. With different fields of knowledge, we academics can see how the subjects of our research are active agents in the making of their own *historias,* their own life stories.

Necessary Equipment

Three absolutely essential cooking utensils are a large cooking receptacle, a sharp knife for peeling, and a good set of tongs for separating. The receptacle needs to be large enough for feminism*s* rather than a singular feminism to fit in it. The cooking container needs to have room to accommodate the fact that there are different "cultural-based subjectivit[ies]," and as Aihwa Ong says, not all women conduct their lives according to one "particular" feminist "vision of the future."[4] To this I add that we should recognize a woman's unique and specific life situation whenever possible. Women, even as members of a single family, do not carry out their daily lives in homogeneous ways. Therefore, a container large enough for cooking multiple possibilities of social change rather than a grand single theory is key equipment for preparing this recipe. Chicanas theorizing about feminisms take this approach by developing strategies that "are context-dependent and largely the result of lessons learned from their daily lives and the daily lives of women around them."[5] Theories, like philosophies, come out of culturally specific realities; they come out from people's way of knowing the world.[6] The second necessary tool is one that helps us peel off the thick skin that keeps theory-making within the realm of academia so that we can find theories in nontraditional places. Sonia Saldívar-Hall lists some of these places as "the prefaces to anthologies, in the interstices of autobiographies, in our cultural artifacts, our *cuentos.*"[7] To this I add our cooking practices. The third cooking gadget crucial for the creation of this recipe is a set of tongs to enhance our efforts in removing the layers of oppression and victimization in women's lives so that we can present women's moments of agency. These three tools are necessary to begin preparing a methodology from the ground up where working-class women's culinary epistemologies, along with their poignant practical and emotional articulations, express themselves as subjects, as agents of their own lives.

The Basic Ingredients: Dedication, Recognition, Humility, and Collaboration

For my version of this recipe, I first used a genuine and generous portion of dedication that took me from wanting to conduct and control culinary interviews to sharing and learning by engaging in *charlas culinarias* (culinary chats). The change took place during the first interview in 1996. Only ten minutes sufficed to discover the contradictions embedded in the methodology I was using to hear how women use the kitchen and cooking to express themselves. In my effort to conduct objective empirical research true to its disciplinary field led me, then a Ph.D. student in comparative literature, to solicit the guidance of an anthropology professor to structure a questionnaire appropriate for ethnographic research. Armed with it, I set out to interview my mother, Liduvina Vélez, to find out what she had to say about her relationship to *foodways*. Yes, I used the proper academic discourse such as foodways, and I even defined it by quoting Lucy M. Long: "a network of activities and systems— physical, social (communicative), cultural, economic, spiritual, and aesthetic."[8] I went on to say that foodways are deeply embedded in the formation of personhood and nationhood. Needless to say, the very structure of the questionnaire limited what my mother could and would share. She would answer my questions with a simple "yo no sé hablar" (I don't know how to say it). She also avoided the topic I hoped to discuss by singing a song: "Allá en el rancho grande, allá donde vivía, tenía una rancherita que alegre me decía, 'te voy hacer unos calzones, te los comienzo de lana y te los termino de cuero." The very structure of the interview led her to avoid answering my questions, which asked for specific events, dates, people's names, and culinary methodological procedures using a discourse that she did not recognize. During this first interview, I even referred to her with the Spanish formal pronoun of *usted*. Yet my siblings and I simply call her *'amá*.

Ingredients in a recipe must complement one another. This often happens by accident, as it was with the case of my recipe. A good dose of self-recognition allowed me to taste the flavorless meal that my own overzealous academic ambition was beginning to create. Fortunately, still in the early stages, I realized that for kitchen talk to function as a vehicle by which women share forms of their subjectivity, their "flesh and blood experiences" expressed in their *sazón*, the second ingredient has been for me to undergo a process of *con-scientización.*[9] In this process I learned to speak *with* my mother and not *to* her. I learned to listen to what she wanted to say and not worry about following a preconceived methodological research agenda. In the process of *conscientización,* I recognized the irony embedded in the initial phase of my research. My academic, intellectual interest focuses on finding out how working-class women subvert the pre-conceived ideological gender implications that define a kitchen as a woman's *place* by converting the kitchen into a woman's *space.* Yet the questionnaire I presented to my mother also had a preconceived assumption on my part: a subtle academic bias that often believes that only when a person is well-read and well-educated in a formal institution of higher learning are articulation and knowledge her domain. Fortunately, my mother also subverted these erroneous notions by shifting the structure of my questions. The concept of *charlas culinarias,* rather than a formal, structure questionnaire, is the result of my process of *conscientización.* A successful interview became a *charla.* The informality of the *charlas* rather than a formal interview creates a level of comfort and *confianza* (trust) among the participants, myself included.

This book is as much my mother's project as it is mine. The the-oretical inquiries explored in each chapter are those suggested from the original *charla* with her. She has gone from "yo no sé hablar" to actively engaging in a number of subsequent *charlas,* telling her friends about the project, and asking them to partici-pate. In this process, I have often become a note taker. I used to say that it was no small feat for a woman with only two years of formal schooling to become the assistant in her daughter's journey of con-ducting academic research. But now I say that for a Ph.D. to be an assistant to a woman with limited formal studies is, as Smith tells her students and researchers, "a humble and humbling activity."[10]

Humility in the context of conducting academic research mani-fests itself as an awareness that allows us, the researchers, not to assume "that we are the experts" and to recognize that "we have a great deal to learn from others."[11] To see others as active agents of knowledge places us in a situation of sharing knowledge as well as in a position of apprenticeship. As academic cooks, due to our well-educated cosmopolitan exposure to international cuisines, we might often think of spices such as galangal, ajowan, saffron, annatto, asafetida as rather significant. But humility in a metaphorical culinary context within this study represents those food items so ordinary, like salt and pepper, that help bring out the rest of the flavors in our food. Because of their common presence in every kitchen (or most), they are easily taken for granted.

I learned my first lesson in humility during the first *charla* my mother set up with two of her oldest friends, María Luisa Villicaña and Irma Vásquez. During this *charla,* I realized how at the inceptive stages of my project, my desire to hear working-class women's voices had clouded my own knowledge of traditional ways of common courtesy. Academia trained me well in the process of conducing ethnographic research, so I thought. Before the visit, I made sure that the tape recorder worked; I made sure I had enough tapes and batteries, paper and pencil. I also took some books because I wanted to share a few images about food's sensual and sexual implications in case such subjects did not simply enter into the *charla*. My mother also took something that never crossed my mind. She brought two plants and offered one to María Luisa and another to Irma as a gesture of gratitude for *their* generosity in giving us some of their time. And then there was the surprising supper María Luisa had waiting for us, since the *charla* took place in her house. In the academy of life, my mother has learned things that I, in my zeal for obtaining objective knowledge, was beginning to forget in the academy of higher learning.

As I learned to listen to women's voices in the kitchen—90 percent of all these conversations took place sitting in the kitchen sharing a meal—I recognized how these working-class women are grassroots theorists and their *charlas* reflect social and philosophical theories from the ground up. The methodology of the *charlas,* free-flowing conversations, creates a dialogue where unconventional fields of study, of knowledge, come together. As a methodology, it demonstrates how there is not just one history but many stories, how there is not just one intellectual form of knowledge but many ways of knowing and being intellectual. *Charlas* are about vertical thinking, not horizontal, meaning that researcher and women in the field are intellectually on the same plane. The praxis of this methodological paradigm, the analysis, focuses on thought-provoking moments that illustrate the gaps within master narratives of patriarchal and capitalist ideologies, where these women *do* speak and theorize about their lives. The *charlas* alter Gayatti Spivak's question "Can the Subaltern Speak?" to the statement "How the

Subaltern Speaks." Within Spivak's theoretical paradigm, subalterns, colonized women, cannot speak because they hold no political or economic power. This book, however, shows that working-class women have been speaking all along, but perhaps not in political or economic conventional discourses. Their theories from the ground up open the door to ask different analytical and philosophical feminists questions about women's subjectivity and acts of agency.

Women participating in the *charlas* do not speak of "differential consciousness" as does Chela Sandoval, or "decolonial imaginary" as does Emma Pérez, or "interstitial" gaps where moments of power and knowledge are found, as Michel Foucault argues. Oftentimes, however, they speak of concepts not too different from those developed by academic theorists. Their discourse about social, political, economic, and gender issues, however, differs drastically. The preparation and descriptions of everyday meals do have political and economic ramifications. In the *charlas,* we can hear the life stories of women's social consciousness and quest for change; the conversations provide a way to hear the voices of those who lack not only a room of their own but paper of their own as well.

Humility blends into collaboration. The theoretical concepts of women from the *charlas* interconnect with those of academic scholars, at times to elaborate on a similar issue by speaking of it with a different language and set of examples, at others to add a more in-depth complexity to social relations. The collaboration in this book blends academic scholarship from the areas of anthropology, philosophy, geography, architecture, literature, cultural studies, and folklore with the everyday life scholarship of Mexican working-class women. For example, the *charlas* have led me to formulate the following questions in response to feminist geographer Linda McDowell's observations that "it is often women who have the most spatially restricted lives." [12] While most of us would agree with this observation, I ask whether the kitchen is always a site of entrapment, or whether it is also a space, particularly for women with restricted economic resources, of survival as well as an identity-affirming process. For many of the women in the *charlas,* the latter is the case.

Voices in the Kitchen juxtaposes the *charlas* and literary texts, primarily but not exclusively by Chicana and Mexican women writers, to argue for the interpretation and analysis of the *charlas* as a literary genre. After the transcription of each *charla,* I proceeded to read it as if reading a short story, giving close attention to the nuances of language, the metaphors, and the symbols women use while engaging in a culinary dialogue. The *charlas* represent personal narratives, testimonial autobiography, and a form of culinary memoir. Texts are not just verbal expressions inscribed in written form; they are actions, practices, and even silences. Texts are embodied as well as inscribed. In this book, while women speak of specific life *herstories* through the seasoning of their cooking, what gets expressed goes beyond the kitchen and cooking per se. Memory, emotions, and history are all evoked and shared within the discourse of the *sazón,* the sensory-logic of cooking, which is highly personalized but socially charged. The fact that the same recipe prepared by two people yields different results further shows the personalization of the *sazón,* or what I call in this study, women's own *chiste* (twist), which reveals particularities of her life. Ketu H. Katrak analyzes a person's *chiste* as she writes, "I tasted anxiety in the onions fried a bit too brown and tension in the too many dark burned spots on the roasted *papads.*"[13] For Gloria Gonzales, "papas fritas" as a form of sharing *chistes* can cure any depth of loneliness or sadness.[14] In this book, the *chistes* we will hear the most relate to Liduvina Vélez's life; we will see them by reading direct transcriptions of our *charlas* or as the source of the theoretical inquiries explored in each chapter.

The theoretical anchors supplied during the transcription of the first *charla* with Liduvina Vélez structure the organization of the book. With the original questionnaire aside, my mother and I began to remember aunts, sisters, and grandmothers. Once she and I were chatting, she shared her own notions of subjectivity as she explained the value in the ownership of the *space* that made up her first *cocina propia* (her own kitchen). The kitchen as a woman's *space* rather than a woman's *place* is the topic of discussion in the first chapter, "A *Place* of Their Own: Appropriating the Kitchen *Space.*" My mother then took me into a sensual field of knowledge based on the *sazón,* the sensory-logic that prevails in the practices of cooking and in the language of the kitchen. She took me there by describing recipes created by feeling measurements in her hand, by touching food's texture, by looking at the food's color as it cooks, by tasting it and smelling it. The focus in chapter 2 is the *sazón* as the epistemology of the senses. The joy she expressed at remembering her beautiful hand-made tortillas when she was sixteen led to an exploration of aesthetics in *el arte culinario casero* (home culinary art). Chapter 3, "*El arte culinario casero:* Cooks-as-Artists," engages in the politics of cooking as art. The description of her recipes and invaluable anecdotes connected to them show a critical understanding of her social and cultural milieu as she writes parts of her life embedded in her cooking practices. Again, due to her stories full of personal and cultural histories, folklore, wisdom, and courage, the theme of chapter 4, "Kitchen Talk: Cooks-as-Writers," is the life stories surrounding a recipe. The kitchen as a woman's *space, sazón* as an embodied knowledge, and stories in recipes give the theoretical frame for the literary analysis in the last chapter, "The Literary Kitchen: Writers-as-Cooks."

As a whole, the book creates a space for bringing together the grassroots theorists, the women in the *charlas,* and academic feminists on issues of subjectivity and acts of agency. The bridge it builds represents my attempt to put the theory of decolonial methodologies into practice by the very structure of the book. One of these efforts is not to think of women in the *charlas* as "informants" for my research agenda, but as critical thinkers in their own right who use the language of food to formulate their theories. As a gesture of professional courtesy and respect, when referring to the ideas others have published, even when they happened to be our friends, we refer to them by their last name. The convention of using the last name represents a formal public symbolic act of respect and acknowledgement to someone whose ideas influence our thinking. With this same intention, I refer to all the women, including my mother, by their last name, except in the transcriptions of the *charlas* that form part of this book. In the shift between these two writing techniques, I hope to capture the different discourse of two fields of knowledge. In consideration of non-Spanish speakers, this book offers within the text English translations of the *charlas,* which took place in Spanish. Yet to keep some flavor of these women's voices, short quotes consisting of a few words or a sentence are in Spanish, followed by an English translation. This editorial format also applies to literary text originally written in Spanish. All the translations are mine unless indicated differently.

● ●

Women in the *charlas*

All the *charlas* began with my mother, Liduvina Vélez, in 1996 and continued through 2004. The first conversation took place in Vélez's house in Menlo Park, California, when she was—well—I do not believe I can reveal her age. Her response to her age is always the same, "esas cosas nó se preguntan" (you do not ask those things). Vélez was born in Michoacán, Mexico, lived there until she had five children, then lived in Nuevo Laredo, Tamaulipas, Mexico, for a number of years where she gave birth to two more children. Now California is home. She has been divorced twice. When she immigrated to the United States, she took five of her seven children, the oldest being fifteen and the youngest two. The other two children joined her three months later. No one spoke English. Her occupations have ranged from selling food, to making curtains, to washing dishes, to cleaning houses. Since Vélez is known by her friends and family as Duvi, within the transcriptions I will refer to her as Duvi.

Alma Contreras is my oldest sister. The *charlas* with her were always a three-way conversation with our mother. All of them took place at our mother's kitchen table with the special sound and aromatic effects of something cooking on the stove. Contreras has been married twenty-four years, and has four children ranging from twenty-three to nine. While still living in Nuevo Laredo, she attended an academy where she received a Bilingual Secretary Certificate, yet she spoke no English. Even with her nonexisting English, within a year of moving to California she was working at Bank of America. Now, she works as a housekeeper. She explains that this work allows her to have flexibility of time. She is her own boss, a sentiment shared by Vélez. Most of her adult life, she has lived in the same house where the small, no-counter-space, blue-and-white kitchen is located at the back of the house.

Esperanza Vélez and Guadalupe Flores are Liduvina Vélez's two sisters. In order to avoid confusion with the same last names, when the reference is to Esperanza Vélez I will use her full name. Esperanza Vélez loves to cook, and she is known in our family for her *buen sazón*. When she had her house constructed, she told the architect, "la cocina la quiero grande porque es donde más me agrada estar" (I want a spacious kitchen because it is where I most enjoy being). The first of our four *charlas* took place over the telephone. The subsequent conversations were held in her house in Puebla, Mexico, usually in the kitchen while cooking together. Her kitchen is roomy with space for a breakfast table. Esperanza Vélez has been married for over forty years and has three children. When her children were small, she began selling clothes by going to people's houses; now she has her own boutique, which is located in the first floor of her house.

For many years, Esperanza Vélez has hired someone to help her with the household duties, except for the cooking. This remains her domain.

Guadalupe Flores, unlike her sister, does not like to cook. But when she cooks, she does it with love for her family. Again the first kitchen talk with her took place over the telephone; the second *charla* was held in her house in Laredo, Texas. The kitchen in her house does not have a definable space of its own; it simply forms part of the dining room. The third conversation took place in a restaurant in Nuevo Laredo, Mexico. In the transcriptions I refer to her as Lupita. Flores has been married for over thirty years, and she too has three children. For many years, Flores was a housewife who dedicated herself to raising her children, but there came a point in her life that she defines as *su depresión* (depression), which she overcame by carving out a career for herself as a Mary Kay consultant, later becoming a director. Now, she travels to places she never imagined she would ever go. Proudly, she shares with me that she has had four company cars.

Irma Vásquez and María Luisa Villicaña are the first two kindred spirits Liduvina Vélez met soon after her arrival in California. Both Vásquez and Villicaña come from the same town as Vélez, such a small town that Vásquez and Vélez are distant relatives. Their friendship goes back over twenty years when they first met working in a sweatshop making curtains. Of the three women, only Villicaña remains in the curtain business, but now she is a designer. Both Vásquez and Villicaña are married; Vásquez has three children and Villicaña none.

Imelda Silva and Guadalupe Flores's friendship goes back over forty years. Vélez suggested that speaking to Silva would widen my understanding of daily life activities in Aguililla and Apatzingán, Michoacán, their native birthplaces. During this *charla,* Silva, her mother, and I made *tamales amarillos* at Silva's house. With Silva, I learned much about Redwood City's Mexicanization over the past thirty years. Silva is married and has three children, two living on their own and one still at home. She works cleaning rooms in a hospital.

The conversation with Alicia Villanueva, Licha, took place at Vélez's dining table. Villanueva is in her mid-fifties, the mother of five children whose ages range from twenty-one to thirty. She is mother and father to her children; she got divorced when her younger son was about five. Villanueva's ex-husband is Contreras's brother-in-law, thus her connection to women in my family. When Villanueva moved to the United States also from Aguililla, Michoacán, she did not speak English. In order to support her children and herself, she has worked in a laundry, cleaned houses, and now babysits her grandchildren.

I met Hilaria Córtes, or Yaya, while living in Los Angeles, California, from 1991 to 1994. Back then we were neighbors, so I knew that she sold food on the weekend to supplement her income. Years later when I asked her if she would like to be part of this study, she responded, "pues sí, a mi me encanta platicar" (of course, I love to talk). The *charlas* with Córtes took place in the house of mutual friends in South Pasadena, California. Córtes was born in Jalisco, Mexico, where she finished only a few years of elementary school. In her words, "sí fuí a la escuela pero no aprendí. Fuí re burra" (yes I went to school but did not learn. I was a donkey). She moved to the United States in her early twenties, shortly after she married and had four children. For all intent and purposes, she has raised her children on her own. In addition to selling food, occasionally she irons other people's clothes to make some extra money. For fifteen years she rented a house, but with her hard work and efforts she now owns her home.

Erika Morales became part of the *charlas* on the recommendation of a friend in graduate school. During the time of the conversation, Morales was living in Sacramento, California, and she was working as a cook for my friend. She shared many of her family culinary stories and recipes typical of Veracruz cuisine, her native state. Her *compañero,* Cesar, also participated in this conversation. They had been together for just a few years and had a six-month-old baby. They were both in their early twenties. Since then, Morales has moved back to Veracruz and is now the mother of two. During the season of harvesting, primarily tomatoes, Cesar returns to California to work for a few months.

Alma Welty's culinary talk took me to an extensive history of Puebla's culinary arts. She has been a housewife all her adult life. The limitations of her economic circumstances were such that the kitchen where the *charla* took place did not have a sink, and she cooked on an electric one-burner stove. One of her children, years back, had an accident that left him in a wheelchair for the rest of his life. Welty carries the responsibility of taking care of him. I met

Welty thanks to Ángeles Herrera, my sister-in-law's mother. When I went to Puebla in 1999 to have a *charla* with Esperanza Vélez, I also spoke with Herrera, who suggested that Welty was "una excelente cocinera y ha tenido una vida muy dura" (an excellent cook who has had a hard life).

During this stay in Puebla, I also met Susana García viuda de Melo thanks to my aunt Esperanza Vélez's recommendation, who felt her *comadre* García viuda de Melo would be an excellent person to talk with since she makes a living selling food. García viuda de Melo runs a *mini-cocina* from her house, where she serves *comidas corridas* and *a la carta*. In a front corner section of her house, she has her mini-kitchen, which is big enough to hold three tables, each with four chairs. Her private kitchen, the one inside her home, is larger. At this kitchen's breakfast table, our visit took place. Chapter 1 discusses much of García viuda de Melo's life.

Verónica Abarca, my sister-in-law, became part of the *charlas* when Vélez suggested that as our family increases I should continue to gather its history. We spoke while sitting in Vélez's dining table. Back then she had been married for less than a year, left her family in Puebla and moved with my brother, Juan Abarca, to California immediately after the wedding. Now she is a stay-at-home mother of two living in Sacramento, California. We spoke when she was twenty-three.

Norma Salazar's inclusion in these *charlas* deviates from working-class women who are in one way or another connected with my family. I met Chef Salazar, head instructor of the California Culinary Art Academy, in South Pasadena, when one day in June 2003, I walked into the academy and asked if I could speak to someone about the influence Latino food has had on California cuisine. A few days later, Chef Salazar shared with me not only California's history of Latinized fusion cuisine, but also the history of her life in the kitchen, which began when as a little girl she made cookies with her mother. Chef Salazar began working in professional kitchens when she was eighteen.

What brings Lucy Fischer-West into this book are the ongoing *charlas culinarias* we have had since we met in 2001. Since we both love to cook and garden, people who knew us separately would tell us that we needed to "hook up." Married for over thirty years, she has one son, with whom she enjoys kitchen time. Every meal Lucy offers to her friends and family represents a celebration of life.

Those fortunate enough to eat at her table receive spiritual nourishment from her meals, from her hospitality, and from her storytelling. In *Child of Many Rivers: Journeys to and from the Rio Grande* (2005), Fischer-West offers a literary repast honoring life's experiences.

Voices in the Kitchen offers feminists within academia new areas (yet old practices) for developing theories about women's lives, experiences, and knowledge. What this research offers the women from the *charlas* is public recognition, acknowledgment, admiration, and respect for their lives, their struggles, their knowledge, and, above all, their *coraje* (courage) grounded in the mundane activities of everyday cooking. I would like to close by saying that *los chilaquiles de mi 'amá,* as a metaphor, is the gift that I present not only to all the women who have participated in the *charlas* but also to all those women who do narrate their lives in the daily preparation of each meal, formulating theories from the ground up as they assert their subjectivity and acts of agency. To them I say, *a sus órdenes.*

CHAPTER 1

● ● ● ● ● ● ● ● ● ● ● ● ● ● ● ● ● ● ● ●

A *Place* of Their Own

Appropriating the Kitchen *Space*

Liduvina Vélez, my mother, at the age of eighteen had her first kitchen, which she describes as follows:

> After two years of marriage, your father had already bought a little piece of land and had a little house built. There I had my own kitchen. It was just a chimney, [made] all of clay.¹ But I plastered my little room [with] something made of adobe—you don't even know what adobe is. I used adobe mortar to plaster all the walls and the floor too, by hand. I plastered the floor every day because as you walk, dust from the dirt floor loosens; therefore, every day you have to replaster. When I already had my house, my kitchen, I felt independent, with something of my own.²

For Vélez, her *cocina propia* (her own kitchen), a single room with a chimney and a dirt floor she cleaned by hand every day, represented independence. The freedom she describes is from a matriarchal household governed by her mother-in-law and sisters-in-law where she lived the first two years of her marriage. That small room with dirt floors freed her from feeling "como una arrimada que le hacen mala cara. Se siente horrible vivir de arrimada" (like an uninvited guest who continuously feels rejected and humiliated. It feels horrible to live on the mercy of someone). As Vélez's words suggest, the kitchen is more than just a functional, necessary room within a house's architectural design.

Feminists advocating women's rights, however, do not always perceive the kitchen as representing women's independence. On the contrary, a kitchen stands for a woman's mandatory duty once she says, "I do." Alma Contreras, Vélez's oldest daughter and one of my sisters, attests to this notion when she recalls her first encounters with cooking: "Actually, it happened when I was married. Because I had to, because I didn't have anyone else to do it. I had no other choice. My mother was not there so that she could cook. I had to cook. But I don't remember cooking when I was single. Cooking, never."[3] In a mother's absence, a wife cooks. Contreras's comment, perhaps without her full awareness, alludes here to what some material feminists from the nineteenth century, the 1960s second-wave feminists, and contemporary feminists insist constitutes women's oppression: the kitchen. In particular, this is the case when the kitchen (the house) represents a hegemonic site of women's social and natural rightful *place.*

The juxtaposition of the kitchen's two meanings as a *space* of freedom for Vélez and a *place* of obligatory labor for Contreras encapsulates the theoretical exploration throughout this chapter. As a woman's *place* the kitchen can imply a site of mandatory wifely and motherly duty to her family, culture, and even nation, a servitude that makes her financially dependent on her husband's salary, for her life revolves around mainly performing unpaid domestic labor. In this context, many feminists argue that the kitchen represents the locus of women's emotional, physical, spiritual, and economic vulnerability. These concerns address the ideological meanings that produce the notion of *place.* In the fields of architecture and geography, traditionally, to a great extent a patriarchal and capitalist agenda defines the social meaning of *place* as usually representing the physical and stable boundaries of a location. The production of the geographical scale, according to feminist geographer Linda McDowell, defines one place as different from another. Yet such differences "are defined, maintained, and altered through the impact of unequal power relations."[4]

The kitchen as a woman's *space,* though, can represent a site of multiple changing levels and degrees of freedom, self-awareness, subjectivity, and agency. The social interactions of daily life that unfold within a given *space* define its significance.[5] Vélez understands how spaces acquire different meanings by recognizing the difference between her daughter Alma's and her own feelings about the kitchen. In a *charla* among the three of us, Vélez says: "mi'ja la cocina la mira como un martirio. Como que si ella pudiera mandar borrar la cocina de su casa, lo—" (*mi'ja* sees the kitchen as a kind of martyrdom. If she could have the kitchen erased from her house—). Contreras interrupts her and enthusiastically finishes the sentence: "¡sí, la eliminaría!" (Yes, I would eliminate it!). With her new free space in the house, she would have "a hot tub, with warm water and a glass of wine. Just be there, relaxed. If I had a housekeeper, if I was rich, oh how wonderful. Someone to cook; someone to iron."[6] Vélez's transformation of the kitchen into an empowering *space* does not automatically transmit to her daughter. Yet Contreras momentarily changes the kitchen form and function into an imaginary *space* of relaxation and romance. A short-lived imaginary *space,* but this fleeting moment shows the social meaning she wishes to inscribe into her kitchen. In this chapter, I am particularly interested in how working-class women symbolically and/or literally transform the ideologies embedded in the construction of the kitchen as their *place* into their own social *space.*

•••••••••••••••••••••
From Place to Space

Due to the binary thinking fundamental in Western philosophy, what gets coded male manifests itself in actions, constant changes, explorations, creations, or as feminist geographer Doreen Massey says, of always "Becoming." What is coded feminine are the opposite of these qualities.[7] In the context of this book, if the kitchen *is* a woman's place, its walls limit her social, economic, and personal mobility, which derives from conceptualizing *place* as a fixed, unchanging, and nostalgic location.[8] Massey underlines the gender complications contained within this theoretical paradigm of *place.* She argues that the characteristic connected with *place* as "stable . . . resonate with ways of characterizing" the social role of women in our culture. *Place* as "comfort of Being" rather then as a "project of Becoming" (of changing) is coded feminine. In other words, women are in a constant state of simply "Being" while men are in a constant state of creating, of changing, of "Becoming." For Massey, place "in this formulation [is] necessarily an essentialist concept which . . . [is] interpreted as the comfort of Being instead of forging ahead with the (assumed progressive) project of Becoming."[9] Since *place* lacks progress, the feminist rejection of the kitchen as a woman's *place* re-jects situating women in the nonprogressive but stable *place* found within a kitchen. A woman's liberation from the kitchen as her *place,* therefore, would mark her right to divorce herself from the limita-tions embedded in the daily, and often mundane, responsibility of quotidian work. Once divorced from this constrictive place, a woman will engage in the "project of Becoming."

Both *place* and *space* interconnect in kitchen politics. The con-nection of *place* with home, the *place* of home, centers the discussion that follows. The main concerns are the association of home with a nostalgic view and moral social values that must remain fixed throughout time ("the comfort of Being") in order to combat the un-predictable, competitive, and aggressive lifestyle produced in the public sphere of the workplace ("the project of Becoming"). Further-more, home becomes a location of leisure and comfort, at least in ideological terms, seemingly making the *place* of home a fixed and stable site. Feminist architects and geographers today work with a more complex notion of *place;* they see it not as "a set of coordi-nates on the map" but as "contested, fluid, and uncertain," which is defined by its "socio-spatial practices and power relations." [10] None-theless, home retains its Victorian legacy as the *place* of both leisure and the threshold of social moral values where women re-main responsible for providing both. A home's ideological currency as a stable *place* of relaxation is evident by its absence from philos-opher Michel Foucault's influential theory on the concept of "Other places," where he explores social sites that might subvert institu-tional policing and control over citizens. Foucault's theory excluded the house, for he sees it as a place of rest. But we must ask, rest for whom? For Guadalupe Flores, Liduvina Vélez's younger sister, her life placed her in a situation of asking such a question in a rather poignant manner. In the first *charla* with Flores, she refers to a pe-riod of "coming out of her depression," a depression caused in part by a complete lack of appreciation for the labor done within her house. "I am going to tell you something, when you are working, and working, and working, and no one acknowledges anything you do, you feel like you are being used, right? Like a robot that only works, works, works. But no one appreciates anything you are doing. And then there comes a moment when you get fed up. And you say, 'the hell with picking up shoes, underwear, everything.'" [11] But now Flo-res is happier and feels self-fulfillment from dedicating her time and effort to her work as a cosmetic director for Mary Kay. When home is a mandatory social *place* for women, to provide a site of rest for others, this construction makes it a *place* policing and controlling women's movements.

Because *place* does carry this patriarchal ideological baggage, when women define the kitchen as their *space* they engage in their own everyday acts of agency. Sherry Ahrentzen quotes Barbara Cooper who argues that "thinking about how women move through space, . . . 'may help feminist theorists find a new and revitalizing point of entry into the question of female agency.' . . . [W]omen contribute to the gradual transformation of gender relations not simply through conscious manipulation, resistance, or protest but also through the active spatial positioning in which they engage in their everyday lives in an effort to define themselves socially and to improve their lives materially." [12] In the opening quote of this chapter, Vélez asserted her agency through the ownership of her kitchen *space* in a number of ways. In her small adobe kitchen she experienced freedom from having to share the kitchen with a mother-in-law and sisters-in-law; she was generally in control of not only when but also how things were done, to the point that she designed and built her own *chimenea* (wood burning stove). Furthermore, Vélez's agency, in her rather patriarchal milieu, extended to the very construction of her first home, where she had this first kitchen. In one of the numerous telephone conversations we have had as I interrupted the flow of my writing to read her parts of the analysis and hear her own interpretation of it, she often adds more information about life's trajectory. In June 2004, she shared a part of her life unknown to me, another moment of her enactment of agency:

> *Doña Virgina, your grandmother, had a brother who would get sick on certain occasions. He got crazy. One of his obsessions was that he wanted to kill Felix. Felix was about six months old. I was always very afraid that he would kill my baby boy. One day when Juan [your father] was gone, I took my little boy and went to my father's house. He was living in the United States and I had keys to his house. When your father came back, he wanted to take me back to his mother's house. I refused to go back. I told him that I would not go back. I needed him to give me a place to live. I would just not go back to his mother's house. When this happened, he already had a piece of land. So he went and began*

to construct a little room in that piece of land. He built a little
room, more like an overhang. The kitchen was at the end of this
overhang. As you walked in, first there was a little table and
then the stove. I lived two years in that little house. Chava was
born in that place. But after two years, he [your father] took me
back to his mother's house. He took away my independence be-
cause I went back to live de arrimada!¹³

Vélez created her first *space,* her first home and kitchen, by literally
escaping her mother-in-law's house. While this *space* of independence lasted only two years, it does show her efforts to define herself
socially and improve her life not just materially, but psychologically
as well. "Although the house and the home is one of the most
strongly gendered spatial locations," as geographer Linda McDowell
says, "it is important not to take the associations for granted, nor to
see them as permanent and unchanging."¹⁴ The fact that Vélez's
husband took her independence from her does not falter her quest
for it, as the last section of this chapter shows. Shifting the kitchen
from a woman's *place* to a woman's *space* requires that we think of
new forms to the very concept of home itself.

The acts of agency, which transform the kitchen from a woman's
place into her *space,* take multiple forms. Before I move on to a theoretical discussion of how these terms are negotiated within academia, the field of architecture, and capitalist interest, I want to offer
one more example of how Esperanza Vélez, Liduvina Vélez's middle
sister, clearly sees the kitchen and cooking not as socially mandatory women's labor but as celebration and affirmation of her talent,
knowledge, and affection.

For Esperanza Vélez, an act of agency is the way she tena-
ciously sustains her sense of self by validating her emotions and
claiming the right to her own *sazón,* culinary knowledge and talent
based on the epistemology of the senses. When Esperanza Vélez
serves her *comida en la mesa* (food on the table), she offers her love
and culinary talent as a gift: "It's a way of showing love. At least this
is how I feel about it. And I feel that you also see it this way. And
you like the kitchen. And I believe that you understand me because
you also—I have seen that when I come you cook or [when] someone that you love comes, you cook for them. Because you also like
the kitchen. We enjoy cooking."¹⁵ Not only does Esperanza Vélez address the importance of her emotions toward her family with the

offering of food, but she also connects the gesture of self-giving as a communal act of emotional expression. Self-giving here becomes a communal act of showing gestures of love through plates filled with food. The agency in her act of giving does not follow the traditional implication of religious self-sacrifice: the denial of our own individuality for the benefit of our family or community. On the contrary, cooking for either Esperanza Vélez or me, as she says, is not an obligatory performance but rather an occasion to celebrate her affectionate nature with her culinary creative expression.

Through the organization of what follows, divided in four parts, I explain the engendering implications, both in theory and practice, of *place* and *space* as they apply to notion of home. First, through a feminist perspective, I highlight some gender associations connected to *place* rooted in the ideologies of separate spheres, the private and the public. I call this section the "Feminization of Place." The focus of the second part, "Place in Architecture," illustrates how historically in the field of architecture the place (the design) of a house has been influenced by dominant economic and political needs, which continue to *place* women in the home for the benefit of a capitalist and patriarchal society. Due to this continuous manifestation of place, feminists, in the social sciences and humanities in general, have underscored the way social power relations (economic and political) work to *place* people in particular types of homes or leave some homeless. The third part looks at how the notion of *space* helps counterbalance some of the social meanings associated with *place* by introducing my concept of a borderless boundary zone where the separation of spheres blur, where the ideologies of *place* and *space* interconnect. As one of my students once said, "where women take their own *space* in the kitchen *place*." What creates the meaning of a borderless boundary zone is the "presence of individuals in [a] space" for they "determine its nature."[16] Through the process of appropriating the kitchen's *space*, a woman, like many of the women from the *charlas,* converts the kitchen from her seemingly prescribed natural *place* into her own self inscribed social *space,* by constantly redefining the meaning of the kitchen and cooking. For a woman, the significance of her kitchen's *space* changes throughout her life. The inscriptions Vélez gives to the many kitchens she has had represent different stages of her life, as we will see in the final section of this chapter and throughout *Voices.*

• •
Feminization of Place

The kitchen as a woman's rightful *place* becomes problematic when
place connotes either a stable, unprogressive, static, or nostalgic location. Within this paradigm, some feminists argue that the kitchen
represents a stifling setting for a woman's intellectual, economic,
and personal growth, thus making the kitchen a site of social entrapment. Ruth Hubbard, a feminist scientist, expresses this sentiment when she vehemently criticizes Arlene Voski Avakian for
complaining in an anthology, *Through the Kitchen Window* (1997),
about women's kitchen stories. Hubbard writes to Avakian: "I was
irritated at the idea of collecting a set of feminist writings about
women and food, including recipes. Haven't we had enough of women
being viewed through the kitchen window. . . . I cannot help but feel
that it is self-indulgent to put together a United States collection on
'women and food,' when women and feminists are confronting so
many problems and engaged in such important struggles in this
country and elsewhere."[17] The catalyst creating such response exists in seeing *place* as static and nonprogressive, in fact, seeing it as
oppressive.

I do not wish to deny that the kitchen can be a place of oppression and aggression toward women. Philosopher Uma Narayan indicates one particular form of violence against women that generally takes place in the kitchen, dowry-murder by fire. Quoting Veena
Talwar Oldenburg who speaks on this matter, Narayan writes, "It
virtually destroys the evidence of murder along with the victim and
can easily be made to look like an accident. It is also relatively
simple to commit. It occurs in the kitchen, where the middle-class
housewife spends a large amount of time each day. Pressurized
kerosene stoves are in common use in such homes; a tin of fuel is always kept in reserve. This can be quickly poured over the intended
victim and a lighted match will do the rest. It is easy to pass off the
event as an accident because these stoves are prone to explode . . .
and the now ubiquitous but highly inflammable nylon sari easily
catches fire and engulfs the wearer in flames."[18] The aim of this example is not to indicate that such torture only happens in third-
world countries due to their cultural practices that keep women
extremely oppressed. This event came to mind because when it happens, it takes place in the kitchen. But I agree with Narayan who

points out that violence against women happens all over the world. Perhaps in the United States, the absence of a cultural term such as "dowry-murders" blinds many to the domestic violence that results in death. Much of the sociological research on violence against women identifies the house as the site where such aggression occurs. As a matter of fact, in "1990 in the United States, about 40 percent of all female murder victims were killed by their husbands or boyfriends. For many women home is a battleground not a sanctuary."[19] I imagine that Hubbard's reaction to Avakian's project, *Through the Kitchen Window,* in part reflects a rejection to the kitchen as a *place* where patriarchal ideology governs its operation. Thus, a book celebrating women's relationship with food might seem counterproductive to feminists' liberating social efforts.

While Hubbard might not be speaking of such severe forms of violence or oppression, her tone and particularly the phrase "women being viewed through the kitchen window" reveal that she speaks from the position of an outsider looking in. Her location outside from those women "being viewed" asserts her subjectivity. Following Hubbard's frame of thought, she creates her agency by her position as an onlooker, while the women "being viewed" remain silenced because their voices are not heard. While Hubbard's critical remarks speak for liberating women from the kitchen, ironically, her tactics for women's active and visible sociopolitical participation silences those women who physically remain in the kitchen doing the cooking. Consequently, she risks the possibility of denying some women the right and the power to narrate their own experience from their kitchen *space.* The simple act of speaking from the kitchen makes it a *space* of shared *confianza* (trust) where taboo or other difficult issues can be unveiled. The act of speaking creates collective agency.

Women like Liduvina Vélez and Alma Contreras through their view of the kitchen express the peculiarities of their individual lives. Kitchen talk among them serves as a moment of critical reflection and affirmation. For instance, in my family, topics on sexuality and conjugal relations are often not broached. Yet in a *charla* Contreras with a quasi-serious tone brings up an issue that our culture trained us well never to explore: the right over our own bodies. This takes place when Contreras imagines the substitution of her kitchen for a "hot tub." Contreras's last sentence in this particular moment of our *charla,* in addition to wanting a housekeeper to do the cooking and ironing, says, "¡Hasta quien hiciera lo otro! No te digo más porque estás grabando" (Someone who would do the other thing! I don't tell you more just because you are recording). Contreras says enough for the three of us to understand. Contreras alludes here to what she conceives as her conjugal duties, to which Vélez responds, "eso no es trabajo que tengas que cumplir, mi'ja" (it is not a chore that you have to fulfill, *mi'ja*). In this exchange, Vélez and Contreras engage in a critical reflection that challenges dominant ideology of the female body as cultural economy.[20] This conversation, which begins with the exchanging of the kitchen *place* for an imaginative hot tub *space,* seems rather humorous and inconsequential. But with this imaginative architectural reconceptualization, Contreras expresses her desire to free herself from the constraints of a social role that keeps her in a position of servitude due to economic dependency, for if only she had money she would hire someone to do house chores. While she expresses her entrapment within economic constraints, and her solution would *place* another woman in an awkward predicament, Vélez's comment rejects such views by offering a different one. For Vélez, a woman's body, regardless of a woman's economic limitations, belongs to no one but herself.

In order for a person to change the oppressive, less-than-satisfactory circumstances of her life, this person needs first to know what has led her to that predicament. In Contreras's case, she identifies economic limitations as the boundary keeping her in a less-than-satisfactory setting. Vélez uses this moment in the *charla* to invite her daughter to reach the level of *conscientización* that Vélez has clearly obtained. In the next chapter, we will see how Contreras does embark on a journey towards *conscientización,* particularly with her affirmation of her creative culinary practices.

There are other ways a kitchen offers a *space* to speak with *confianza* about how women do experience a level of subservience and endurance of a spouse's unacceptable behavior. Hilaria Cortés, when recalling the reasons for her own marriage, says, "Yes I got married . . . because loneliness is rather ugly. I was rolling from here to there from there to here . . . like a billiard ball. . . . And I said to myself, 'I will get married. Maybe my destiny will get better.' And it was worse. It was worse!"[21] Vélez also alludes to the gender power relationship with her husband as she remembers how after experiencing two years of independence living in her own home, having her own kitchen, he took her back to his mother's house. Clearly, these women are aware of the complexity of their situations. But to answer one of Hubbard's comments to Avakian, mentioned above, the feminist struggle for human rights begins at the personal level. Personal changes always have a communal effect, for our sense of self is woven by our relationships with others. As anthropologist Suad Joseph says, we are "never without a family, without relationships, outside the social body."[22] I do not intend to romanticize the lives of the women from the *charlas*. I wish, however, not to silence them, if they desire to speak, by taking away their right to articulate and share their stories. The act of sharing our stories is in itself an act of agency.

Through a correspondence with Avakian, Hubbard recognizes the risk of silencing others and realizes how the kitchen can become a woman's *space* of agency, for herself:

> *I found your letter very helpful. I now have much more understanding for why any number of friends of mine love to prepare meals for their friends, or even just for themselves. I have never thought about the really quite obvious fact that preparing a meal can be a sign of caring and of loving communication, because food just has never been an avenue of communication for me. It would be more correct to say, a positive avenue of communication. The fact is that as I have thought about the subject since our correspondence began, I have realized that I have quite negative connotations with food.*[23]

Here, Hubbard views herself from the inside of her own kitchen *space,* and the history of social relationships associated with it. While Hubbard's recognition is not positive, nonetheless, to be cognitive and express what the kitchen and cooking means for her, she makes the kitchen her own *space.* Without opening the kitchen's window to hear the voices coming from within, the kitchen from afar could be seen only as a social site that keeps women as subordinated second-class citizens. Some women from the *charlas* admit that they do not like to cook, yet they still make the kitchen their *space* as they articulate why they dislike cooking.

Hubbard's initial concerns, however, need not be dismissed, since the kitchen as a woman's *place* has been viewed as a source "of stability, reliability, and authenticity."[24] In and of themselves these social qualities are not negative, yet ideological complications arise when such qualities are coded female, giving women the responsibility of remaining stable, reliable, and authentic, particularly as these qualities are deemed necessary as the result of shifting economies from that of an agrarian system to the development of capitalism. The economic changes caused by industrialization, urbanization, and a competitive market created an ideology of separate spheres that "rhetorical construction . . . responded to changing social and economic reality."[25] In the public sphere, the growing competitive market of early capitalism brought constant uncertainty and turmoil. The home became the "embodiment and the environment of stable values. Maintaining a site of permanent value . . . facilitated" a traditional life that was "increasingly subject to the caprices of the market."[26] The separation of the spheres protected traditional family values against the often callous, ambitious, and material values of the workplace. Tradition, nourishment, morality, and spirituality were social values that home provided. Within the ideologies of separate spheres, women's nature *naturally* made them into the ideal providers of such values. Thus home became associated with womanhood.

The kitchen as the *place* for women's social functions finds its roots in the early capitalist system with its integral ideology of separate spheres. With the separation of spheres, the capitalist system determines the value of women's roles in society. Geographers Mona Domosh and Joni Seager in *Putting Women in Place: Feminist Geographers Make Sense of the World* (2001) explain that as capitalism began to emerge, "the separation of a masculine world of work and production from a feminine world of family and reproduction was essential to" the structure of capitalism. "This system required a commitment to hard work and competition in the marketplace, and at the same time required the behind-the-scenes care and nurture of family and children and the unpaid maintenance of the physical (and psychological) needs of the workers."[27] Needless to say, women throughout history and throughout different parts of the world have contested this so-called natural place behind-the-scenes.[28] What gets challenged is the correlation between home, family values, and stability as an essential characteristic of being female.[29]

When women from the *charlas* admit that they do not like to cook and only do so for their children, they clearly question the naturalness in homemaking activities and their sense of self. Flores states it succinctly in our *charla* when she says that she really cooks more for her family than for herself: "Actually, one cooks for them. I am going to tell you something. As for me, for how much I eat, a tortilla would be enough. But when you cook, you cook for them. So that we can all eat together, right. And you feel horrible when they complain about everything you have cooked."[30] *Voices* does not essentialize the cooking as women's second nature. It simply hopes not to undermine the knowledge that does exist within the kitchen *space.*

The capitalist separation of spheres values a woman's social role as "the comfort of Being," preventing her from "the project of Becoming." In other words, capitalism values women for the benefits they provide to its operation within the home. Paradoxically, capitalism also devalues women's housework for its failure to produce capital. Jeanne Boydston points out that, "over the course of a two-hundred-year period, women's domestic labor had gradually lost its footing as a recognized aspect of economic life in America. The image of the colonial goodwife, valued for her contribution to household prosperity, had been replaced by the image of the wife and mother as 'dependent' and 'non-producer.'"[31] Prior to capitalism, women did (and still do) produce capital by selling items made in their domestic *space:* food, drinks, quilts, baskets, clothing, and other such things. While this work still takes place on some scale, rather prevalently in working-class communities, most women's production of material goods for use in an exchange economy system or to sell for monetary compensation has been taken from their hands. The separation of spheres *places* women at home, and the gradual consolidation of capitalism as the dominant economic system removes domestic productions away from women's hands and into the factory.[32]

The industrialization of tortilla making in Mexico during the late nineteenth and early twentieth century exemplifies this process. In Mexico, this effort became the replacement of the Aztec blender, *el metate,* with mechanical mills. Don Luis Romero Soto, "one of the most colorful and inventive figures in the development of the tortilla industry" at the beginning of the century, saw his mission in life to "redeem the women of [the Mexican] nation from the slavery of the *metate.*"[33] Romero Soto was one of the first inventors to obtain patents for a tortilla machine in 1899; he also formed a corporation for his new invention and called it La Malinche. The new Malinche was to free indigenous women from the long hours of laboring on the *metate* in order to make tortillas. The mechanical mills were introduced with an official discourse of liberating women from the *metate.* Both Jeffrey Pilcher in *¡Que vivan los tamales!* (1998) and Bert Kreitlow in "The Culture of Maize" (1999) indicate that the investors and government officials' motives for introducing modern technology in rural areas were to improve the well-being of peasants.[34] With the mechanical mills, a large portion of women's daily time was rescued from the chore of making corn dough for tortillas.

In "Del metate al molino" (1983) Dawn Keremitsis argues, however, that mechanical mills only led to the development of factory-made tortillas, which marked a class, racial, and gender division in various ways. The process of tortilla making, a task that for centuries had belonged to rural (indigenous) women, shifted to the hands of businessmen. Women owned neither the mills nor the *tortillerías*. As a matter of fact, Keremitsis points out how special syndicates were formed to keep women from owning *tortillerías,* thus, from having some control in the industry. Gender also divided labor distribution within the industry. Men usually worked at the mills making two or three times more than women who sold the tortillas. Keremitsis's study, which looks at the evolution of mills and factory-made tortillas during the first three decades of the twentieth century, concludes by stating that, while many women were no longer slaves to the *metate,* they became slaves to a capitalist society. The owners of the mills needed cheap labor to run them and sell the tortillas. The industry of corn mills and factory-made tortillas became one of the most profitable in the country. Modernization, argues Guillermo Bonfil Batalla in *México profundo* (1996), forces many indigenous people into a monetary labor-exchange economy.

The factory-made tortilla, according to Hilaria Cortés, has not eradicated home tortilla making entirely. For instance, Cortés explains why most women in the small town of San Miguel del Zapote, Jalisco, make their own tortillas. She says:

> *Because all these women are used to making their* nixtamal, *to grind their maize, and to make their own tortillas. Factory-made tortillas, if you eat them warm, they are good. But by the next day, they are no longer good because they get hard. On the other hand, the ones we make [at home], they are good for two or three days. You heat them up, and they are soft, flavorful. Not the factory ones. They are stiff.*
> **Meredith:** *Why do you think they are that way?*
> **Yaya:** *Because people say that in the tortilla factory, they add* olote *to the* nixtamal *[dough for making tortillas].*

Meredith: *What is* olote?

Yaya: Olote *is from where the maize is threshed. The center [cord]*
from where the maize is threshed.

Meredith: *Why do you think they do this?*

Yaya: *Just to save money. So that they can get more from the corn.*
Because you must know, that the maseca *is rather dry. Because*
from the maize, people derive many products. Mazola oil comes
from maize, other kinds of oils [too]. So by the time they are ac-
tually ready to make the maseca, *what is there left of the maize?*
All of its oily moisture, of its juices is all gone. It has no flavor
left. Therefore, the maseca *has no flavor. And that is why I don't*
like maseca.[35]

Cortés addresses a number of issues in her comments on the
process of tortilla making. Homemade and handmade tortillas for
the women of San Miguel del Zapote, Jalisco, according to Cortés,
define a cultural value based on aesthetics of custom, taste, and of
working-class efficiency. In her discussion, Cortés theorizes on how
the lack of prime quality material in the production of factory tortillas is due to monetary profits. Due to the better quality prime
material used by working-class women of San Miguel del Zapote,
their work produces better results. Ironically, the mill, La Malinche
invented in 1899, functioned within the same negative image as the
historical figure, Malintzin, the young indigenous woman Hernan
Cortés took as his mistress. This woman is known in Mexicans' collective consciousness as La Malinche, who assisted Cortés in con-
quering the Aztec capital of Tenochtitlán in 1521. According to
Mexican philosopher Octavio Paz, by bearing Cortes's children, La
Malinche must be held accountable for the creation of an illegiti-
mate mestizo race.[36] Due to her connection with Cortés and the con-
quering of Mexico, the name Malinche has become synonymous
with traitor. The (perhaps aptly named) Malinche *tortillería* machine thus compromises the tortillas' savory and nutritious value
because its operation focuses on economic profit. Factory-made tortillas, while they might save women's time from the long process it
takes to make them at home, do not taste as good and do not last as
long, creating, if nothing else, a financial burden for the poorest of
all—rural indigenous women.

The separation of the workplace and home has forced women to
be active participants in both locations, oftentimes learning to cre-

ate a thirdspace that I refer to as a borderless boundary zone. I will elaborate on this later in the chapter, but for now suffice it to say that such a zone speaks to women's ability to carve out a public setting from the privacy of their home *space.*

• •
Place in Architecture

Place and *space* are gendered in many ways, which vary between cultures and over time. The kitchen as a woman's natural and rightful *place,* however, retains much of its currency. Its consistency generally derives from the fact that a society's economic system preinscribes a kitchen's social and cultural function as it determines its location within a house's floor plan. Another reason lies in the reality that men and masculine ideologies dominate the field of architecture. In 1999, only 17.5 percent of architects and only 15.8 percent of architect faculty in the United States were women.[37] Within this male domination, *place* represents a fixed "theoretical model that describes and explains certain aspects of" a built structure.[38] The abstract theoretical model depoliticizes, neutralizes, and universalizes the forms and functions designated to particular places.

Yet, as feminist architect Diana I. Agrest indicates in *Architecture from Without: Theoretical Framing for a Critical Practice* (1991), such a theoretical model configures "spaces beyond" their "form and functional aspects."[39] The functional aspect of the kitchen within the overall house's design, for instance, serves as the place where food is stored, prepared, served, and often eaten. Historically, economic, gender, racial, and class motives have shaped the form (design) of the kitchen beyond its basic functional aspects. Where is the kitchen situated within the overall design of a home? Who does the cooking? How is the kitchen designed? Exploring these questions shows feminists' concerns regarding the form and function of the kitchen's *place* within the structure of the house and the *place* it serves within society at large. The theoretical model can, therefore, downplay the fact that what defines the form and function of a particular *place* are the ways individuals conduct their daily lives in any given setting.[40] Places inhabited by humans gain meaning by the social life within them, a life that "consists of exchanges, encounters, conflicts, and connections with one another; and where human interaction is not that of abstract citizens or economic agents but of

individuals relating to each other in the flow of daily life."[41] Architectural designs, as we can see, are never free of ideological (economic) governing assumptions.

"Architecture picks a site in nature and transforms it to the political realm by means of symbolic mediation," explains French philosopher Henri Lefebvre in his study of *The Production of Space*
(1974). The symbolic mediation, argues Lefebvre, establishes a
form of "knowledge and power" by prescribing divisions of gender
production and dictating gender (and class) social codes.[42] Lefebvre
calls such divisions the "realization of the master's project."[43] Feminist architects tracing such symbolic mediation within the design
of contemporary housing demonstrate "that rooms associated with
men are always focused at the front of the house—the high-status,
'public' section of the house—while rooms which have historically
been associated with women, such as the kitchen, are hidden away
at the rear of the house."[44] The dichotomy of front/back, public/pri-
vate articulates gender relations, which in turn manifests the ideological boundaries women face in their effort to emerge from their
socially "hidden away" *place* at the rear of patriarchal houses.

Feminist architects and geographers approach the concept of
place differently since they consider how a person experiences a
sense of place through their body, their sensual and affective knowledge. They create spaces that offer "experiences that correspond to,
provide models for, the experience of the body, give validity to a
sense of the self as bodily—a sense that may be shared by both
sexes."[45] Deborah Fausch, art critic, explains how in a feminist approach to space, space is "situated within [the] large-standing opposition between vision and the other senses." Fausch goes on to argue how "an architecture that required that it be experienced by
senses other than vision in order to be understood could be claimed
as a strategically feminist architecture. It would merit this desig-
nation if it fostered an awareness of and posited a value to the experience of the concrete, the sensual, the bodily—if it used the body
as a necessary instrument in observing the content, the experience."[46] The way women from the *charlas* appropriate the kitchen as
their *space* represents a concrete practical manner of making the
kitchen into a feminist *space* by experiencing it with all the senses.
This point will become more evident in chapter two, "*Sazón: The
Flavors of Culinary Epistemology*," where I argue that knowledge of
cooking, the *sazón,* is a corporeal knowledge.

In the field of architecture, Agrest points out the importance of incorporating the female body within the theoretical designs of places and practical occupation of spaces. Agrest explains that a traditional male approach to architecture represses the female body by an "ideological apparatus that has systematically excluded woman, an exclusion made possible by an elaborate mechanism of symbolic appropriations of the female body."[47] Three symbolic appropriations Agrest offers include suppression, repression, and replacement. The female body is suppressed since "it is man's body— that is, according to the classical texts, the natural and perfectly proportioned body—from which architectural principles and measurements derive." The repression comes from the fact that "women's unique quality, that of motherhood, is projected onto the male body. Thus woman is not only suppressed, but indeed her whole sexual body is repressed." Therefore, the female body is replaced by the "figure of the architect." The male, through what Agrest calls "a transsexual operation, has usurped the female's reproductive qualities in the desire to fulfill the myth of creation."[48] Due to this history, feminist architects work makes the body the locus of architectural developing. While Linda McDowell in *Gender, Identity and Place* (1999) does not make an explicit reference to the female body, she argues that the body as a theoretical focus helps blur the division of public/private spheres since it is deeply personal and the subject of public comment. The body also does not allow an association of *place* with a concept of stable, fixed-in-time. The body "has a plasticity of malleability which means that it can take different forms and shapes at different times."[49]

These concepts of the body and architecture enter into the notion of homes in the ways feminist architects conceived of homes' meaning. Homes should not be ideologically located in the private sphere, and as a place of rest from the public world of economic battles. Since homes "are the essential institutions that root people in a place and a culture, . . . the creation of communities [should be] the ultimate goal of housing development . . . informal housework economy and domestic work, both controlled by women, [need to be recognized] as the most valuable economic activities of developing societies."[50] Since the female's body has been suppressed, repressed, and displaced, a woman by making the kitchen her *space* regains her body as she determines the functions of her kitchen, through the *sazón,* the knowledge of the senses.

Without dismissing the gender architectural and ideological associations between home and women, *Voices* argues that a blanket rejection of the kitchen overlooks the ways some women, particularly working-class women, have made the kitchen their own *space* of social, economic, and personal mobility. Besides, even with scientific advances, a breakfast, lunch, and dinner pill has not yet been invented, thus, a literal divorce from the kitchen is not possible, even if it is desired. Moreover, as Vélez explains in the opening of this chapter, the kitchen for some women is not necessarily a stifling social entrapment. For some women, the kitchen is one of the *spaces* in their "project of Becoming." Listening to the women from the *charlas* we hear how they challenge dominant ideology defining the kitchen as a woman's *place* by making the kitchen into their *space*. Instead of a kitchen containing a woman's identity, a woman can create her own identity by reconfiguring the social function of *her* kitchen, by making the kitchen her social *space*. In the kitchen as a social *space,* a woman inscribes a feminist epistemology where she takes ownership of *her* body.

To understand the kitchen as a woman's own *space,* I use the metaphor of a *borderless boundary zone.* The metaphor captures the array of different social *spaces* created within the kitchen by women's own manifestation of their particular needs in accordance to their own milieu. Borderless is meant to represent the many types of social relations women can create from within their kitchen. By boundary I refer to the economic and cultural power relations that do affect the flow of women's spatial mobility, regardless of their economic or marital status, age, or ethnicity. These two spatial concepts, borderless as *space* and boundary as *place* overlap to form the zone where all of us carry out our daily social life. *Borderless boundary zone* as a feminists' conceptual tool helps define *space* as the *place* "where social life consists of exchanges, encounters, conflicts, and connections with one another."[51] Women's ways of making the kitchen their *space* undergo a continuous process of negotiation, or of combining different ingredients, to reflect their specific social needs and their own taste for change, which remain determined by what their daily lives offer.

While many women continue to challenge the ideological limitations imposed on their lives, to say that these social conditions can be completely erased, or transcended, negates the acute tension many of us feel as we struggle to negotiate (and sometimes distinguish)

between our rights and our obligations, between our privileges and
our responsibilities, between our desires for modernity and our grip
on tradition. Because we live "spatially restricted . . . lives in a home,
in a neighborhood, in a city, in a work place, all which are within the
nation-state," the tension results from the fact that "these sites or
places are constructed through sets of complex, intersecting social
relationships that operate at a variety of levels and which are affected by beliefs, and attitudes, images, and symbols that are themselves increasingly variable and complex."[52] Aihwa Ong makes a
similar argument as she explains how "non-Western woman as a
trope of feminist discourse is either [seen] as nonmodern or modern,
she is seldom perceived as living in a situation where there is a deeply
felt tension between tradition and modernity."[53] The constant negotiation, between a woman's individual needs—the kitchen as her
space—and the social demands on her, the kitchen as her *place,* creates the *borderless boundary zone.*

Since the kitchen is an area that the majority of women cannot
entirely escape, regardless of our class or marital status, profession,
ethnicity, or political views, it offers most of us a *space* for a common
practice where we can negotiate our different forms of subjectivity.
The *borderless boundary zone,* which is my metaphor, not the
women's from the *charlas,* represents a pragmatic manifestation of
theoretical concepts such as "thirdspace epistemologies," "decolonial imaginary," "decolonizing methodologies," or "methodologies of
the oppressed."[54] In one way or another, all these theoretical concepts deal with ways of finding spaces where those who have been silenced by long histories of colonization speak from, or of finding the
gaps between structures of domination where the underclass finds
moments of empowerment. I use the term pragmatic to resonate
with the philosophy of pragmatism, which focuses on the notion of
"things in the making." Joan Ockman, in *The Pragmatist Imagination: Thinking about "Things in the Making"* (2000), defines pragmatism as "zones that stimulate new thinking, new ideas; it deals
with uses rather than interoperations, with our relation to those
things still in the making that provoke us to think, to imagine, and
so to act, create, transform, in new ways."[55] Many of the women in
the *charlas* make and remake their kitchen *space* constantly.

A perfect culinary analogy for the production of distinct social
spaces is the composition of a recipe. Any good cook knows that
a recipe's composition, as Debra Castillo says, "is not a blueprint.

It is less a formula than a general model; less an axiom of unchanging law and more a theory of possibilities."[56] A knowledgeable
cook informed by the sensory logic of the *sazón* always knows how
to combine different and new ingredients when those previously
used are no longer desirable or available. Just as there are multiple
combinations of ingredients, there are also multiple manifestations
of *spaces* created within the kitchen. The concept of *borderless* cor-
relates to the recipe as a theory of possibilities that leads to an
overall savory meal: women's rejection of their so-called natural
state of silence, submission, and economic dependency. In part, economic and social structures as well as cultural patterns create the
boundary. The *borderless boundary zone* as a thirdspace epistemology with its "theory of possibilities" reveals the different levels and
degree of subjectivity and agency many women *do* articulate within
their kitchen *spaces*.

Women from the *charlas* speak of this rejection not in terms of
rejecting the actual kitchen, though some do, as do Flores and Contreras, Flores in her dedication to her career, and Contreras in her
creative substitution of the kitchen for a hot tub. Women reject the
idea that in the kitchen they lose their agency, particularly their
economic agency and their assertion of knowledge. Susan García viuda de Melo, for instance, as she converts her kitchen into her *space*
of economic resource, enacts her agency. In our *charla*, García viuda
de Melo explains how her kitchen *space* became her source of economic substance:

> *My profession was not actually cooking. What happened is that
> once I became a widow, well I had to change my type of work
> from [selling] milk to cooking. Because I had daughters to sup-
> port on my own, since I was a widow. The milk business was no
> longer useful. . . . I used to sell milk, I would make cheese, and
> everything. But, unfortunately, the truck in which I transported
> milk and everything else, was stolen from my daughter. . . . And
> I was left absolutely handicapped. Then I began to sell food. To
> support my daughters—so that [they] would finish [their] stud-
> ies. How else was I going to support myself other than from sell-
> ing food? But boy, it is an enormous job. . . . And then that's how
> I started, little by little, little by little. And well, now, blessed by
> God, it is what I support myself with because I didn't have a pen-
> sion, and I didn't have money in the bank to support myself.[57]*

García viuda de Melo does not conceive of the kitchen as a limitation but as the source of courage to face the world without the moral and economic support of a husband. As she says, "lo importante que yo tengo es que me gusta mucho guisar" (an important thing about me is that I like to cook very much). Throughout our *charla*, she did mention more than once that her main concern has always been to put her daughters through college: "That's why I have always said, even when I became a widow, 'no, my daughters have to study; they have to study. They have to finish their studies, because what is going to happen to them when I am no longer here? The same as me? Shifting from one place to another.' I wouldn't mind being a dishwasher. I wouldn't care. I wouldn't mind ironing other people's clothes. I wouldn't. As long as they finish their studies."[58]

For García viuda de Melo, the kitchen and cooking are a means to an end. She transforms the kitchen into her *space* of business, which helps offer to her daughters opportunities new and different from what she had for herself. She breaks the cycle of women in her family having to support themselves with manual labor. "If I had not begun this business of cooking, I don't know what my life would have been. Because . . . I don't have a formal education. I only finished elementary school. Because, unfortunately, my parents were very poor and they could not send us to school."[59] She tells me how her own mother made a living: "What my mother did for a living was to sew for other people. She sewed beautifully; she didn't learn that formally. She didn't study to be a seamstress. She made dresses without patterns."[60]

García viuda de Melo breaks the cycle of manual labor for her daughters. Her oldest daughter, as she tells me, has "su profesión. Ella es educadora. Ella trabaja en El Colegio de la Paz" (her profession. She is an instructor. She works at the College of the Paz). Her youngest daughter has recently completed her baccalaureate degree. Manual labor, however, is not something of which García viuda de Melo is ashamed. She only aspires to something different for her daughters. She opens the window to such aspirations by converting the kitchen as her *space* of business. García viuda de Melo's subjectivity expresses a motivation to offer different life paths for her daughters.

For working-class women, the appropriation of their kitchen *space* becomes particularly crucial since they can rarely afford to leave their kitchen work to someone else. The social and economic limitations found within the boundaries of a traditional patriarchal kitchen's design as a woman's *place* are transformed by a woman's active initiation. This active initiation makes women the principal agents converting the kitchen site into their own *space*. As the *charlas culinarias* unfold, each woman's agency manifested itself not only through their conceptualization of a kitchen's function but also by their critical and reflective act of self-representation.

•••••••••••••••••••••

Liduvina Vélez's Kitchen *Spaces*

What follows are aspects of Liduvina Vélez's acts of agency, which show how her independence and self-belief increased throughout the years as she appropriated the kitchen as her *space*. Her culinary narrative goes from describing her first *cocina propia,* to her life now in the United States where she first supported herself by working as a dishwasher and now as a housekeeper. Throughout her life, Vélez's personal relation to her kitchens has gone through constant transformations, which reflect her shifting priorities and needs. Vélez transforms the ideological notions that construct the kitchen as a site that puts a woman *in* her *place* as wife and mother, a *place* of mandatory labor and often submission to a male order, by modifying it into her social *space* as she carves out a public zone from within her private kitchen. Vélez expends and negotiates the *borderless boundary zone* of her kitchens to work within and against the grains of dominant social powers.[61] In her case, the powers of dominance display themselves in forms of gender and class discrimination, which she attributes to the result of "la ignorancia y la pobreza" (ignorance and poverty).

In order to fully understand Vélez's sense of independence as she recalls her experiences of her *cocina propia* at the age of eighteen, as mentioned in the opening of this chapter, we need to learn more about her life. Vélez, as she says, was born into "ignorancia y pobreza." Her mother, Aurora Larios Cárdenas, at the age of thirteen was literally stolen by Federico Vélez, who two years later became Liduvina's father. Two years after, Larios gave birth to a second daughter, Esperanza. Then she miscarried. When Liduvina was five, Larios gave birth to her third and final child, Guadalupe. In a *charla matrimonial* (matrimonial chat) with Larios, she recalls the event of her "kidnapping" as following: "Me acuerdo que estaba en

la huerta piscando y Federico me llegó de sorpresa. Me jaló de las
greñas y me llevó" (I remember I was in the orchard picking fruit.
Federico arrived unexpectedly. He pulled me by the hair and took
me with him). Liduvina Vélez has few memories of life with her parents since they separated when she was only eight years old. After
her parents' separation, the youngest child stayed with their father,
the oldest and middle children were sent to live with a maternal
aunt who lived in Atlisco, Puebla. Unfortunately, this aunt, *la tía*
Dora, turned out to be physically, verbally, and emotionally abusive.
After Vélez received the first beating, she left the house. As a child
and young teenager, Vélez never had a home of her own.

By the time Vélez was fifteen, her paternal grandmother had
passed away, and she returned to live with her father, to take care
of him. She remembers this episode as following:

> *When my grandmother died, I didn't want my father to bring a*
> *woman into the house, because it was known that he had a lot*
> *of women in the* cantina. *Once grandmother died, he would take*
> *a woman to live permanently in the house. That's why I wanted*
> *to learn how to wash, how to iron, how to cook, because accord-*
> *ing to my way of thinking, my father would not bring anyone to*
> *the house. But nonetheless, he still brought a woman from* la
> cantina *to the house. Someone by the name of Carmelilla. We*
> *used to fight a lot [Carmelilla and I]. That's why I think I didn't*
> *spend much time in the kitchen in that house. She used to hide*
> *the food from us, so that Lupita and I wouldn't eat. That's why*
> *I would go stay with my uncle Mayolo; my aunt Celia was a good*
> *woman, and my uncle a good man.*[62]

Only a year after the return to her father's, she found herself married to a man she hardly knew. At some point during the course of
one year, the man who was to be my father, a man she scarcely liked
and never loved, began to court her. A marriage contract between
her father and mine brought Vélez to the altar when she was not
quite sixteen.

Interestingly, however, Vélez had planned to escape the marriage, or at least the religious ceremony.

> *Oh well. By the time that the civil marriage took place, there was*
> *no time to think of anything because everything took place dur-*
> *ing those same days I was still mad. But the religious ceremony*

did take more time because the admonitions had to be read be-
fore the marriage. They had to be read, I don't know, three or
four Sundays in case there might be an impediment for the mar-
riage. And yes, it was then that I said, "No, what am I doing; I
am stupid. Why am I going to get married?" But under the civil
law, I was already married. And then I thought of leaving before
the religious ceremony. I thought about leaving the house. Just
like that, all of a sudden I said, "I won't marry, and I won't
marry, and I don't want to get married because I don't love him."
I planned on leaving the house the night before the wedding. I
planned to escape. But I overslept. And that was it—I got mar-
ried. And that's the end of this story. There was the marriage.[63]

The catalyst of her anger and going along with the civil marriage
was the result of a gift, a jewelry box and some candy, that the man
who became my father gave to Vélez's younger sister, Guadalupe
(Lupita). Because the nature of the gift did not seem appropriate for
a ten-year-old, their father believed the gift was meant for his oldest daughter, Liduvina. Not accepting his daughters' word, he used
corporal punishment on his youngest daughter to "get the truth"
about who was the intended recipient of the gift. In her effort to stop
such treatment, Vélez falsely admitted that the gift was for her.
Somehow, a jewelry box and some candy, in the mind of Vélez's father, took a symbolic representation of an engagement ring. Vélez's
father met my father on the street and questioned his manhood for
not having the courage to formally ask for Vélez's hand in marriage,
never mind the fact that they were not dating. An arrangement between both men, on the street, led to Vélez's marriage at the age of
not quite sixteen. Considering Vélez's life story prior to her marriage, and the fact that the for first two years of it she lived with her
in-laws, it is no wonder that she remembers her first *cocina propia,*
as mentioned in the opening of the chapter, as a period of independence in her life.

The relationship that Vélez has had with her kitchens is complex, and not full of romantic nostalgia. The description of her first
kitchen, however, does bring forward what on the surface seems
a contradiction in terms. While she conceives of her first kitchen as
affirming her independence, she testifies to the tremendous
amount of work involved in keeping it clean: "But I plastered all the
walls and floor of my little room. It is the same thing as sweeping

and mopping but you do it by hand. You also have to clean the chimney because with the masa—just imagine the mess you end up with! And then you have to clean the *metate* with a little brush that makes you splatter masa everywhere and it looks like *zopilotes* shit all over. Therefore you have to clean everything all over again so that everything is in order."[64] An initial reaction after reading this passage might make us wonder why anyone would think fondly of a kitchen where the walls and floors need daily cleaning by hand. Yet for her, the *space* she created within her kitchen goes beyond the hard physical labor of maintaining it. Vélez's sense of independence, pride, and eventually self-belief are easily understood within the politics of location. This process requires a contextualization of what comes before Vélez had her first kitchen. As mentioned above, Vélez is the oldest of three daughters, whose parents divorced when she was only eight. Due to "la ignorancia y probreza," as she would say, neither of her parents was able to keep either of the two oldest girls with them. Consequently, Vélez's formal education reached only to second grade because she had to fend for herself working as a *nana* (babysitter) for well-to-do families.

Vélez makes the kitchen and cooking her *space* by enacting her agency in a number of subtle ways. For example, throughout the *charlas* only rarely does she relate her cooking practices to wifely responsibility to cook for her husband. One of these occasions when she does refer to her husband takes place while living with her in-laws. While Vélez does not fully remember who cooked there, she says, "Yo pienso que yo cocinaba según para el marido y ellas cocinaban para ellas" (I think I would cook, supposedly for the husband, and they cooked for themselves). Her choice of expression was yet another way of asserting agency. She undermines the cultural *placement* of women in the kitchen to serve (to cook for) their husband. Vélez downplays such patriarchal assumption with her dismissing tone in "según para el marido" (supposedly for the husband). The two dismissing aspects in this phrase are the adverb *según* (supposedly)—presumed to be true, real, or genuine, especially on dubious grounds—and the use of the article *el* rather than the pronoun *mi* (my husband). I do not make this observation on any linguistic principles that would argue that in Spanish it is or it is not common for a woman to use the phrase "mi marido" (my husband). I make this observation of Vélez's dismissal, not of cooking but, rather, of the husband. In all the *charlas,* and Vélez has participated in many of them, she always refers to her husband as *el marido* (the husband).

While feminist geographers deconstruct gender divisions of *places* and *spaces* through their theories, Vélez also deconstructs them through her own pragmatic theory of remembrance and re-thinking the significance of her kitchens. When Vélez speaks of her kitchens, she subverts the male architectural design since she only speaks of her kitchens in relation to other women: her mother-in-law, sisters-in-law, and neighbors. In connecting the kitchen to other women, Vélez helps me increase my own *conscientización:* women are not always in competition with one another. My first inclination when she affirmed her desire to be a good housekeeper and connected such desire to her neighbors was to read this moment of our *charla* as her sense of pride and competition. In the same *charla* when Vélez describes her first *cocina propia,* she also says, "I feel that when I got married, I don't know why, but I became interested in being a good *ama de casa* (housewife). Because, boy, with the neighbors, boy! The one who would go sit outside of her house to sew was because she had already finished with her household chores. I would go, I don't know, at five in the morning, I think, with my *nixtamal* to the mill. I would come back, make my fire and make my tortillas. Then I would clean my chimney. I would make breakfast and give it to my children. I would clean them up. Then they would go play and I would go embroider."⁶⁵ One morning while sharing a cup of coffee and some muffins, I thought of asking why she made that reference of wanting to be the first neighbor sitting outside her house embroidering. Vélez says, "There is always a sense of pride in knowing that you are clean, that you are a hard worker. But more than that, I think it was the idea of sharing. We would go outside the house to embroider and share different embroidering techniques. We would learn from each other. Over there I would share my embroidering, here I share my books."⁶⁶ While I was inclined to interpret the relation to her neighbors as competitive, she grounds that connection in mutual sharing and socializing. Years later, while living in Nuevo Laredo, Tamaulipas, neighborly sharing was part of a daily exchange of food with *la güera,* her neighbor: "I remember that *la güera* and I would share each other's food. . . . Yes, whatever she would make, she would send me, and I would send her some of what I had made. I think we did this every day, depending on what we had cooked for dinner."⁶⁷ The kitchen space and cooking become for Vélez resources to gain community, mobility, and independence.

Vélez's first kitchen as her *space* initially represented her independence from a matriarchal household, yet this taste of independence led her to make the kitchen (and cooking) her *space* of survival politics. Carol Hardy-Fanta defines survival politics with four basic principles: (1) a class-linked concept—working class; (2) struggles outside political institutions; (3) individual, personal efforts that go behind the scenes; and (4) an informal, private, and individualistic process.[68] None of these principles is difficult to identify as Vélez appropriates the kitchen as her *space*. For Vélez, survival politics are the acts of agency that allow her to both create new spaces and move to existing ones in her life as her sense of independence increases and she becomes an economically self-sufficient woman.

Carving out a public *space* from within her private *place* represents the first stage of Vélez's survival politics and her first negotiations in maneuvering inside her *borderless boundary zone.* The rage she felt seeing her children's hunger and shabby clothing led her to transport the kitchen to the front door of her house. Vélez, as does Susana García viuda de Melo, at one point in her life sold food to help her feed and clothe her children: "[In Aguililla] every afternoon, I would put my little table there in the street, at the door of the house, without chairs or anything. People would eat standing up there or would take the food to their houses."[69] The issues motivating her survival political agenda, selling food, were the literal necessity of feeding and dressing her own children. Her *puestesito,* the table she located outside her door, does not constitute a conventional "political institution," and the struggle within this site represents an economic one. Vélez's limited resources provoked her individual initiative, though not behind the scene. "When I already had many small children—you know that one needs to buy them clothes, underwear—I began to put my little stand right out there at the door of the house. I would make *morisqueta:* white rice and meat with chile. Lets see, what else would I sell? Tostadas. I would make *pozole.* . . . It occurred to me to sell food there in the house, well, because I wanted to make some money; I wanted to have some money to buy things for my little ones. And that was the only way. I started selling food right there at the door. Yes, I had customers. . . . Yes, yes, I would make a profit, because from the money I would make, I would buy more groceries, and I would still have money to buy things for my little ones, food, or clothes."[70] As Vélez carved out a *space* for herself, her kitchen became her social, cultural, and economic mobility.

The informal economic practice helped increase Vélez's assertiveness in stating her opinions. After the inauguration of her food stand, *the* husband wanted to move to another city; Vélez's response shows her fight to keep her new form of independence: "After I already had my selling stand in Aguililla, [the] father of my children wanted us to move to Apatzingán. I would tell him that he should go, because from selling my food I was making enough money to feed the children. He still took me with him. But later, when we were already in Apatzingán, he [the husband] also started asking the workmen if they wanted to *asistirse* to the house to get their meals. Therefore, he brought me people from his work, and they gave me, I think, ten pesos daily for the meal. But I think that there were six or seven, so I would get seventy pesos. But with twenty I would prepare the food. I would feed them, and I would still have fifty pesos left. And what's more, the food I would prepare was also enough to feed my children."[71] At this point in Vélez's life, home became the social body where her motherhood, wifehood, and businesshood were all simultaneously negotiated as she moved through her kitchen *space*.

Vélez's mobility within the boundaries of her zone helped her gain a confidence and self-esteem that helped her change her *destino* (destiny) as well as her children's. Once she learned that she could support her children on her own, she planned a second escape, this time a successful one: "I didn't have money for the ticket; I asked my mother for it. But she didn't want me to leave the husband. She didn't want me to have a broken marriage. But she sent me money to buy clothes or toys for my children. . . . But with that money, I bought the tickets. He had gone, well, to sell his sandals at the market. I went to wait for the bus, not at the terminal, but to a place called the *glorietas*. I left with all my little children. We went to wait for the bus. I was fearful because I thought that all the people who saw me knew what I was going to do, and they would go tell him. But no, the husband had asked me to bring him dinner in the afternoon, and I left him waiting for the food that never arrived."[72] We can notice once again that here too, Vélez never refers to her husband as "my" husband but instead only as "the" husband.[73]

When she finally escaped from the husband, Vélez moved to Nuevo Laredo, Tamaulipas, where she worked on the restaurants

that by then her mother owned. There, she had a public kitchen
that her children took as their private kitchen and ate to their
heart's content: "There, whatever they would ask for, the children
would order *a la carta*. We could not give them whatever food we
had made for the day. Oh no, one wanted one thing, the other something else. Thanks to my mother, they ate like royalty."[74] At this
level of quotidian practice, of the mundane, Vélez's actions of selling food illustrate how the appropriation of her *cocina propia* led to
a level of self-esteem and self-belief about her capacity of earning a
living for her children and herself independent of her marriage
with a man who "liked to drink a lot. . . . Yes, he was a *macho*, a
Mexican *macho*. Drunkard, abusive, and a womanizer. And everything. And I think that everything has a limit. There comes a moment when you say, 'I can't take it any more.'"[75] The ways in which
Vélez has maneuvered herself through her kitchen *space* show that
while "women do not control physical or social space directly does
not necessarily preclude them from being determinants of, or me-
diators in" shaping the meaning of *spaces*.[76]

As mentioned above, another way of manifesting acts of agency
when a woman appropriates the kitchen as her *space* is by making
it a site of *confianza* (trust), sharing stories that have little to do
with actual cooking. Vélez, who has been divorced from *the* husband for over thirty-seven years, rarely speaks of their conjugal life.
She once said that regardless of what happened between the two of
them, he is still our father and if one day we want to meet him, help
him out, or live with him, we should be entitled to make that choice
independent from her feelings and memories of him. But as I say,
the *charlas* serve as a platform for issues beyond cooking. During a
charla with Vélez and two of her friends, Irma Vásquez and María
Luisa Villicaña in 1999, Vélez recalls an episode of her marital life:

Duvi: *I remember one time I went to visit my godmother Felipa, and
she gave me corn, and I don't know how many other things.
Would you believe that this blessed man got very mad . . . he
made me return them. Can you imagine how embarrassed I was
having to tell my godmother, "He did not want these things!"*
Irma: *And did you return them, Duvi?*
Duvi: *Yes, [I returned them]. He beat me so hard from chin to ear.*
Irma: *And yet, you still call him "blessed man," Duvi? Can you even
call someone like that human?*
Duvi: *I would get so mad, since my little children were hungry.*[77]

Vélez's rage at seeing her children hungry answers feminist geographer Massey's question, which asks if it is possible for a sense of *place* to be progressive, and not self-enclosing and defensive, but outward looking.[78] Vélez's answer is yes, by filling the *space* of a *place* with courage.

Many years later and twice divorced, what keeps Vélez from doing what she finds most self-fulfilling, to be an *ama de casa,* is the necessity of supporting herself in a country whose official language she does not speak well. Usually *ama de casa* translates as housewife, but making a literal translation it means "lover of home." To be an *ama de casa* would free Vélez from the obligation of supporting herself financially by performing the physical task of cleaning other people's houses. While she still maintains interest in her latest kitchen, its function along with her desire and ability to cook has changed.

Duvi: *I like my kitchen a lot, but I like it clean. And just look at it. To walk by here and see everything clean. That's how I like it.*

Alma: *Mom used to cook lots of wonderful things when we were little, and now she hardly cooks.*

Duvi: *Well yes, then I had to, I had small children.*

Alma: *There it is, "had to." That's where I am too. . . . I have never liked to cook. It was after I got married that I had to make myself cook. I had no other choice.*

Duvi: *If I'm at home, why not [cook]? What I don't like is to come home now, tired [from work] and have to cook. But if I'm home, I like to do laundry, iron, clean my house, cook dinner. . . . Yes, I tell Panqui, "take me out of work and you will see if I won't cook again." I believe that I can be a good* ama de casa, *and I like doing it. What I don't like is that now I come home tired to go and fix dinner. If I have so much work, such a mess everywhere, do you think I want to be in the kitchen![79]* [When this *charla* took place, Panqui was the oldest remaining son still living in her house.]

While Vélez's personal connections to her kitchens have undergone constant change, she has maintained this desire, to be a good *ama de casa.* What does it mean for a woman to say that she can be and that she likes to be a good *ama de casa?* For Vélez, the answer to this question is found within the context of her experiences. For Vélez, *ama de casa* means lover of the house and not housewife, with the social connotations this term carries. Her constant reference to her great ability and desire to be an *ama de casa* have never been for the pleasure, duty, or fear of *the* husband. Her kitchen *space* is about her own identity. The way Vélez uses the phrase *ama de casa* captures an understanding that "people construct houses and make them in their own image, so . . . they use these houses and house-images to construct themselves as individuals and as groups."[80] With *Voices,* Vélez's kitchen *space* became the site of ethnographic research.

Vélez's appropriation of her kitchen and especially the consequences of this action resonate with bell hooks's argument that the homeplace is a site of resistance for women who have never had a home. Speaking of the legacy of slavery, hooks says, "I want to speak about the importance of homeplace in the midst of oppression and domination, of homeplace as a site of resistance and liberation struggle."[81] The oppression and domination hooks expresses is that felt by black people living under a white supremacist society. "Black women," says hooks, "who for the most part worked outside the home serving white folks, cleaning their houses, washing their clothes, tending their children, . . . returned to their homes to make life happen there."[82] Vélez has made and continues to make life happen in her kitchen *space*. As grandchildren come into her life, she returns to the wisdom of her *sazón*, the corporeal knowledge of the senses.

•••••••••••••••••••••

CHAPTER 2

Sazón

The Flavors of Culinary Epistemology

Irma: The rice needs to be fried, but only until it is light brown. Then, once the rice has reached its exact degree of frying, you just add the tomato sauce and water. Well, you have to know how much water to add, because if you add too much water the rice will have a watery texture. And if you do not add enough water, then the rice will not cook.

María Luisa: How do you know the amount of water?

Irma: Well, I think that is something you learn because I never measure anything. I just add water, and the rice comes out perfect. I guess I learned well. I feel it. I stir the water in the frying pan, and I know.

Meredith: You can calculate just by seeing the water, right?

Irma: No, I think it is in my hand because I just mix the rice [with a spoon] and I know when it needs more water or when it has enough. When I add the water, I stir it. I know. I don't know how I know. That, I could not explain to you.[1]

By using her hand as the measuring utensil, Irma Vásquez knows how much water she needs so her rice cooks to perfection. While confident in the efficiency of her *sazón*, a sensory way of knowing, Vásquez cannot explain the intrinsic logic of her touch. She only knows it works. Vásquez's sensory utensil, in this case her hand, reflects an epistemology based on the faculty of all of the senses: the *sazón,* the language spoken in the kitchen. Once practiced by individuals, the *sazón* becomes their culinary discourse to conceptualize and articulate aspects of their personal and social cultural environment. The kitchen and the *sazón* represent a form of a "sitio y lengua," to quote Emma Pérez, that offers a site of power (the kitchen) and a discourse of empowerment (the *sazón*) to those historically silenced by colonialist, imperialist, and patriarchal social mechanisms.

Yet, finding ways to theorize the *sazón*'s conceptual process, a nonverbal cognitive logic, creates something of a challenge. Speaking metaphorically, a cook's *sazón* is like a gardener's green thumb. With this metaphor, we can understand that the *sazón* refers to the ability someone has to create a rather savory meal out of the simplest ingredients, just as a person with a green thumb can make anything grow. This metaphor, however, does not explain the ability a cook has to know *how* to create a meal out of the simplest ingredients. I am not referring here to the creative/artistic process of cooking; that topic is explored in chapter 3. The question at hand is twofold: how do women guided by their senses, as Irma Vásquez says, know if a meal is cooking at the right temperature, if it has enough water, if it has enough salt; and how do their culinary epistemologies reveal personal aspects of their life stories?

What exactly is the *sazón*? Liduvina Vélez in a number of our *charlas* defines other people's *sazón* as "un don" (a gift some people are born with). For Imelda Silva, what contributes other people's *buen sazón* is their ability to cook non-traditional working class Mexican meals. Talking about her cousin Alicia, Silva says, "My cousin taught me to make ham with pineapple. Macaroni salad. Ribs in barbecue sauce. These are things that I would have not learned because we don't eat them from where I come from. For me, my cousin was a very good cook. I considered her as a very good cook."[2] For Raquel Merlo, it is "la mano de la experiencia" (the hand of experience), and Erica Morales defines it as "el sazón de la mano" (a hand's knowledge).

If having a *sazón* is a gift, perhaps Liduvina Vélez's inclination to humility prevents her from seeing her own *buen sazón* as such. At the age of twenty-three when she sold food out of economic necessity, she says, "Sí tenía clientela. Nó sé, que les gustaba mi sazón. Malaya para el sazón que haya tenido yo, pero sí les gustaba" (Yes, I had customers. I don't know, they liked my *sazón*. I don't think I had a good *sazón,* but they liked what I cooked). Modesty does not keep Vélez from seizing moments of agency by embracing her *buen sazón.* One of the few occasions in which she admits to having a good *sazón* is in the process of making masa for tortillas. When she speaks of making good tortillas, she expresses pride in her expertise. She shares this pride as she tells me how when she was first married, her sisters-in-law were rather surprised that she knew how to make tortillas by hand, from preparing the masa to serving warm tortillas in a basket: "Well, *mi'ja,* it has to do with knowing how to do something well. Even though I was not from the town, that even though I came from where tortillas were not made at home, where you go and buy them, right, well [your father's sisters] were very surprised because they didn't believe that I would know how to make tortillas."[3] Throughout the *charlas,* this is one of the few times that Vélez openly admits to actually having *buen sazón.* The implication of the *sazón* as a *don* (gift) differs not only from one person to another, but at different periods of an individual's life, as is the case with Vélez.

Esperanza Vélez attributes her own "forma del buen sazón" (good ability to cook) to an external religious intervention. Whenever she adds salt to her meals, she says:

> *When I add salt I take it with my fingers, [and] I say in the name of God, and add it to the food in the form of a cross. With my fingers, I can calculate perfectly. I always say, "in the name of God." I do it unconsciously. It's just a habit of mine. I always invoke God. He is either blessing my meals or my ability to calculate. I am so stupid [to cook well on my own] that I need to say, "in the name of God." It is something I do; no one taught me to do so. Maybe because I was so young when I started cooking in my aunt's house, I was about seven when my mother left me there. I had to use a stool, a little wooden chair to reach the stove and the pan. In the* metate, *I would grind tomatoes, or whatever was needed for the soup or other meals of the day. I think that this experience with my aunt is where the gesture of making the cross comes from. Maybe my fear of not doing things well was so strong because if I did things wrong my aunt would hit me. Therefore, unconsciously, I would say, "Oh, dear God, let this come out right." I used to have such fear! Only God could help me so that I would not fail in doing the recipe as my aunt had told me.[4]*

In Esperanza Vélez's explanation of adding salt to food in the form of a cross, she conceptualizes and shares a personal aspect of childhood. The *sazón* in these particular moments of the *charlas* with Esperanza Vélez seems grounded in some source of divine intervention. Since *Voices* speaks about the knowledge these women reveal through our *charlas*, I believe it important to indicate that Esperanza Vélez introduces her "stupid" self-reference with laughter that she knows dismisses the potential claim that she lacks in her cooking abilities.

Her family and friends know Esperanza Vélez for her *forma de buen sazón*. For instance, she says, that while cooking frijoles is one of the simplest things to make, "todo el mundo dice que pa' frijoles los míos, nó" (everyone says that to eat good beans you must have mine, yes). Esperanza Vélez's self-assertiveness reflects her own belief in the ability of her *sazón*. The culinary authority she derives from her *sazón* comes from years of recognition of her gastronomical talent, a recognition she receives from family and friends. Due to Esperanza Vélez's *sazón*, many people ask her to open a restaurant. "People have told me, 'you have a good *sazón*; why don't you open a food business?' No, I don't like that. For me, cooking for a restaurant, for people I don't know, is something I am not interested in doing."[5] Esperanza Vélez cooks because she loves it. "Clases de cocina nunca tomé. Lo que pasa es que a mí me gusta guisar. A mí sí me gusta guisar" (Cooking class, I never took. What happens is that I like to cook. I do like to cook). The assertiveness in talking about or making something she is quite capable of doing well lets her to describe the procedure of cooking beans in a matter-of-fact tone, asserting her sensory knowledge.

I put my beans on the stove; I only put a bit of oil, a piece of onion, and enough water. Enough water so when the beans are cooking you won't need to add any more, at all! Because the trick is that the water you added at the beginning be enough for the beans to cook. Therefore, I add the right amount of water, and I cover them, and then just leave them there. When they are cooked, I check them one more time. When they are almost cooked, I take my salt and I add it to the beans making the sign of the cross. I taste them, if they need more salt, another cross. I taste them again, and let them cook for just a little bit longer, and I turn the stove off. You eat a plate of frijoles de la olla *and*

they would taste wonderful. And if you cook them in the pressure
cooker, they don't have the same flavor.[6]

Esperanza Vélez's knowledge is indicative of someone who believes
in her *sazón*. The *sazón* here captures the notion of *saber* rather
than *conocer*. *Saber* is at an epistemological level while *conocer*
relates more to the technical operation of cooking. These two concepts are not mutually exclusive, and Esperanza Vélez's cooking involves both.

Whether the *sazón* is a *don* (a divine gift) and whether the
meals prepared by those who have it are considered healthy or not,
having a *sazón* certainly involves an acute awareness of a sensory epistemology. The *sazón* captures the finesse, the nuances, the
flair of something that involves a specific chemistry between the
relationship of food, its preparation, and the person preparing it,
a relationship that leads to philosophical everyday observations.
Within the context of Mexican women, the efforts to define the
sazón carry a long history. As a way of illustrating this, I offer the
most prevalent and relevant example. Sor Juana Inés de la Cruz,
a seventeenth-century Mexican nun known nowadays in Mexico
as the intellectual mother of Mexican women, places the kitchen
and cooking as a discursive "sitio y lengua" (space and language)
for women's knowledge, especially in a society, like hers, that denied
women the right to university studies. She indicates that within
the often-mundane practices of cooking, a woman's labor, lies a
wealth of knowledge: cooking offers lessons in chemistry, physics,
and philosophy.

> *Well, and what then shall I tell you . . . of the secrets of nature that*
> *I have learned while cooking? I observe that an egg becomes solid*
> *and cooks in butter or oil, and on the contrary that it dissolves in*
> *sugar syrup. Or again, to ensure that sugar flows freely one need*
> *only add the slightest bit of water that has held quince or some*
> *other sour fruit. The yolk and white of the very same egg are of*
> *such a contrary nature that when eggs are used with sugar, each*
> *part separately may be used perfectly well, yet they cannot be*
> *mixed together. I shall not weary you with such inanities, which*
> *I relate simply to give you a full account of my nature, and I be-*
> *lieve this will make you laugh. But in truth . . . what can we*
> *women know, save philosophies of the kitchen? It was well put by*
> *Lupericio Leonardo [sic] that one can philosophize quite well*

while preparing supper. I often say, when I make these little ob-
servations, "Had Aristotle cooked, he would have written a great
deal more." [7]

Sor Juana uses the kitchen and the practices of cooking as one of
her many tactics to "unmask the semantics of repression" toward
women's knowledge. [8]

Most of the references I have read about Sor Juana's expression
of kitchen philosophy in connection to women's knowledge do not
mention that Sor Juana employs the kitchen and cooking rhetori-
cally. I underscore this observation neither as a criticism of Sor
Juana's quintessential work, which does unveil different ecclesias-
tic and civil layers of repression against women's intellectual freedom, nor to suggest that Sor Juana did not cook, but to illustrate
how in Sor Juana's discursive kitchen space the sense of sight dom-
inates over the other senses. The first obvious reason for the omission of the rest of the *sazón*'s senses is that, unlike the *living*
kitchen of the *charlas,* Sor Juana's kitchen is a *rhetorical* space she
writes about in *La Respuesta* (1691). Perhaps a less obvious reason
is Sor Juana's goal: the right to pursue an intellectual life within
the world of science and literature, which she felt, was *her* calling.
This is a form of knowledge perceived, understood, and conceptualized, for the most part, through the sense of vision. Sor Juana's observation of culinary knowledge, just like Esperanza Vélez's reason
for evoking God when she adds salt to her food, also expresses an
aspect of Sor Juana's own life story: Her personal quest for a textually based intellectual life. The difference between a *rhetorical* and
living kitchen lies in the kind of sensory knowledge used to operate
within such space. Neither Sor Juana nor I define the kitchen as
women's proper place of knowledge. The *sazón* involved in the living
kitchen simultaneity usages of all senses. The argument here illustrates how the knowledge that exists in the process of cooking all
too often gets ignored as irrelevant.

• • • • • • • • • • • • • • • • • • • •
The Historical Division of the Senses

The significant academic attention foodways presently enjoys in the
social sciences and humanities is not prevalent in the area of philosophy. Two reasons account for the absence of philosophical studies

on foodways. First, food and cooking challenge notions of objectivity due to their continuously varying nature. Food and cooking habits change constantly within cultures, regions, families. Second, the responsibility for preparing most meals historically has been the work of women, slaves, or labor workers. In part, these two social issues presumably render food and cooking philosophically insignificant and unreliable for developing theories applicable to all, at all times. These notions reflect the dualism between mind (the objective) and body (the subjective). The separation of mind and body, deemed necessary to achieve knowledge, raises a problematic question, as philosopher Lisa M. Heldke points out: "how can we *knowers* ever know anything which is *that* separate/different from us?"[9] Some philosophers, like Lisa M. Heldke, Deane W. Curtin, and Carolyn Korsmeyer, speculate that if cooking had received more attention from the time philosophies about human nature were beginning to develop, the distinction between theory (mind) and practices (body) might not have taken root. Philosophy, as "a culturally located critique of widely held beliefs using resources, methods, and attitudes present in the culture," argues philosopher Scott L. Pratt, should include as philosophical activities storytelling, ceremonies, treatise-writing, practices accessible to most. Philosophy, states Pratt, is not something only for an elite class of specialist.[10]

The chapter's opening dialogue between Vásquez, Villicaña, and me raises the issue of the senses' ability to transform sensations into forms of knowledge. It also illustrates how Western philosophy, unconsciously perhaps, influences Vásquez and me. Vásquez places her sensory knowledge on *la mano*, her touch, even without having a language to explain such practice. Yet my own inclination privileges sight, as I suggested to Vásquez that she calculates the amount of water when cooking rice by seeing its level in the pan. Our emphasis on different senses as the sources of knowledge reflects the compartmentalization Western thought gives to the senses according to their epistemological faculties.

Anthropologist Paul Stoller in *The Taste of Ethnographic Things* (1989), a study that examines the vital role senses other than vision play in the lives of the Songhay of Niger, offers an explanation for Vásquez's preference for touch as the sense of knowledge and my own quick preference for sight. Hegel, states Stoller, created the lead in "separating the intelligible from the sensible" senses. The "intelligible" incorporates only the senses of vision and hearing, known as the "higher senses"; the "lower senses," by contrast, are taste, smell, and touch. The fundamental distinction is that the "higher senses" are conceived of as objective, whereas the "lower senses" are subjective.[11] The different senses Vásquez and I favored, within Hegel's theory, places touch at the lower level of knowledge and sight at the highest. My suggestion here is not that Vásquez's knowledge is sense-driven and mine logic-driven. Using my own experience, I hope to prove this assumption not to be the case by demonstrating how Western thought influences our relationship to the senses. My academic training leads me to select the sense of sight; Vásquez's culinary experiences lead her to ground her knowledge on a bodily sense.

From the beginning of Western philosophy, the senses were divided in terms of higher and lower, separating sight and hearing as those which contribute to the "highest achievement of human efforts: knowledge, morals, and art."[12] Within these two, sight, for Aristotle, came first. In his words, "All men by nature desire to know. An indication of this is the delight we take in our senses; for even apart from their usefulness they are loved for themselves; and above all others the sense of sight. . . . The reason is that this, most of all the senses, makes us know and brings to light many differences between things."[13] Sight and hearing are distal senses that operate by perceiving and processing world experiences directed outward, away from the immediate body. Seemingly, the detachment from the immediate body makes them sources of objective information, for one can see or hear something "without entering into a relationship with it."[14] With the emergence of scientific culture, the idea of personal detachment in order to gain objective information was further advanced by the emphasis on empirical knowledge. Empirical knowledge, says Stoller, "raised sight to a privileged position," neglecting the other sensory-logic, particularly, touch, taste, and smell.[15] Nietzsche expresses a similar concern as he argues, "Over the course of history, the visual has increasingly taken precedence over elements of thought and action deriving from the other senses (the faculty of hearing and the act of listening, for instance, or the hand and the voluntary acts of 'grasping,' 'holding,' and so on)."[16] Nietzsche goes on to say that the privilege of sight extends to the point "that the senses of smell, taste, and touch have almost completely [been] annexed and absorbed by sight."[17] The consequence of these philosophical views places sight and hearing as the only senses necessary for forming rational, reflective, and theoretical concepts, fundamental in the development of universal truths.

The lower senses—touch, taste, and smell—in contrast to the higher senses, perceive and process world experience in the body. The fact that they are bodily senses renders information gained through them subjective because such sensations vary from person to person. In addition, the senses of taste and smell are considered "primitive." Carolyn Korsmeyer attributes this view to the fact that these senses "evolved for protective purposes necessary for life and to some extent still function that way." While this is true, Korsmeyer points out the negative implications in conceptualizing some senses as "primitive." For one thing, it suggests that they have not progressed beyond their early stages. Also, since they function in a similar manner in lower life forms as in humans, "they are unworthy of extended" philosophical attention. "The danger of the term 'primitive' when applied to taste and smell," argues Korsmeyer, "is that it is very easy to slide from the sense of 'early,' 'basic,' to the sense of 'uncivilized.'" When this takes place, Korsmeyer suggests, "we are back in the territory of the theorists who classify the bodily senses as less worthy from the higher ones on moral grounds." [18] Overindulgence in the bodily senses, closely connected to the desire and pleasure of food, drink, and sex, creates the immorality of the lower senses, for they distract an individual from the path's journey to universal truths. Everything associated with bodily desires that might clutter reason requires control. Consequently, within this dualistic aspect of Western thought, the lower senses connected with the body are easily dismissed as lacking credibility and as not providing empirical forms of knowledge. They are, in the words of Suzanne Langer, "reason's disgrace." [19]

The argument that the so-called lower senses—smell, touch, and taste—have no epistemological value only devalues people's corporeal ways of knowing. Yet this has not always been the case. In *Aroma: The Cultural History of Smell,* Constance Classen, David Howes, and Anthony Synnott (1994) explain that in the premodern West, smell held a different epistemological status that actually challenges modern linear worldview. They explain that "odour was thought of as [an] intrinsic 'essence' revelatory of inner truth. Through smell, therefore, one interacted with interiors, rather than with surfaces, as one did through sight. Furthermore, odours cannot be readily contained; they escape and cross boundaries, blending different entities into olfactory wholes. Such a sensory model can be seen to be opposed to our modern, linear worldview."[20] Since smell and taste are essential in conceptualizing the structures of some societies by taking an outer reality and experiencing it in the body, these senses have been "marginalized because it is felt that [they] threaten the abstract and impersonal regime of modernity by virtue of [their] radical inferiority, [their] boundary-transgressing properties and [their] emotional potency."[21] Stoller, in *Embodying Colonial Memories* (1995), echoes this same argument.[22] The marginalization of the bodily senses dates to the late eighteenth century and early nineteenth century when philosophers and scientists decided that "sight was the preeminent sense of reason and civilization, [and] smell was the sense of madness and savagery."[23] Furthermore, the sense of smell in the nineteenth century became feminized, as it was associated with intuition, sentiment, homemaking, and seduction. The division of the senses, therefore, relates to the philosophical split between thought and practice, the eternal and the temporal, the universal and the particular, the mind and the body, that which is masculine and that which is feminine. As a matter of fact, an implicit gendering separates the senses: "the ability to transcend the body to govern the senses, to gain knowledge, is a masculine ability that when exercised well will keep one embodied as a male. [T]herefore, . . . the higher, distal sense of sight and hearing paired up with the controlling intellect of a virtuous man, and the lower, proximal senses [paired up] with the appetites and the dangerous pleasures that are in one way or another associated with femininity."[24] Such separation is purely philosophical because the faculty of the senses operates the same way in both men and women. What this indicates, however, is a "split between some rather vague concept of femininity associated with the bodily senses and actual females, a split that is responsible for a great deal of incoherence in conceptual frameworks where gender lurks."[25]

Elizabeth Grosz argues that the source of the "crisis of reason" experienced in the twentieth century "is in part a consequence of the historical privileging of the purely conceptual or mental over the corporeal."[26] Even with the basic fundamental differences between the senses, as shown above, sight and hearing projecting reality outside the body and the other senses taking an outer reality into the body, all the senses are connected to a subjective and emotional person.

The *sazón* highlights the conceptual difficulty of the seeming necessity to separate mind and body in the quest of knowledge.[27] In the realm of food and cooking, the *sazón*'s sensory epistemology shows the interconnection of all the senses as cognitive devices. Since food is experienced through all the senses and taken into the body, it rejects the separation of mind and body. Developing spaces for a sensory-logic, for the logic of the *sazón,* alleviates the "crisis of reason" and shows how the "lower senses" are not "reason's disgrace" because the body is a source of cognitive and intuitive knowledge. Stoller suggests that such spaces, within the field of ethnography, are found when researchers do not make the Eurocentric mistake of believing that sight is the only orientation in conceptualizing the world. In some cultures "the senses of taste or smell are more important than vision."[28] A sensory-logic demonstrates that sight and hearing achieved their higher status due to political and economic power and not on their capacity for objective, disembodied epistemologies.[29]

●●●●●●●●●●●●●●●●●●●●●
Food's Social and Scientific Conceptual Knowledge

The *sazón* is a corporeal, sensual knowledge. Yet to understand its epistemology, we must first find ways of gaining back the body as a center of knowledge. The *sazón*'s sensory-logic, inseparable from food, thus inseparable from the body, values the ordinary, as the activity of cooking and eating, which in turn lead to regain a sense of ourselves as cognitive bodily creatures. If one way the mind controls the body is through the denial of food, which extends to the denial of corporeal knowledge, in embracing food as central to the development of philosophies, the body becomes a source of knowledge.[30] Since food is the "most common and pervasive source of human experience," food as a source of knowledge goes beyond an individual's likes and dislikes.[31] To understand the *sazón*'s corporeal knowledge, philosopher Michel de Certeau's concept of a "science of singularities" is useful since it studies the relationship of everyday practices to particular circumstances, and the local networks that are constantly affected by social-economic constraints.[32] We can say, then, that the corporeal knowledge involved in the practice of everyday cooking offers a way of thinking about food, as philosopher Uma Narayan says, that "can help reveal the rich and messy textures of our attempts at self-understanding, as well as our interesting and problematic understanding of our relationship" to and with others.[33] These are relationships experienced in the body.

In *Food, the Body, and the Self* (1996), Deborah Lupton theorizes about the interaction among food, embodiment, and subjectivity. Lupton argues that this interaction combines cognitive discourses and "non or pre-discursive sensual and embodied experiences [by which] individuals come to understand themselves, their bodies, and their relationships to the food they are eating. Touch, taste, smell, hearing, and sight are our entrées into culture. Food, of course, has a supremely physical presence, and we interact with this presence through our senses: we smell, taste, see, and touch food, and sometimes hear it (for example, the sizzling of frying food). We do not necessarily need language and discourse to experience food. However, language and discourse are integral to the meanings we construct around food—how we interpret and convey to others our sensual experiences in preparing, touching, and eating food—which in turn shape our sensual responses."[34] Sensual responses, a combination of cognitive and embodied experiences, inform philosophies that come out from people's specific cultural and historical realities. The grassroots theorists from the *charlas* place food and sensory logic, the *sazón*, at the center of culinary knowledge, calling into question how much the so-called lower senses have in fact been annexed and absorbed by sight, as Nietzsche suggests.

Hilaria Cortés, in a brief moment of our *charlas*, indicates that perhaps sight only absorbs the other senses when a person does not have, as she says, "la costumbre" of using and valuing all the senses as sources of knowledge. When Cortés and I broached the topic of cookbooks and recipes that call for exact measurements and procedures, first Cortés admits to not owning any cookbooks, then she says, "It depends on people's custom. Here, Americans are more civilized people; it's the correct way, right? The measurement. But when you don't have time to measure or when you don't have the curiosity to measure, it doesn't matter. Because you have the measurement in the feel of your hands and in your precision of vision. All you need is your eyes and your hands. But if you don't have the right feeling in your hand, or the right sense of vision, well then you will need to measure. But if you have such [forms] of calculating [with your hand and eyes], you don't need measuring utensils."[35] Cortés's comments question the validity of adhering to just one form of epistemological understanding. Cortés acknowledges that cooking with scientific precision involves money and time. To cook with scientific precision, women are expected to employ every machine, device, or apparatus as these become items of *necessity*. The concept of time, feminist geographer Massey reminds us, "is aligned with history, progress, civilization, politics, transcendence, and [thus] coded masculine. And it is the opposite of these things which have . . . been coded feminine."[36] Cortés echoes this association in terms of nationalities as she connects the measuring utensil with the correct civilized form employed by American people. The marketing strategies of consumption, the ideologies of first world superiority (Americans) over third world inferiority (Mexicans) control scientific culinary methodologies and not the sense of sight in and of itself.

Scientific discourse, with its precise culinary measurements that rely on the sense of sight, aims to legitimize itself as the only efficient culinary practice, thus eliminating the *sazón*'s sensory-logic, based on all of the senses. Cortés's comment indicates the fallacy of such an assumption by placing in a parallel continuum both sight *(el ojo)* and touch *(la mano)* as forms of sensory epistemology. Cortés bases this form of knowledge in "la costumbre," a continuous participation in the culture of the senses. For Cortés, one only needs measuring utensils if one does not have *el tantéo* (the calculation of the hand); thus she provides a distinction between the efficiency of material utensils and dexterity. If a person lacks understanding of the epistemology of all the senses, then such a person must depend on material apparatus. Cortés emphasizes culinary methods and procedures that differ according to culture and class. This correlation of all the senses is found throughout the *charlas*.

The *sazón* relies on an interconnection of all the senses, sight always included but not necessary privileged. The grassroots theorists from the *charlas* do what some contemporary academics suggest the study of food and cooking illustrates: the inseparability of the senses and their collective cognitive function. Yet some academics, including me, continue to draw a separation due to our tendency for binary thinking despite our best intentions to do otherwise. For example, in the first *charla* with Vélez, once again it was I who privileged sight over the other senses. As she describes the process for making masa for tortillas she says:

> To let the ears of corn became maize, you don't cut them from the plant. Leave them there until they turn yellow, until the leaves

*are dry. Then you can cut them. Then you remove the grains
from the cob, and you make the corn dough. You cook the grains
in water to which you add some unslaked lime. But you have to
know how much unslaked lime to add; you need to know how
strong it should be . . . because if you add too much lime, the
masa would turn out yellow, and it would taste bad. Therefore,
you have to know how much unslaked lime to add to the water.
And you also have to know what is the right degree of cooking.
To know if the grains of corn are cooked, take one and if its skin
comes off, then it's done. Then you take it off the stove. You leave
it sitting in the water until the next day. The next day, you drain
it and grind it.*[37]

Since Vélez mentions the importance of knowing exactly how much
unslaked lime one must add to the water when soaking corn to make
masa, I asked her how I would know the *quantity*, empirical means
of knowledge, of unslaked lime to add. She looked at me with an expression that made me feel I had asked a rather obvious question.
She did answer my question. Extending one of her hands, she
showed me her palm while with the other she made a gesture as if
gathering unslaked lime out of a sack and pouring it into her open
palm and said: "te la pones así, la sientes pa' calcular" (you put it
in like this; you feel it in order to calculate). Vélez's culinary knowledge goes beyond touch as the necessary sense for making masa.
Not only "la mano" determines the amount of lime but also smell.
Touch, to weigh the unslaked lime, and smell, to determine the right
potency, correspond in importance with the sense of taste and sight.
Too much lime and the tortillas turn out yellow, and they taste bad.

Contreras not only affirms the equality of the senses, but she
also questions my own insistence in determining quantities by a
process of using measuring utensils. While giving me a list of "add
this and add that" to a boiling pot in the process of making *pozole*,
I stopped her and asked for quantities:

Meredith: *And quantities, how do you know? You say, "I put this
and I add that." But how much? Portions. How do you know?*
Alma: *I don't know about quantities because that is something I just
calculate.*
Meredith: *How do you calculate? How do you know?*
Alma: *Well, depending on how much I am making. Onion. I use
a whole onion if I am making a big pot. I add salt, and that*

*is determined by taste. Everyone can determine the amount of
salt according to their taste. Some people like food more salty
than others do. Chile. Normally one bag. If I want it very spicy,
two bags.*³⁸

Once again, as with other women in the *charlas,* for Contreras cooking by calculation does not mean just touch but an integration of
different senses. As the women from the *charlas* describe their culinary practices, it is evident that they have not forgotten the importance of the so-called lower senses.

The *sazón's* cognitive sensory-logic involves foods' chemical reactions learned from many years of experimenting in the kitchen.
After Contreras shares her two ways of making American or Mexican beans, she says that for beans not to turn brown, if they need
water while cooking, the water must be hot. Hilaria Cortés,
Liduvina Vélez, Guadalupe Flores, Alicia Villanueva, and Esperanza Vélez confirm this process when we broach the topic of cooking beans. Throughout the *charlas* there are numerous examples
revealing a sophisticated awareness of food's chemistry. María
Luisa Cárdenas learned from her mother, who would grow her own
vegetables, that in the process of preparing cabbage for tostadas
one must chop it early in the day and add baking soda. According to
Cárdenas's mother, this was "para materle los animalitos" (to kill
all the insects it might have). We have already seen some chemical
culinary understanding in Liduvina Vélez's knowledge of adding
unslaked lime to water for soaking maize.

Esperanza Vélez expresses a similar knowledge when she gives
me a recipe for making *pipián verde* (pumpkin-seed sauce). When
making this sauce, she says that one must add enough oil to the frying pan and add salt to the pan, "para que no te brinquen tanto
porque es un brincadero tremendo" (so that the seeds do not scatter
all over the place). One must know to what degree the seeds must
be fried, if they over fry "se te amargan" (they taste bitter).

Meredith: *[If you over fry them], do they taste bitter like garlic does?*
Esperanza: *Correct, the seeds have the same reaction as garlic. If
they are over fried, they will taste bitter; they will burn, and the
seed will have a different color and a different taste. It does not
require much [time or ingredients] to prepare* pipián *and it is so
good. Whenever I have to visit someone and bring a dish, people
say, "Oh,* señora *you have to bring the* pipián verde." "Esperanza,*

you have to bring the pipián verde?" *Why? Because everyone
loves [my]* pipián verde.
Meredith: *Have you eaten other people's* pipián?
Esperanza: *Yes.*
Meredith: *And does it come out different?*
Esperanza: *Well, it is not the same thing.*[39]

Perhaps one reason many people like and request Esperanza
Vélez's *pipián verde* is because she knows yet another chemical reaction involved in preparing it. She explains that this sauce separates if the hands of different people get involved in the process of
cooking it. In Vélez's words, "Es que es un guisado muy especial que
no permite que otra gente le meta mano" (It's a special dish that
does not let other people stick their hands in). Erika Morales
shared a similar observation when we discussed the process of making *barbacoa Veracruzana.* A key ingredient for this Veracruz-style
barbecue, made either with beef, pork, or chicken, is a leaf called
"acuyo." *Acuyo* comes from a tropical tree native of the region of Veracruz, similar in taste to avocado leaves. Morales says that "no más
no debe de pasar [el punto de cocerse] de la hoja porque es muy
hostigoza" (you must know the right amount of time to cook the leaf
because if overcooked it tastes cloying).

Why does adding salt to a frying pan prevent the squash seeds
from bursting out of the pan? Why does the *pipian* sauce separate if
someone other than the cook stirs it? Why does overcooking *acuyo*
make it taste *hostigozo?* Why when cooking *maíz* to make masa, as
Liduvina Vélez mentions above, is it necessary to know the right ra-
tio of unslaked lime and water to soak *maíz?* None of the women from
the *charlas* gave me a specific scientific explanation for these chemical reactions. But nowadays, in the case of soaking *maíz* with unslaked lime when preparing it for making masa for tortillas, scientific research proves that this process of dissolving unslaked lime
in water increases "the calcium content to at least twenty times that
in the original maize while possibly increasing the availability of certain amino acids."[40] The tortilla eaters of Mesoamerica have been the
only group of people to use *maíz* as their main item of diet who have
not suffered from the plague of pellagra. Arnold J. Bauer explains
that "among dedicated corn eaters the sole exception to the plague of
pellagra were the people of Meso-America and the humble tortilla
claims substantial credit. Maize is low in pellagra-preventing niacin

and, moreover, what is present exists in a chemically bound form. The addition of lime, however, frees the bound niacin so there is some evidence for the beneficial effect of this treatment. More important was the practice of eating tortillas in conjunction with beans and chiles, which provide protection against pellagra."[41]

Bauer is not convinced that the pre-Columbian people were consciously adding lime for nutritional reasons for *maíz*. Liduvina Vélez, like millions of peasant people throughout the years, however, without conducting laboratory studies and without the scientific discourse of pellagra-preventing niacin, guided by her sensory-logic developed a fairly well balanced diet gathered from both *la costumbre*, a sensory culture, and her limited local resources.

The *sazón*'s cognitive aspects also involve a social dimension. Multiculturalism, for instance, according to food historian Donna Gabaccia, in *We Are What We Eat: Ethnic Food and the Making of Americans* (1998), is something we experience *in* our bodies by the foods we are willing to eat. Gabaccia states that for Americans "multicultural is not so much its many separate culinary traditions as it is Americans' desire to eat a multi-ethnic mix of foods, and to make this mix part of themselves."[42] In this case, the experience of multicultural politics takes place *in* the body. In the *charlas,* something similar takes place when women define aspects of their cooking practices in terms of ethnic or national politics. A number of women from the *charlas* express some effects of this form of multiculturalism in their process of cooking and the intake of such foods. For instance, Contreras expresses two forms of cooking beans as Mexican and American; their distinction is not only in terms of color but also in how much time it takes to cook them. Contreras prepares either "güeritos" (white) beans or "prietitos" (brown) beans by simply altering the cooking method.

Alma: *I never measure the water. But the recipe so that beans don't turn out brown is that once they begin to boil you must turn the heat down and cover them. Slowly they cook by themselves; I don't add more water. Therefore, they take longer to cook, but they come out white. Therefore, when I feel like having American beans, I do them this way. When I feel like having Mexican beans, I do them fast. I keep adding and adding water so that they cook fast and they come out brown.*
Meredith: *But why some American and some Mexican?*

Alma: *The Americans are white and the Mexicans are brown. . . .* *Therefore, it depends on how much time you have [to cook them].*[43]

In the process of cooking beans, Contreras differentiates between American (white) beans and Mexican (brown) beans. American beans, "güeritos," are associated with a certain amount of excess time. Mexican beans, "prietos," are associated with a lifestyle "on-the-run." The pigmentation of beans and this supposed representation of national identities reflects a racial stereotype. Contreras, as a Mexican woman living in the United States, however, does not adhere to the divisiveness of the stereotype. In her description of cooking beans, Contreras does not select one over the other. She cooks beans using both procedures, and she eats them both, a culinary symbolic acceptance of both cultures. Her cooking habits are not traditional in the sense that she eats Mexican food. As a matter of fact, while she has a habit of eating out a lot, she rarely goes to Mexican restaurants. She prefers to go, as she says, "a la comida china, las pastas, las ensaladas" (Chinese food, pastas, salads). But she also has a genuine appetite for "enchiladas, pozole, albóndigas, and sopitos."

Cortés speaks of yet another way of how through her cooking process she appropriates the food of "los americanos" (the Americans) and makes it "comida de la raza mexicana" (food of Mexican people). This dialogue takes place as I asked her about the time she used to sell hot dogs.

Meredith: *Tell me, how did you do selling hot dogs?*

Yaya: *Sometimes good, sometimes bad. Well, selling hot dogs you can make some good money if you find the right place to sell. If you find a good place where there are Hispanics, but mainly Mexicans because if they are Salvadoran, you won't sell hot dogs.*

Meredith: *Why do you think that's the case?*

Yaya: *Because Salvadorans only buy traditional things from their country. Pupusas, fried bananas with beans. All those things. You can't sell hot dogs to them. But if there are Mexicans, hot dogs sell well.*

Meredith: *But why if hot dogs are not our own food?*

Yaya: *No but they are "perros calientes" of our country. Just change the name from hot dogs to "perros calientes" of our country. . . . Before, I used to sell a lot of hot dogs. Now, I have not sold them* *for a long time. Since I now live in a new place, and there are mainly Salvadorans where I live.*[44]

The inversion of "hot dogs" to "perros calientes" takes away the symbolic American association of this food, making it Mexican, especially since they are cooked with a strip of bacon around them, grilled onions, and a salsa of cooked tomatoes, onion, and *serrano chiles* instead of ketchup. Here, Cortés also indicates that multiculturalism's ability to enter our bodies has its limits; Salvadorans from her neighborhood in Los Angeles are not as open to accepting "perros calientes" as Mexicans are. Food's social conception is one that every chapter of *Voices* explores in different forms.

The *sazón's* sensory-logic is not constrained to an unchanging methodological or conceptual paradigm. Contreras stresses the particularities and subjective elements of sensory knowledge as she says "cualquiera puede calcular al gusto" (anyone can calculate to their taste). The social meaning of the *sazón* changes *al gusto* (to the taste of each person). By acknowledging people's own understanding of *al gusto,* Contreras admits that sensory knowledge *is* subjective and a matter of perspective. Using *al gusto* as a feminist culinary theoretical concept, we can clearly illustrate that knowledge is always subjective and not based on a separation between the mental and the physical. Elizabeth Grosz argues that "to admit that knowledges are but perspectives—points of view on the world—is to acknowledge that other, quite different positions and perspectives are possible." Grosz goes on to say that one must accept the diverse series of influences, "some rational, some not, some universal, some highly particularized" in the production and nature of knowledge.[45] The *sazón* as a corporal knowledge is not an inversion of the senses' higher/lower status. What most of the grassroots theorists from the *charlas* change is the senses' hierarchical, vertical paradigm into a concept that places all five senses in horizontal parallel lines.

The grassroots theorists' concept of *al gusto* resonates with postmodern and poststructuralist discourses of subjectivity. Generally speaking, postmodernism inclines "toward the unstable, fluid, fragmented, indeterminate, . . . for that which resists definition, closure, and fixity."[46] Likewise, poststructuralist theory examines the social construction of the nature of knowledge. It emphasizes the centrality of language in understanding social interactions without forgetting the fluidity in the meaning of language as a source of communication. Poststructuralists influenced by post-modernism provide a theoretical lens to see that our identity is not a unified self but rather a multitude of fragments that make up our subjectivity. The term subjectivity describes "the manifold ways in which individuals understand themselves in relation to others and experience their lives. Subjectivity is a less rigid term than identity, as it incorporates the understanding that the self, or more accu-rately, selves, are highly chargeable and contextual, albeit within certain limits imposed by the culture in which an individual lives, including power relations, social institutions and hegemonic dis-courses."[47] *Al gusto* suggests this particular concept of subjectivity, since food habits reflect much about our sense of self. When the wo-men from the *charlas* say that *al gusto* one adds salt, chile, onion, garlic to one's cooking, they speak of people's notion of a fluid sense of self using terms of the *sazón*'s sensual-logic of subjectivity.

The *al gusto* embedded in the *sazón* is where individuals' life stories are revealed. The *sazón* with its *al gusto* subjective, corporal intrinsic logic leads to investigations of "life stories of individuals as opposed to totalizing investigations."[48] Such type of investigation enables us to understand how individuals are able to assert agency even when their lives faced social, economic, or gender challenges. The *sazón*'s element of *al gusto*, using Luce Giard's words, can be defined as how each woman creates "her own style according to how she accents a certain element of a [cooking] practice, [of] how she applies herself to one or another [method of cooking, of] how she creates her personal way of navigating through [already] accepted, allowed, and ready-made [cooking] techniques."[49] To this list of defining a woman's *sazón*, I add invention, or piecing together, of new cross-cultural and geo-social culinary techniques. In this new-ness, subversion to establish social "norms" takes place.

During the *charlas,* for example, all the women speak of the im-plications of modernization and how technology can, does, and must alter cultural and traditional practices. In the *charlas,* Mexi-can traditions and cultural practices can be spoken of as culture-in-transition. One reference to this transition is the use of microwaves or toaster ovens in order to expedite Contreras's own process of making enchiladas. As Contreras explains her process of making enchiladas, she indicates how many people, in order to sit down and eat together, normally would make a lot of enchiladas and put them in the oven. Later they put everything on the table and they eat. Contreras, however, does not like them this way.

Duvi: *Well, it is more work to be making them as people are eating. But they taste better; their steamy flavor.*
Meredith: *But with the other way, everybody can sit together.*
Alma: *Yes, but I don't like them that way. I like the enchiladas to be almost crisp. Not soggy.*
Meredith: *And when do you eat?*
Duvi: *At the end.*
Alma: *At the end. When everyone is done, I prepare mine. Or I try to make them fast so that there might still be one person eating who would eat with me.*
Duvi: *And in the micro, mi'ja. Maybe in the micro it would work.*
Alma: *No, where it would work very well is in those little toaster ovens. Maybe in those ovens, it might work because they would be the same. I have heated tamales in the little toaster ovens and they are good. Better than if you use the microwave.*[50]

In this segment of our *charla,* both Liduvina Vélez and Alma Contreras believe in a certain methodological process of making enchiladas to achieve a perfect *al gusto* taste, texture, and flavor that is characteristic of Contreras's own *sazón.* This moment of our *charla* shows how the interconnection of some modern techniques in the process of making enchiladas does not significantly alter Contreras's own *al gusto* style of enchiladas, known in my house as "las famosas enchiladas de Alma" (Alma's famous enchiladas).

Another dish discussed in a number of *charlas* that indicates personal stories as people add their own *al gusto* are *chilaquiles. Chilaquiles* is a rather simple meal, nothing more than fried tortillas, salsa, cheese, cream, and, if they are to be authentic, one must add a few leaves of epazote. Although *chilaquiles* are simple to make, it is not simple to make them with *sazón.* Verónica Abarca, my sister-in-law, for instance, tells me that although her mother makes wonderful *chilaquiles,* she herself cannot: "Mi mamá hace los chilaquiles ¡deliciosos! Nó, nó, yo nó sé hacer chilaquiles. Nó sé por qué, pero nó me salen" (My mother makes delicious *chilaquiles.* No, I don't know how to make them. When I make them they don't turn out well). Abarca explains her mother's procedure in making *chilaquiles;* therefore, her inability to make them is not based on not understanding culinary technicalities. In her case, the lack of her *sazón,* as she explains in our *charla,* is perhaps based on her own disinterest in the discipline of culinary studies, a discipline where her own mother finds much pleasure. Abarca says, "Well, cooking is something that my mother enjoys. Something that I don't enjoy. Well, when I lived at home, she would tell me, 'come and see so that you can cook when you get married.' I hated the kitchen. I have never, never liked to cook."[51]

When Vélez speaks of her own *chilaquiles,* she says that "la gracia de los chilaquiles es que te queden las tortillas doraditas, pero no fritas" (the trick of the *chilaquiles* is in frying the tortillas to the right degree). Vélez's *sazón* for *chilaquiles* is not obtained by following a prescriptive culinary method, after all, Vélez claims that everyone has their own style of making *chilaquiles,* their own *al gusto.* In the particular case of Vélez's *chilaquiles,* her *sazón* captures and articulates the sense of her working-class roots. Vélez always categorizes her *chilaquiles* as "la comida de uno de pobre" (the food of we the poor). When I taste the *sazón* in "los chilaquiles de mi 'amá," I am always reminded of her intelligence, ingenuity, and, most of all, her courage, all of which she reveals in her *sazón* as she cooks *la comida de uno de pobre.* The trajectory of Vélez's culinary knowledge and her personal use of it, as discussed in the last section of the previous chapter, demonstrate the acts of agency embedded on the *sazón.* In my own making of *chilaquiles,* my *sazón* serves as a savory expression of my feelings toward my adopted families, the only ones with the reserved privilege to enjoy my *chilaquiles* as they are an integral part of my life. Each person's *sazón,* therefore, carries personal, cultural, and social messages that exceed the preparation of a meal.

The *sazón*'s sensory-logic manifests itself through bodily techniques. The *charlas* demonstrate how "doing-cooking," Luce Giard's words, is in fact as much a mental activity as it is a manual labor. Giard defines the activity of doing-cooking, as one that requires intelligence, imagination, and a twofold memorization: one of gestures and the other of senses. A study of women's process of doing-cooking, as we have seen, and will continue to see throughout *Voices,* leads to a study of women's "subtle intelligence which is full of nuances and strokes of genius."[52] Understanding such intelligence involves an awareness of the memory process necessary for a culinary production. Giard categorizes memory into three distinctive processes: apprenticeship, programming, and sensory perception. Memory of apprenticeship refers to "the witness of gestures"; a programming memory operates the astute calculation of both preparation and cooking time, and a memory of sensory perception is more important "than the theoretical cooking time indicated in the recipe; it is the smell coming from the oven that lets one know if the cooking is coming along" as it should be.[53] The memory of apprenticeship requires the performance of two specific culinary gestures, technical and expressive, which involve the "movement[s] of the body as well as the mind." Technical gestures are "inhabited by a necessity (material or symbolic), a meaning and a belief." Whether a technical gesture requires a tool, as a knife, or only the bare hands, it "calls for an entire mobilization of the body," therefore, it is a body technique. The technical gesture expresses "invention, tradition, and education to give [gestures] a form of efficacy that suits the physical makeup and practical intelligence of the person who uses [them]."[54] Of expressive gestures, Giard simply says that they "translate a feeling or a reaction."[55]

In the *charlas,* both technical and expressive gestures are inseparable. A number of women mentioned the *metate* and the *mano,* a sort of mortar and pestle, used to grind corn as well as chiles, nuts, chocolate, and other things. The *metate* is a wide, flat rectangular surface that resembles a three-legged table with the front two legs shorter than the back leg; the *mano,* the hand, is a long semicircular stone, both usually made of basalt rock. The *metate* itself, in many households, is a symbol of familial history. Alicia Villanueva says that part of her inheritance, of the legacy her mother is leaving to her, is "el metate." Villanueva will inherit her mother's *metate* since she is the youngest daughter. Cortés, when speaking of the history of her aunt's *metate,* the one her mother has always used, says, "The *metate* my aunt has belonged to her grandmother, my great-grandmother. It's like a hundred and thirty years, or more! If my aunt is ninety, and her grandmother gave it to her. Imagine!"[56] One can only imagine the stories engraved in those two pieces of stone with the *sazón* of all the women who have used it in the course of a hundred years—or more![57]

When women in the *charlas* speak about the use of the *metate,* commonly referred to as the Mexican blender, they address how their mothers have mastered the bodily technique involved in using the *metate.* While Alicia Villanueva's mother masters the skill of the *metate-mano,* her own leaves much to be desired: "My mom . . . knows how to make a very good red sauce. She grinds everything using the *metate*. When all of us went in 1990, I tried to help her. She made *mole* for all of us. I tried to help her grind. I saw how easily she would grind using the *metate*. I told her, 'let me help you, *amacita*.' I was not able to grind anything! The chile kept coming out whole. I would put pressure on it and move the *mano* of the *metate* in different ways, and the chile would remain whole. When she did it, everything would be finely ground."[58] As Villanueva remembers her mother's ability to make the chile into powder, she brings one of her hands toward her mouth making a sound with her lips as if giving a kiss, and says, "de acordarme qué rico le sale el mole" (just to remember how delicious her *mole* is).

Irma Vásquez offers an explanation that reveals the uniqueness of her own mother's technical and expressive gestures in using the *metate*—a uniqueness that explains Villanueva's own savory gesture as she remembers her mother's *sazón* for making *mole*. When Vásquez shares her mother's recipe that she likes the best, she immediately says, "Meat with chile sauce. She would fry the meat, and she would always grind chiles *guajillos* and also chile *pasilla*. She would grind them with the *metate*. I think that's what gave it its special flavor, that she would always use the *metate*. Even if she had an electric blender, she would always grind her chiles, and corn for making masa with the *metate*. I think this is what gave her *mole* its special flavor. Because otherwise, the meat with chile sauce is the same thing we make. Clean the meat then cook the chiles. But the only difference is that we put it in the blender. She doesn't. She would always make it with the *metate*."[59] The sense of touch involved in the process of grinding spices in the *metate* reveals "the complexity of the gastrula realm [which] embraces an essentially indefinite . . . variety of codes."[60] For Vásquez and Villanueva, with each gesture of pounding the *mano* into the *metate,* their respective mothers transmit an essence of themselves into the sauces they prepare. Marcel Mauss in *The Gift* argues a similar point in relation to an economy of reciprocal gift giving. Mauss says that "to give something is to give a part of oneself. . . . [O]ne gives away what is in reality a part of one's nature and substance, while to receive something is to receive a part of someone's spiritual essence."[61] When Vásquez and Villanueva eat or remember the taste of their mothers' *mole*, a part of their mothers enters their own being. The use of the body, of the hand, converts their mothers' food into soul food. The expressive gesture that transmits a feeling would get lost if instead of the *metate* and the direct use of the bare hand, Vásquez and Villanueva's mothers would use an electric blender. Vásquez and Villanueva's mothers' *sazón* and their daughters' remembrance of it is given and received through the sensual, corporeal knowledge of the *sazón*. Villanueva certainly feels strongly about this matter: "When we go, . . . she loves to make *mole* for us. And she uses the *metate*. Now she has an electric blender, and she is also getting old. But she loves to grind using the *metate*." [62]

While both Vásquez and Villanueva's mothers have electric blenders, when making *mole* for their families, they refuse to deprive themselves of their *sazón* and refuse to become what Giard calls "*unskilled spectator[s]* who watch the machine function in [their] place." [63] Giard's argument carries a tone of lamentation. She feels that modern technological instruments deny a cook the ability to use her dexterity and display her ingenuity. The connection I see between the *sazón* and bodily movement, the use of the hands without many industrial appliances, is that heavy dependency on such equipment diminishes our ability to rely on all of our senses as the guide of our culinary knowledge, a guide of social interactions and philosophical observations. Technical appliances primarily demand that we use our sense of sight and for the most part ignore the rest of the senses. The ultimate effect, therefore, is that many people begin to forget the sensory-logic and discourse of the *sazón*, which is based in the interconnection of all the senses.

One effective way of forgetting such an interconnection of all the senses is to rely too much on textually based knowledge. The more a person relies on textually based knowledge, as following directions in a cookbook requires, the more the cognitive sensory-logic of the *sazón* and confidence to cook *al gusto* gets lost. The more a person depends on cookbooks that rely on the sense of sight, the less that person grounds her/his knowledge within the epistemology of the other senses and body techniques or gestures. Contreras indicates this effect on the senses in relation to the two of us when she questions my reliance on textually based culinary knowledge. Contreras says, "I never write down measurements. You also cook only by calculating. Or do you use measurements? I don't think you go and look at the recipe. [I] don't base my cooking on a book and having to look at what must be added next in a recipe." [64] Her question to me, which suggests a suspicion regarding measuring utensils, and her answer reflect a validation of her *sazón*. Interestingly, Contreras can only recreate *al gusto* those recipes learned through her *sazón*'s sensory-logic and the memory embedded in body gestures but not those recipes described and prescribed on a written text. When she recalls a carrot and orange cake that once she loved to make and made it a lot, she says:

> *The ingredients. Well, you prepare flour, egg, and this thing so the cake can rise. You add carrots and orange, the skin of the orange. And you put it in the oven. And it turns out really good.*
> **Meredith:** *And where did you learn this recipe?*
> **Alma:** *From a recipe in a book. But ask me to make this cake again, I don't remember how to make it that well. But I used to make it a lot.*[65]

Much culinary literature indicates that baking, unlike other forms of cooking, does require the precision of measurements. While this could explain Contreras's example, other women from the *charlas* also indicate that recipes initially learned from cookbooks can only be recreated by looking at the written text again. Yet those recipes learned through their sensory-logic remain guided by the *sazón*. On numerous occasions throughout the *charlas*, the *sazón*'s corporeal knowledge remains more important than cookbooks' inscribed knowledge.[66]

Many grassroots theorists do participate in the network of sharing recipes, yet, while some of them are shared in written form, many are not. Even those recipes shared in writing often omit exact quantities. As a matter of fact, many of these women do not have an index card container filled with recipes or a collection of cookbooks. After Esperanza Vélez describes the procedures of numerous recipes that range from cooking beans, to *pipián verde, pipián rojo, chiles en nogada, pozole, tinga, el mole verde, sopas de cremas, adobado,* and so on, I asked her about the collection of recipes she has gathered throughout her lifelong practice in culinary matters.

> **Meredith:** *Tell me, all these recipes, do you have them written in a book or you know them by memory?*
> **Esperanza:** *No. I know them by memory. I don't have them written down. I know them by memory.*[67]

Like Esperanza Vélez, Liduvina Vélez, who in Mexico once sold food outside her house and later managed a restaurant where the menu changed daily, did not collect or depend on written recipes. When I ask Liduvina Vélez about written recipes she says, "Here with you is where I came to see cookbooks. Here in the houses where I'm working. And in the restaurant where I was working, the Bay Window [in California]."[68] When I asked Susana García viuda de Melo, owner of a small mini-cocina situated within the property of her home, if she had a recipe that she would call her own, one that she has invented, she addressed my question by asking her daughter to answer.

Meredith: *If is okay with you, could you speak to me about your recipes?*
Susana: *To speak of my recipes, yes of course.*
Meredith: *Do you have a recipe that you have invented? Something that you say, "This is mine?"*[69]

García viuda de Melo smiles a little, asks me to wait and calls her daughter, Vero, and asks her to answer my question:

Vero: *She invents everything!*
Meredith: *She invents everything?*
Susana: *Tell her.*
Vero: *She can invent anything. The other day she made ribs in barbecue. She put a thousand things in it. Whatever she has at hand, she adds and complements flavors. She uses whatever she has, whatever she has bought.*[70]

Almost as a way to prove her ingenuity, her subtle intelligence, García viuda de Melo gets her daughter to testify to her inventive nature. While she did share very specific recipes with me, she recalled them all by memory. The source of García viuda de Melo's inventive *sazón* is her skillful business sense. As she says, she has to cook food that goes a long way since people like to eat a lot for very little money. Susana García viuda de Melo gives us yet another social manifestation of her *sazón*'s sensory-logic.

I close this chapter by changing the question I asked at the beginning: "What is the *sazón?*" to "How does one develop a *sazón?*" The *sazón* is the ability to "seize power over one part of oneself" through the epistemology of all our senses, which in turn helps us regain the body as a center of knowledge.[71] The power of the *sazón* to conceptualize and articulate aspects of social reality has been overlooked by privileging the faculties of sight and hearing. These faculties *are* of fundamental importance in a textually and visually based society like ours. Yet, to categorize the faculties of smell, taste, and touch as less valuable blinds us to the richness and complexity of the ordinary aspects of life, such as food, that make our personal and collective lives meaningful. The epistemologies of all the senses are not only important when studying non-Western societies, they are crucial when studying all societies. Taste and sound and smell, Stoller points out, "are all part of one's experience, [of] one's knowledge of the world, knowledge every bit as important—sometimes more so—than the facts one articulates mentally or verbally."[72] In numerous theoretical and philosophical arguments contesting the privilege sight has had in Western thought, theorists and philosophers formulate their analysis in a model of binary oppositions: the so-called lower senses, taste, smell, and touch, and the "higher" ones, sight and sound.[73] The first set expresses living experiences while the latter is viewed as the senses that assist in obtaining scientific proof; thus, sight is needed for discursive textual expression. The grassroots theorists from the *charlas* participate actively in the culture of the *sazón,* which rejects the binarism of higher and lower senses.

Liduvina Vélez (Duvi) preparing *chiles rellenos* with goat cheese for her daughter's (Meredith E. Abarca) birthday dinner. Meredith's kitchen in El Paso, Texas, 2004. *Photo by Lucy Fischer-West.*

Alma Contreras getting ready to go eat at a restaurant. Alma's home in Menlo Park California, 2000. *Photo provided by Contreras.*

Esperanza Vélez
serving a plate of "love"
to her mother, **Aurora
Larios,** while visiting her
sister, Guadalupe Flores.
Guadalupe's kitchen
in Laredo, Texas, 2003.
Photo by the author.

Guadalupe Flores drying
dishes after a large family
meal gathering at her
house. Guadalupe's kitchen
in Laredo, Texas, 2003.
Photo by the author.

Hilaria Cortés (Yaya) chopping cilantro
to flavor and garnish her meal. Yaya's
kitchen in Los Angeles, California, 2003.
Photo by the author.

María Luisa Villicaña and **Irma Vásquez** eating a tossed salad and *mole poblano* and drinking *agua de orchata*. Duvi's kitchen in Menlo Park, California, 2003. *Photo by the author.*

Susana García viuda de Melo and her granddaughter making *chiles en nogada*. Susana's kitchen in Puebla, Mexico. *Photo provided by García viuda de Melo.*

María Luisa Cárdenas eating grilled salmon at Guadalupe's house. Guadalupe's kitchen in Laredo, Texas, 2003. *Photo by the author.*

Lucy Fischer-West, center, frying tortillas for *huevos rancheros* and **Meredith E. Abarca,** left, frothing chocolate with a *molinillo*. Lucy's kitchen in El Paso, Texas, 2002. *Photo by John Martin West.*

Alicia Villanueva visiting and drinking coffee at Duvi's house. Duvi's kitchen in Menlo Park, California, 2003. *Photo by the author.*

Imelda Silva making salsa to serve with tamales. Imelda's kitchen in Redwood City, California, 2003. *Photo by the author.*

Verónica Abarca and her mother, **Ángeles Herrera.** Verónica's kitchen in Fremont, California, 2003. *Photo by the author.*

Chef Norma Salazar in her office at the
California Culinary Art Academy. South
Pasadena, California, 2003. *Photo by the
author.*

•••••••••••••••••••••

CHAPTER 3

Homemade Culinary Art
(*El arte culinario casero*)
Cooks-as-Artists

Alma Welty in a *charla culinaria* held in her home's kitchen in Puebla, Mexico, defines quotidian cuisine as *el arte culinario casero*. "I have always said that culinary art is an amazing thing. How wonderful when you see that what you have cooked is eaten with such pleasure. . . . And truthfully [cooking] is easy. All that is needed is for you to like it, to enjoy it. . . . But I must say, I see cooking as a ritual. . . . It's a ritual how things come together. . . . When you eat a *chile en nogada* it has already gone through a fantastic, fabulous process. . . . You can cook a sauce, a sauce that anyone else can cook, but yours will taste better if you do it with joy and love. . . . Cooking is an art. Home cooking is an art."[1] For Welty, the art of quotidian cuisine is *maravilloso* (a marvel). It is an art form based on ritual, inspired by joy, pleasure, and love. The aesthetics of *el arte culinario casero* are captured in the expressions of enjoyment from those who eat, which in turn delights the artist by recognizing her talent.

But Welty does not simply theorize about *el arte culinario;* she combines theory and practice during our *charla*. She would not simply talk about food without eating it. Welty, whose income resources are significantly limited, nonetheless prepared an array of *antojitos poblanos* so that I could sample some of Puebla's culinary art made at home. Welty's creation took place in a tiny kitchen; she cooked on an electric one-burner portable stove that she placed on top of the

counter. Physical space limitations did not get in the way of Welty's
arte culinario casero.

Artistic expression comes in multiple forms, and one of them is
food; its social and cultural importance is indicated in food scholarship as the following titles suggest: *Art, Culture, and Cuisine: Ancient and Medieval Gastronomy* (Bober, 1999), *Feast and Folly: Cuisine, Intoxication, and the Poetics of the Sublime* (Weiss 2002), *The
Good Life: New Mexican Traditions and Food* (Cabeza de Baca,
1982). And culinary art is emphasized in films like *Mostly Martha*
directed by Sandra Nettelbeck (Germany, 2000), *Like Water for
Chocolate* directed by Alfonso Arau (Mexico, 1992), and *Babette's
Feast* directed by Gabriel Axel (Denmark, 1987). The voices of the
working-class women of the *charlas,* academics, and the interpretive
lenses of film directors show how the transformation of food into an
artistic meal takes place within multiple social forms and settings.

In this chapter, I address those moments in the *charlas* where
women transform their quotidian cooking into artistic culinary creations inspired by an array of emotions. Everyday culinary art reveals itself through the senses, through the rhythms of the body
while cooking, and by the effect caused by the process of sharing a
meal. To pay tribute to the artistic talent of the women of the *charlas,* throughout the remainder of this chapter I will refer to them as
cooks-as-artists who demonstrate an appreciation for their own
culinary creations as well as their mother's and grandmother's.
They are cooks-as-artists whose creative energy transforms their
quotidian cuisine into artistic meals in order to feed their soul.

My aim is to share the ways in which the cooks-as-artists' culinary creations have invited me to explore some theoretical issues
behind the politics of what is art, what constitutes the difference
between art and craft, who has the right talent to create art, and
who has the privileged knowledge to judge if a given production is
worthy of being called art.[2] What sets this theoretical exploration
in motion is the result of listening, seeing, smelling, and tasting
how the cooks-as-artists theorize about the aesthetic value of their
culinary artistic creations.[3] I must admit, however, that most of the
twenty women who collaborated in the production of *Voices,* with
the exception of Welty and Raquel Merlo, would not use the word
art to describe any of their cooking. As a matter of fact, my own use
of such a word in reference to their cooking practices might seem
inappropriate to them.

The absence of the word art from the cooks-as-artists offers a moment of critical reflection. At first glance it might suggest that the cooks-as-artists have internalized the idea that housework activities do not merit the name of art because the routine of domestic tasks requires no special skills or talents. This is an ideological assumption with a long history that can be traced back to the founding fathers of Western thought, particularly Aristotle and Plato. Activities carried out at home, by women's hands, such as cooking, gardening, sewing, and weaving are too often not taken as meaningful endeavors of creative and intellectual thought. Yet with a serious examination of housework we can see the countless ways in which creativity is in fact innate and universal. By universal I am not suggesting homogeneous artistic expressions that have transcendental and abstract meanings, but that the desire for artistic expression is part of our human nature. Furthermore, a critical and sensible study of housework will reveal that domestic tasks are not uncreative, repetitive, unskilled, and unthinking habitual functions. "The strength of this approach," as Michael Owen Jones says, "is that it broadens the definition of aesthetics beyond its use in the fine arts to involve those senses not acknowledged by Western aesthetics—smell, touch, and taste—and also a sense of bodily rhythms and patterning, or getting into the 'groove' with a task or a machine."[4] In the realm of housework, quotidian culinary art provides a culturally and historically gender-specific network of skills, knowledge, creative expression, and aesthetic value.

As with other chapters of *Voices,* grassroots theorist Liduvina Vélez planted the seed for this particular analytical probing during our first *charla.* Vélez's remembrance of her experiences of making tortillas by hand at different stages of her life suggests a number of theoretical questions that explore the spaces where female acts of agency take place. These are spaces that continue to be undervalued as sites where power, knowledge, and creativity are negotiated, expanded, and practiced.[5]

I begin this analytical investigation by critically examining one theory embedded in Liduvina Vélez's story of her own handmade tortillas. Vélez broaches the subject of tortilla-making as she recalls her early days as a newlywed: "When I got married, your father's sisters and his mother used to make really ugly tortillas. And when I saw they made some ugly tortillas, I no longer was embarrassed. I remember that I wanted to show them that I knew how to make tortillas better than them. They made really, really ugly tortillas. *Uy*—I would show off making my tortillas; I would put them in a little basket! *Uy,* my tortillas would come out so thin, puffed up so nicely! The ones I would make. I mean, yes, yes; I would beat them at making tortillas, over there. Yes, they would make some ugly, fat tortillas with holes in them."[6] When Vélez noticed her mother-in-law and sisters-in-law's ugly tortillas, she no longer felt insecure. Knowing that her tortillas were better, she says, "Pues me sentía fregona [al saber] hacer algo" (Well, I felt proud to know I could do something). For Vélez, only sixteen, forced to marry a man she hardly knew, and living with her in-laws, the aesthetics of her handmade *bonitas tortillas* offers her an affirmation to assert her-*self* as a teenage-woman and face her life's circumstances. Vélez transforms her life circumstances into the subject matter of her artistic expression: her *bonitas tortillas.*

The main theory Vélez formulates at this particular moment of our *charla* speaks of acts of agency. The aesthetic value of Vélez's handmade tortillas reflects what bell hooks calls "the sense of agency [that] artistry offers; the empowerment"[7] it offers to its creator. Academic feminist hooks and grassroots theorist Vélez, therefore, theorize on a similar issue using a different discourse. In the above expression of making tortillas, Vélez weaves theory into practice.

• •

Creativity in Quotidian Cuisine

In the *charlas,* the culinary artistic expression manifests itself in what I call art-in-process. Art-in-process does not suggest an artifact not yet completed. The artistic creation and aesthetic value is one that emanates not only from the end result, thus the product, but one that is found in the very process of making, of creating, and of eating something. It indicates that the artistic expression reveals itself in the very moment of its creation. In this case, it is that actual moment of preparing, speaking, and/or sharing the meaning of a culinary practice.

Art-in-process resonates with what Raymond William describes as "art of practices," which differs from art of objects.[8] On the one hand, art as objects become commodities, which one can purchase or admire in museums, where their cultural and aesthetic significance

is characterized by their exchange-market value.[9] With arts conceived as practices, on the other hand, those engaged in its making
process define its value. To give an example of this form of artistic
expression, for instance, the editors of *Artists in Aprons: Folk Art by
American Women,* point out that "a woman made utility quilts as
fast as she could so her family wouldn't freeze, and she made them
as beautiful as she could so that her heart wouldn't break."[10] The
beauty of the quilt provides two forms of practical and necessary human value. First, it literally warms the physical body; second, it
nourishes the spirit of the quilt maker. Conceiving of quilt making
as part of an art-in-process helps broaden the cultural meanings of
a quilt's beauty beyond the one given to it once it is exhibited on a
museum wall, an art gallery, or on a wall in our home. Quilts, weaving, crochet, everyday cuisine, and other household artistic endeavors are part of an art-in-process that helps affirm a sense of creative
agency for working-class women who often have no other creative
outlet to nourish their soul.

For Vélez, the artistic value of her *bonitas tortillas* derives from
the act of doing, of making something. Art-in-process of quotidian
cuisine, of tortilla-making, can be expressed in part within Tomás
Ybarra-Frausto's *rasquachismo* and Michel de Certeau's definition
of popular culture. Ybarra-Frausto in "Arte Chicano: Images of a
Community," says that *rasquachismo* is a working-class aesthetic
that attempts to eradicate (the ideological) boundaries between
"fine" art and "folk art." *Rasquachismo* "recognizes that everyday
life and the lived environment were the prime constituent elements
for [a] new aesthetics."[11] Michel de Certeau in *The Practice of Everyday Life* says that arts of popular culture are essentially an "art of
making" and "a way of thinking invested in a way of acting, an art of
combination, which cannot be disassociated from an art of using."[12]

Ybarra-Frausto and de Certeau's concept help to understand
the artistic endeavor of the art-in-process of quotidian cuisine.
Vélez's *bonitas tortillas* as art-in-progress constitute for her both
an everyday practice and a "way of thinking invested in [a] way" of
doing and creating something.[13] Like Ybarra-Frausto, I too am interested in eradicating the hierarchical distinction (influenced by
gender, class, and race) between arts and crafts. With this interest
in mind, I am deliberately referring to working-class women's quotidian culinary practices as cuisine rather than food or simply cooking. In the realm of foodways, the word *cuisine* resonates with high

culture, whereas cooking is what working-class people do with their raw edible material since they are, *supposedly,* unable to transform the raw material into *haute* cuisine. My intent is not to embrace the hierarchical paradigm of fine art versus handicrafts. But situating working-class women's everyday domestic artistic expressions and creations on an even plane with fine art might help break down the hierarchical social value and ideological implication we tend to associate with *art* as opposed to *craft.*

An understanding and appreciation for quotidian cuisine as a form of art-in-process can only take place with a paradigm shift as feminist art historians Linda Nochlin and Griselda Pollock suggest. What a paradigm shift must do, most of all, is lead "to wholly new ways of conceptualizing what it is we study [as art] and how we do" our study.[14] One of the quintessential aspects of creating art is an "affirming part of [our] aliveness."[15] Therefore, art-making is connected to our spirituality and to our sense of self, our sense of culture, and our sense of history as all the Chicana/o artists in *Contemporary Chicana and Chicano Art* (Keller, 2002) indicate is the case for them. The artistic elements of quotidian cuisine carry the potential to capture this same significance. In order to understand the artistic importance of everyday culinary creations as it is expressed and experienced within the practices, remembrances, and descriptions made by the cooks-as-artists, the *re*-consideration of three basic elements related to art must take place: where it gets created, who creates it, and what constitutes an aesthetic form. The changes of conceptual models need to be plural, and they should be broad enough to offer ways of understanding the imaginative energy and creative talent that many working-class women of color have learned to master within their kitchens.

· · · · · · · · · · · · · · · · · · · ·

Rethinking Where and Who Creates Art

The transformation of a raw edible item into gastronomic art has had an erroneous hierarchical assumption to it. To illustrate this postulation, I will quote at some length from philosopher Jean-François Revel's work on gastronomy from antiquity to modern times (nineteenth century). By quoting Revel at length, I do not mean to imply that he is the only one who has taken a position on separating culinary talents by location, education, gender, and class. Other world famous chefs, like Revel, have voiced the assumption that culinary talent cannot be found in the kitchens of working-class women. For instance, French chef Paul Bocuse says, "I intend to repeat my conviction here that women are certainly good cooks for so-called traditional cooking. . . . Such cooking, in my opinion, is not at all inventive, which I deplore."[16] I focus on Revel somewhat extensively since his remarks make clear why I join other feminist scholars from diverse areas of study whose work rebuffs the belief that traditional domestic endeavors inevitably stifle creativity.[17]

For the metamorphosis of raw edible materials to become culinary arts, Revel claims that regional and traditional foods, which he calls "popular cuisine," must enter into the domain of "erudite cuisine." For Revel, "popular cuisine" is "linked to the soil, [it] exploit[s] the products of various regions and different seasons, in close accord with nature. [It's] based on age-old skills, transmitted unconsciously by way of imitation and habit, of applying methods of cooking patiently tested and associated with certain cooking utensils and recipients prescribed by a long tradition." "Popular cuisine" is grounded in peasant traditions. "Erudite cuisine" is achieved only through training and education; it is "based [on] invention, renewal, [and] experimentation." It is "a true international cuisine." Furthermore, the distinction of both cuisines is gender-based: "erudite cuisine" is what "fathers" do in professional kitchens; "mothers" in the home kitchens do "popular cuisine."[18]

While "peasant traditions serve as indispensable raw materials for the creation of haute cuisine," Revel believes "that chefs [have] to transcend everyday methods to realize great art."[19] Raw edible materials in the hands of "mothers" can lead to the creation of some fine "craftsmanship." But "in all fairness," Revel affirms, we must "recognize, however, that, on the whole, Grand Cuisine is a cuisine restricted to professionals."[20] It goes without saying that for Revel "professionals" are men. The separation of popular and erudite cuisine claims, therefore, that the spirit of creativity prevails only in the realm of international cuisines created by the hands of male chefs. As a matter of fact, a chef in order to create gastronomical culinary art "must know how to react against [popular] family cuisine, which clings to its errors" in cooking methods.[21]

Revel's premise foregrounds three crucial elements. First, raw edible materials are a basic necessity for cooking, and when done at home by traditional knowledge and skills they become popular cuisine, which at best might create good craftsmanship. Women generally cook popular cuisine. Second, raw materials cooked in the professional kitchen, with the hands of well-educated chefs who have mastered their skills, have the potential to be transformed into haute cuisine. Finally, his position on these matters is based on objective analysis, or so he indicates. Revel "proves" his observations by explaining how "The history of gastronomy is above all that of erudite gastronomy, for this is the tradition that has left the greatest number of written traces. The great cookbooks are obviously the fruits of study, of invention, of the reflection of a change, rather than the fruit of the everyday run of things."[22] The hierarchical stance in Revel's gastronomical history juxtaposes art against craft, cultivated/educated professional training as opposed to rural traditional skills, international cuisines as distinct from local cooking, and male chefs versus female cooks.[23] Revel's paradigm privileges public institutions, male knowledge, and the written word.

As soon as cooking becomes a socially prestigious commodity, it ceases to be popular cuisine, and it becomes a culinary art that is fostered within public institutions. Yet historically, women have been excluded from entering the professional kitchen via culinary schools or by literally moving up the line: from prep cook, to pastry chef, to sous chef, to executive chef. "As [of] February 1997, of the 2,134 certified executive chefs (currently) practicing in the United States, only 92 are women. That represents only 4.3 percent, a far cry from what one would expect to see in an industry where cooking was traditionally a woman's domain."[24] Even when women have entered the professional kitchen there have been efforts to "forbid women from wearing the chef's hat, the symbol of the profession."[25] Lyde Buchtenkirch, one of the first women to graduate from the Culinary Institute of America in 1972, when she began her culinary studies "was offered a blue dress as a uniform; however, she insisted on and received chef whites."[26] For historian Stephan Mennell, a contributing social factor that keeps the number of women low within the professional kitchen is "the inseparability of women and domestic cooking."[27]

Historically, because women are the traditional cooks at home, the ones with the basic knowledge, their traditional talent acts as a double-edged sword. Tradition provides the foundation for all cooking, but it is also tradition that supposedly keeps women from transforming quotidian cooking into art; it is tradition that keeps women from entering the professional kitchen where raw edible material becomes culinary art. While doing research for a conference paper, "Women Owning the Knife: Women in the Professional Kitchen," I learned of an interesting irony embedded in the foundation of some of the early culinary schools in the United States: women ran them, but their students were mainly men. Frances Roth and Katherine Angell, for instance, founded the Culinary Institute of America (CIA) in 1946. For the first twenty-four years of the CIA's operation, the young culinarians were mainly men. It was not until 1970 "that the first woman was enrolled in the culinary curriculum on a full-time basis."[28] The CIA, now located in Hyde Park, New York, by 1996 had a 24 percent female enrollment.

With this brief historical recap of how the transformation of traditional cooking shifts into culinary art, my intent has been to illustrate a systemic pattern of the appropriation of working-class women's knowledge, talent, and creativity.[29] Just as colonialism, imperialism, and now globalization are structures of political, social, and economic power that take sources and resources from indigenous people, third-world people, and ethnic minorities, the metamorphosis of everyday food into culinary art has followed a similar process.[30] When working-class women's ordinary culinary talents are transported or appropriated by culinary schools and/or prestigious chefs, the physical presence of working-class women disappears, while their cooking skills in the hands of those with more economic resources, both men and women, become a refined talent essential in the creation of culinary art.[31] The assumption that no culinary art is created in a home kitchen, particularly if such a kitchen belongs to a working-class woman, is based on the belief that any activity performed in a domestic traditional setting leads to routine, and routine allegedly throttles creative energy, creative inventions.

Rethinking such attitudes about housework can lead us to ask different and new questions about how *tradition* is conceptualized. With our predominant current Western model, practices carried out under the umbrella of *tradition* by people of color, working-class people, particularly working-class women of color, might be embraced as colorful and might even deserve to be classified as crafts. Yet the term *tradition* can provide the excuse to academic settings — culinary institutes, art schools, or universities—not to credit traditional practices as having thought out methodical processes and intellectual rigor both necessary for opening the door to invention and innovation.

A lack of written records accounts for the fact that many traditional practices have often been delegitimized as serious forms of knowledge, power, and creativity. But, as Linda Tuhiwai Smith writes in *Decolonial Methodologies* (1999), any research that grounds its scholarship only on the investigation of written text enacts an imperialist practice of power and knowledge. Smith demonstrates how the conceptualization of history as an academic discipline is a specifically "Western Enlightenment Project" where the stories that everyday folks tell about their past are classified as traditions and not as history.[32] The separation between these two categories is, presumably, to distinguish *just* stories people tell and the official (written) records of our past.

The one disciplinary area where tradition might not be dismissed as an unsuitable subject of serious study is folklore. But even here feminist folklorists M. Jane Young and Kay Turner argue that while tradition has "infiltrated and informed the script of folklore research," it also operates "explicitly and implicitly to the detriment of women."[33] Tradition as presented by the founding father of folklore studies, Johann Gottfried von Herder, "is passed on from father to son; [therefore] the very essence of tradition is masculine."[34] Tradition, theoretically conceived as masculine, has led to an undervaluing of women's everyday experiences, of women's creative energy, of their culinary artistic expression.

How often do we ask the wrong questions? How often does our research privilege the status quo? I ask this in reaction to art historian Linda Nochlin's article, "Why Have There Been No Great Women Artists?" Nochlin answers her question by focusing on the exclusion of women from art academies. She argues that male artists are not simply born with greatness but that their greatness is the result of a social process. Nochlin highlights the social, political, and economic mechanism that creates great male artists. These are art academy institutions for the training and cultivation of artistic talent; traditionally men are the ones who have had the time and means for attending such institutions. Participation in well-known art academies offers audiences with cultivated tastes to judge and honor art productions, which in turn are converted into commodities.[35] For a scholar like Nochlin, the answer for the absence of "great women artists" lies in the exclusion of women from art academies. A similar argument could be made for the absence of larger numbers of great women chefs. This form of inquiry, however, fails to disclose the hierarchical ideologies of gender, class, and race that encompass the definition of greatness.

The specific reference to Nochlin's work is not to point out its fallacies, for within the world of fine arts much of what she says holds true. But I am using Nochlin's analysis to suggest that we need to rearticulate our questions. While I agree that women, especially working-class women of color, in general are systematically excluded from public social institutions that cultivate particular intellectual and creative talents, I do not agree that it is only through these institutions that the development of art is achieved. Insisting solely that women need to enter in greater numbers those public institutions that cater to the development of artistic creation is accepting that those are the only acceptable and valid social locations where such expression is found. A home kitchen, the culinary social institution *traditionally* assigned to women, does not automatically exclude the transformation of quotidian cuisine into potentially *great* culinary art. The art-in-process of quotidian cuisine offers a theoretical challenge to the social apparatus that legitimizes the greatness of male artists by exposing how within that apparatus there are gender, class, and racial biases.[36] This challenge reveals how the social apparatus that creates the setting for homemade culinary art conceptually parallels Nochlin's construction.

The art-in-process found in quotidian cuisine for the cooks-as-artists involves the basic elements that according to Nochlin are essential for the creation and production of great art and great artists: social institutions to develop and learn skills and techniques, teachers, time for training, and/or a long period of individual experimentation. Within this book, a home's kitchen represents the social institution where artistic quotidian cuisines are created.

Teachers

Most women from the *charlas* testified that they have learned to cook from their mothers, grandmothers, aunts, or other women. Thus, the teachers. When I asked Irma Vásquez when she learned to cook, she quickly responded, "Yo pienso que cuando me casé fué cuando aprendí a cocinar" (I think I learned when I got married). In the same *charla*, María Luisa Villicaña comments, "todas" (all of us), meaning we learn to cook when we get married. Yet, this is really not the case for all of the cook-as-artists, or at least not the case when it comes to their signature dish. As soon as Villicaña says "todas," Vásquez remembers, "en la casa, lo único que aprendí hacer es el arróz" (at home the only thing I learned to make was the rice). As we saw in the previous chapter, this is one of the dishes Vásquez knows how to make to perfection—without the assistance of measuring utensils. Alma Welty learned to cook alongside older women. As she says, "yo tuve mucho roce con viejitas. Viejitas, mis tías, mi abuela, la tía de mi marido que era una monja" (I had a lot of contact with old women. Old women, my aunts, my grandmother, my husband's aunt who was a nun). Erika Morales shares a similar path in her own culinary development: "Cocino lo que veía a mí mamá que hacía. Y luego cuando estuve con mi suegra. Pero más bien era ella la que guísaba. Yo vine a guisar más bien cuando nos venimos para acá" (I cook what I saw my mother cook. And then when I was with my mother-in-law. But really she did most of the cooking. I began to cook when we came to the United States).

"Yo vi a mi mamá cocinar siempre" (I saw my mother cooking all the time), says Imelda Silva. But Silva began doing most of her own cooking once she lived by herself; she would ask other women for recipes. "'Wow, what a good meal, how did you make it?' I had a cousin who I believe was a very good cook. She has passed away. Her name was Alicia. I believe she was a very good cook. She knew how to make different foods. When you are from a town and you are a poor girl, you only know how to cook beef stew, meat with chile sauce. What we call *'morisqueta'* [white rice with meat]. Things like that. You cook *mole.*"[37] Some of these foods were mentioned in chapter 2, ham with pineapple, macaroni salad, ribs in barbecue sauce. Silva would communicate with her cousin by phone to ask for recipes: "'Ay Alicia, a mi me gustó mucho lo que hiciste de comer. ¿Cómo lo hago?' Y, ya me decía" (hey Alicia, I liked what you made for dinner a lot. How do I make it? And she would tell me). Alicia introduced Silva to a different form of cooking.

In this part of the *charla* with Silva, she talks about the limitations of a cooking repertoire in her rural hometown in Mexico. Yet with the help of other women she learns to expand her own culinary selection. Since she learned from her cousin Alicia in Redwood City, California, Silva theorizes about the difference between rural cooking and city cooking. Yet her theorization is not in terms of the sophistication of culinary talent but as a result of limited economic resources of women (girls) from her hometown. The value and pride she finds in her own rural culinary traditions is evident in the meal she selected to prepare for us to eat during our *charla.* When I got to her home, she was preparing typical tamales from her hometown for us to share. "Corundas, así los nombran las inditas de Uruapán" (*Corundas,* that's what Indians from Uruapán call them).

Unlike Vasquez, Villicaña, Welty, Morales, and Silva, who learned to cook as adult women once they were either married or living by themselves, Hilaria Cortés's culinary exploration began at the age of six. Cortés entered the kitchen by working next to her mother in the ranch where she grew up: "My mother made tamales. Sometimes she had me help her mix the masa for the tamales so that I would learn how to make them. I was still very young. She would also stand me on top of a stool and using a big spoon, she would have me turn the tortillas [that were cooking on the stove]. There were times when I would burn myself, and I would tell her, 'I'd rather make them.' And I would make the little balls of masa and place them on the tortilla presser and then I would press them. And the tortilla would come out."[38]

Another way to develop artistic talent, as suggested by Nochlin's work, is through long periods of individual experimentation. This being the case, Liduvina Vélez's *bonitas tortillas hechas a mano* (beautiful tortillas made by hand) enter the realm of individual experimentation. Vélez learned the art of doing handmade tortillas on her own: "I remember that I started making tortillas—all by myself when I lived with my Aunt Celía. I think that's when I learned. In the course of one year. I went [to live with Aunt Celía] at fifteen and I got married at sixteen. But my aunt didn't know how to cook, and we both learned together. We learned everything from how to make *nixtamal,* to grind corn into meal, to grind the dough well. We learned to make tortillas using a round metal mold, but later I started making them by hand."[39] Vélez's experimentation in developing her handmade *bonitas tortillas* takes place as she moves from the city, where tortillas are machine made and store bought, to a rural countryside.

Skills/Techniques

The cooks-as-artists speak of the skills and talents they mastered in order to create culinary art.[40] Quotidian cuisine's art-in-process demands virtuosity, as does painting, music, sculpture, and so on.

In the cooks-as-artists discourse the technical language for this aspect of homemade culinary art is expressed in the concept of "todo tiene su gracia," or "chiste," or "punto" (everything has its charm, twist, or moment). For example, Esperanza Vélez says the following as she gives me a recipe for making *pipián verde* (pumpkin-seed sauce): "You put enough oil in a skillet and also salt so that the pumpkin seeds don't pop as much. Because they pop; they pop all over. You fry the seeds to a *punto bonito;* make sure they don't completely fry because if they do they will taste sour, really. Make sure they come out wonderful. The *pipián verde* has a trick to it. For instance, if I am cooking it, you can't *meterle la mano* because it separates."[41] The *gracia, chiste,* or *punto* is a finesse that interlocks technical skill, quality of product, and the sensory-logic of the *sazón.*

Erika Morales expresses something similar to Esperanza Vélez. Morales tries whenever possible to retain the savory personal value and joy she gets from making handmade tortillas. Morales clearly manifests her joy when she tells me: "I love to make tortillas by hand. They come out well rounded and nicely thin. Whenever you like, come and we will make tortillas by hand. My mother made them fat, and they looked like stars; they were not well rounded. . . . The tortillas come out even nicer and they are easier to make and they puff up more when you roll out the masa in the *metate.*"[42] For Morales, the *gracia* or *punto,* the special skill in making beautiful tortillas, consists of rolling the masa on the *metate.*

Yet according to some cooks-as-artists, who at moments become culinary art critics of others' creations as well as their own, this *gracia* or *punto* within the context of achieving a particular artistic quality is one that not everyone manages to achieve. Cortés admits that while she has learned with her mother to make tortillas "a mano y a máquina, de las dos formas" (by hand and using a metal mold), when she makes them by hand "se [le] aportillan" (they break apart with holes in the middle). Morales references her mother's star-shaped rather than round tortillas. Vélez takes great pleasure and derives much self-worth from knowing that while her tortillas were thin and puffed up rather nicely, her mother-in-law and sisters-in-law's were ugly and fat. And as mentioned in chapter 2, Alicia Villanueva also speaks of her own futile attempt at grinding chiles in the *metate* in her efforts to help her mother make *mole* from scratch. Yet her mother masterfully ground whole chiles into fine powder.

The talent involved in creating art-in-process, therefore, is not one we all learn to master, even when we all have access to the social institution that produces homemade culinary art: a home kitchen. I am not contradicting my own argument, but indicating that everyday cuisine's art-in-process does require a cultivation of talent and skills, which too often are ignored under the pretext of simple traditional housework routine activities.

Audience/Critics

The creation of homemade culinary art, as in other areas of artistic expression, needs an audience. In canonical art forms, the critic is a particular audience who is knowledgeable in a specific field of study and thus holds the privilege to judge the merit of an artistic creation. Collectively, the cooks-as-artists of the *charlas* provide an alternative approach to the method of judging an artistic production and to the notion of what constitutes a field of study. Their way of defining and conceiving how their art-in-process is judged engages in community politics. Cooks-as-artists also express the distinction that Linda Tuhiwai Smith makes between community research and field research. Smith writes: "'Community' conveys a much more intimate, human and self-defined space, whereas 'field' assumes space 'out there' where people may or may not be present. What community research relies upon and validates is that the community itself makes its own definitions."[43] Family and friends usually create the community that provides the occasion for the cooks-as-artists to share their repast, their art-in-process.

The merit of quotidian cuisine's art-in-process is articulated in the delight of pleasure that emanates from those who eat what has been cooked. In the words of Alma Welty this delight is "una maravilla," as she indicates in the opening quote of this chapter. For Imelda Silva, her community forms every time her children, now living on their own, come to her home for dinner.

Imelda: *Look, if I don't go to work, if it is my day off, and let's assume that my son tells me, "I am going to come over for dinner." Then, yes, I like to cook a lot. But if I am going to cook just for Enrique [her husband] and myself, I get lazy.*
Meredith: *And why is that?*
Imelda: *I feel that is just spending too much time just for a meal for two people. But if they are going to come [her children], it gives*

me joy to be all together. If I make a lot of food, I know we are go-
ing to eat it. My son likes mole. *I make chicken* mole *for him,*
and if there is left over, he always asks me to give him some to
take. Making mole *is time consuming and laborious. And to*
make it just for two people is just too time consuming. That's the
only thing. But if I'm going to have company, my children are go-
ing to come over; it makes me happy. I don't even get tired. It feels
like a party, better, like a reunion. I feel that your mother goes
through the same thing. I think that all mothers when we begin
to be alone, we go through the same experience.

Meredith: *I do cook for myself. Not every day but at least three or*
four times per week.

Imelda: *But take notice that you still do not have a family; you don't*
feel the difference to be alone and cook. But we do.[44]

Imelda Silva speaks of community on at least two levels here.
Within her family, community is a reunion that must include her
children. The desire to have her family surround her table gives her
the impetus to create laborious meals. Silva also addresses a form
of solidarity with other mothers whose children no longer live at
home with them. The merit of a culinary creation for Silva is inseparable from the participation of her audience.

Another critical reflection based on the above moment from
the *charla* with Silva, is on the attention I brought to myself.
While Silva does not much care to cook just for two, her husband
and herself, I felt the necessity to tell her that I do cook for myself.
Her response suggests a direct and an indirect theoretical implication on why I cook for myself. Directly, for Silva, I too have a community, which as of now generally consists of myself, a community
of one that also needs the soulful nourishment that creating art provides. Indirectly, by listening how for all the cooks-as-artists the
value of a creating a meal is found within the construction of their
community, I am learning to reconsider if the value I generally find
within the creation of my own meals represents a form of art for
art's sake. It would be erroneous of my part to assume that I have
not accepted some Western values as part of my own.[45] Yet sharing
charlas, not just with the women who participate in *Voices,* but by
reading what my students write about their own families' *charlas*
culinarias, I realize that my culinary artistic inventions are not for
the sake of art itself. The value I now find when I cook and eat by

myself is in the anticipation of sharing my new inventions, on future occasions, with my community of friends, colleagues, students, and family.

In the *charla* held at María Luisa Villicaña's house, the interconnection between audience and artist developed as follows: As we approach the table to find a place to sit, an echo fills the kitchen/breakfast area.

Duvi: *Wow, what a beautiful table.*
Meredith: *Wow, what a wonderful salad.*
Duvi: *Wow, look how wonderful, the table is set.*[46]

As we admire the presentation for the meal that we will soon enjoy, it occurs to me that I should have brought a camera to take a picture. Villicaña's response to such suggestion expresses a sentiment of cultural national pride.

Meredith: *Wow, if I had known we would have such a meal, I would have brought a camera to take a picture.*
María Luisa: *Yes? So they would see that it is Mexican food. So they would see I made Mexican food.*
Irma: *Place the cloth (hand embroidered) napkin,* comadre, *so it would be in the picture.*
Meredith: *But with what camera? I didn't think.*
María Luisa: *Do you want one? Let me look for it.*
Meredith: *Let's place this here for the tortillas. Hey, I could even use this picture for the cover of the book.*
María Luisa: *Uh! Yes!*[47]

Villicaña's response to the suggestion to take a picture of the table setting is significant on at least two counts. First, it reflects a sentiment of cultural national pride on the part of the cook-as-artist, Villicaña. With a tone of pride, she says that a picture would show that she cooked Mexican food. Second, her enthusiastic reaction to the possibility of using such picture as a cover for a book, then in its early stages of development, indicates that the artistic significance of Villicaña's art-in-process is not confined to the domestic space and to those within it. I read the desire of expanding the meaning of such moment as the cooks-as-artists effort (other women made similar remarks as those of Villicaña) to make their voices of knowledge about their milieu, their act of creativity, and assertion of agency heard in the public spaces.[48]

The above examples, and others similar throughout *Voices,* are not intended to reduce the complexity of community by implying that it always comes together in harmonious ways. Moments of competition or exclusion are presented within familial community politics. Liduvina Vélez experiences such exclusion as a result of expectations of who has the knowledge to make handmade tortillas. As mentioned in the previous chapter, Vélez takes pride in the *sazón* of her handmade tortillas in part because it works as a shield against the rejection she experienced from some of her in-laws. As a city girl, Vélez's ability comes as a surprise due to the assumption of who has access to a particular regional or local knowledge. Such assumption, however, cuts both ways.

Since handmade tortillas are associated with provincial, rural women's skill, tortilla making is generally dismissed as having no true aesthetic value, a dismissal born out of a classist social attitude that undermines the knowledge and skill of handmade tortillas, let alone its artistic quality.[49] A handmade tortilla as a working-class quotidian culinary art practice carries with it five hundred years of history that in a fast-paced, high-technological society often gets ignored or conceived of as a sign of backwardness. Since rural women would normally make tortillas, their capacity for creating culinary artistic productions were ignored by the more refined city dwellers. Victor Valle and Mary Lau Valle say that "in Tijuana [Baja California, Mexico], a town far from older class-conscious Mexican cities, *tortillas* occupied the bottom social rungs. Though they preserved the knowledge of their Mesoamerican ancestors in the table's daily pillar of *tortillas,* to call someone a *tortillera* was to accuse that person of passivity, Indian backwardness, and poverty."[50] The social value given to tortillas shifts, depending on the critics' situated lives. If the critics are countrywomen who make them, social and personal pride is invested in their creation. If the critic is a social reformer wanting to modernize the process of tortilla making (and change its very consumption), its traditional technique is seen as backwardness. Conceptually, these views of criticism operate within the perimeters of expertise within a different field of study and interest.

Embedded within the idea of field of research, as Smith indicates, there is a sense of distance and detachment from the practice under study so that rigorous observations are drawn by the one conducting such a study. "Field of study" suggests a foundation of acquired knowledge, and due to such knowledge critical and seemingly objective judgments are made about the value of particular practices. Yet how are the motives of such critical opinions evaluated? For instance, within the field of study of nutrition, affected by the ideology of modernization and scientific knowledge, in 1899 Senator Francisco Bulnes published *El porvenir de las naciones Hispano-Americas (The Future of the Hispanic-American Nations)*. In this work, Bulnes arrived at the following conclusion: people can be divided "into three races: the people of corn, wheat, and rice."[51] According to the nutritional value of each grain, Bulnes states, "the race of wheat is the only truly progressive one." Maize, on the other hand, "has been the eternal pacifier of America's indigenous race and the foundation of their refusal to become civilized."[52] Bulnes's scientific zealous proposition did not take root, yet attitudes similar to Bulnes's left a residue that manifests itself in a class and racial basis.

The art-in-process of everyday cuisine under some theoretical frame of "field of study" runs the risk of being completely overlooked. For instance, Liduvina Vélez also experiences a class-based devaluation of her knowledge and talent. Once separated from *el marido* (the husband) after ten years of marriage, Vélez's tortilla making becomes only an imposed activity she must do as part of her perceived provincial working-class status. She says, "In Atlisco, Puebla, we arrived at Aunt Dora's house. There Aunt Dora would have me do work in order to earn my meals. Since she knew that I came from the country, she told herself, 'This ignorant woman is good to do outside labor.' . . . And since she knew I came from the country, and she also had corn planted, she thought that I should make tortillas for them [Dora's family]. Therefore, I had to prepare the *nixtamal* and take it to the mill, and I had to make tortillas for them. According to Aunt Dora, that work was easy for me. But don't you believe that it wasn't a lot of work."[53] Vélez's new circumstances in making tortillas are perceived by Aunt Dora as a lowly labor worthy of a countrywoman who does not know any better. In this new circumstance, for Vélez, tortilla making does have a social value. It rejects the assumption of her "ignorance and passivity," for she is quite capable of articulating the motives of Aunt Dora's actions. Here, Vélez is speaking of the history of class prejudices. Vélez makes the tortillas that are expected of her, not because she is an ignorant woman, but because she is fully aware of her precarious class situation.[54] As Vélez remembers this episode of her life with Aunt Dora, the tension within her familial community is reflected as she omits the possessive pronoun "my" when referring to Aunt Dora. When Vélez speaks of her Aunt Celía with whom she learned to make tortillas she does use the possessive pronoun "my." Thoughts of her Aunt Celía bring back fond memories for Vélez.

Since the social apparatus where *el arte culinario casero* is created conceptually and practically parallels the one that creates "great male artists," as art historian Nochlin suggests, the cooks-as-artists of the *charlas* offer a different approach in thinking about a woman's domestic tradition. For some cooks-as-artists the tradition of *hospitalidad* (hospitality) becomes a manifestation of their creative energy, which they express in the process of establishing the setting for our *charlas*. For most of these women the idea of simply talking about food practices without actually eating was unimaginable. As the husband of María Luisa Villicaña, Vicente, says, "Acuérdese que a la visitas se les da de comer" (remember we must always feed our gusets). The tradition of *hospitalidad*, however, is not carried out in an automatic routinelike mode. The connection between theory (represented in the discussion of food) and practice (the making and eating of food) is expressed in personalized ways. The cooks-as-artists' *hospitalidad*, which is based on an age-old tradition, does not take away their personal creativity, in transforming raw edible materials into *haute* cuisine.

María Luisa Villicaña displayed her hospitality during our first *charla* with an unexpected meal she prepared for us, her guests. Our *charla* took place during a weekday, adding to Villicaña's creative and efficient culinary talent; Villicaña came home at three-thirty and by six o'clock was ready to share a meal with six guests and her husband. Her guests were Liduvina Vélez, my then four-year-old niece Nichollete Palacios, my sister-in-law Verónica Abarca, Irma Vásquez, her daughter, and me.

Villicaña welcomed us with a table set with her best china, the one that comes out of the china cabinet only on "very special occasions," as Villicaña says. The wine glasses were the ones Vélez gave Villicaña as a wedding gift over a decade ago. The welcoming aromas from the kitchen promised a feast to please our palate. The fragrant tomato-cilantro fried rice enhanced the complementary flavors of the rich and dark *mole poblano*'s spicy and "chocolaty" sauce. Rice and *mole poblano* blended together creating an orchestra of savory delights. The smell of corn tortillas warming on a *comal,* the next best thing to actual homemade tortillas, added to the ensemble of aromas, colors, textures, and flavors. Besides the *mole* and rice, on one end of the table there was a bowl with pasta salad, and a spinach salad was placed on the other end of the table. Of course, beans were not absent from that table. Due to Villicaña's culinary hospitality, in addition to the tortillas she also provided bread to satisfy different people's palates in their preference for eating *mole poblano.* Villicaña's welcoming meal represents one form of art-in-process where the *mole,* tortillas, bread, and salads reflect national, cultural, and personal stories, all which became part of the *charla.*

To explain how quotidian cuisine represents and theorizes reinterpretations of national history, a brief look at the historical implications of *mole poblano* and the "tortilla discourse" merits discussion. While the *mole* Villicaña served came from Gualpa, Mexico, *mole* is a main dish of Puebla. The list of *official* sources addressing the culinary history of *mole* is rather extensive. We find references to *mole,* a Nahuatl word that means mixture, in the written records of the conquest.[55] I will not make an attempt to discuss such sources here. Instead, I share a story I heard about the legend of *mole* while having a *charla* with Ángeles Herrera in Puebla, Puebla, Mexico, in September of 1999. I heard this story as I stood in front of clay cookware and the hearths of the Santa Rosa convent's kitchen, where nuns' hands created *mole poblano.* The legend dates to the eighteenth century and, according to this version, the recipe was born out of a "maldad," which in the context of the story refers to a mischievous deed. The legend goes like this: Once a viceroy came from Spain and visited the convent. As the nuns prepared a meal to feed him, they took a sack filled with dry chiles, all kinds of chiles—*pasilla, ancho, chipotle.* They fried the chiles along with peanuts and made a sauce, adding cinnamon and a lot more spices. Then they took a turkey and cooked it; later a nun poured the sauce on top of it. To garnish it, they added some sesame seeds. The nuns who combined all the chiles did not intend to add chocolate to it. But in the convent there was "una maldocita" (a mischievous nun), and she added chocolate to the sauce. So it was a "monjita" who did the "maldad" and added chocolate. "La maldad" came out good.

I have purposely left in the words "maldocita," "monjita," and "maldad" in Spanish since it is because of these words that I share this story of *mole poblano*. Historically, *mole poblano* is seen as a culinary representation of the marriage of two cultures—Spanish and indigenous. Since the courtship of colonization was what led to this marriage, the concept of "maldad" seems a suitable description with which to talk about the culinary effects resulting from the union. What makes this creation of *mole* Spanish is the number of the spices added to it. Cinnamon's origins are from Sri Lanka. Other basic spices used to make *mole poblano* include cloves, native of Southeast Asia; cumin, which comes from East Asia and is grown in large proportions in India, Egypt, Arabia, and the Mediterranean; and black pepper, which is native of either Indonesia or Singapore. Some recipes also call for garlic and onions, which are thought to have originated in Central Asia. The Spaniards introduced all of these spices into the cuisine of the Americas.[56]

At the risk of over analyzing, the diminutive adjective of the nun, *monjita,* who added chocolate out of a "maldad," suggests a folk narrative of native cultural resistance. I base this particular analysis on three sources of information. First, cocoa is a native of Mesoamerica. Second, in the context of colonialist discourse, native people are described with diminutive adjectives to symbolize their so-called lower status, thus the "monjita maldoza." Finally, for the sake of theoretical speculation, piecing these two facts together hints to an act of resistance against the process of de-Indianization, to borrow Guillermo Bonfil Batalla's term. For Bonfil Batalla, de-Indianization is "a historical process through which populations that originally possessed a particular and distinctive identity, based upon their own culture, are forced to renounce that identity, with all the consequent changes in their social organization and culture. [It is] an attempt to hide and ignore the Indian face of Mexico because no real connection with Mesoamerican civilization is admitted."[57] The action of the "monjita maldoza" (the little mischievous nun) resulted in a culinary affirmation of that which is original to Mesoamerica, chocolate.

In the history of Mexican food, the "tortilla discourse" was another effort in the process of de-Indianization. The "tortilla discourse" reveals another colonialist's courtship effort toward the marriage of two cultures, where the identity of one culture would be lost to the other. This history also makes its appearances in Villicaña's meal by the combination of tortillas and bread. During the Porfiriato era (1877–91) the "tortilla discourse" was an attempt to modernize

Mexican cooking and elevate it to the standard of European cuisine by substituting the use of corn grain with wheat. The "tortilla discourse" represented an effort to colonize people's palate by prohibiting the consumption of corn tortillas. From an elite perspective, it was better to eat wheat bread than corn tortilla. Wheat, after all, had European approval. Wheat, while now integral to Mexican cuisine, has never been able to replace the ever-resilient maize. Even though Villicaña offers both bread and tortillas, she notices that of the eight people eating, only one ate bread.

María Luisa: *Did you notice Vicente that only you like bread?*
   Vicente likes bread.
Meredith: *With mole?*
Vicente: *With mole I like bread.*
Meredith: *But with other food, tortillas?*
Vicente: *Tortillas with other food, but with mole I like bread.*[58]

The story of how *mole poblano* was invented and the combination of both tortillas and bread bring to mind two academic debates about the concept of *mestizaje:* as a historical process and as an act of resistance that rejects a modernization that aims at the de-Indianization of cultural practices. In this particular example of just one moment in just one *charla*, Villicaña's art-in-process marinates two theoretical academic debates in one meal.[59] Villicaña's art-in-process works with a combination of materials that brings together an array of histories, theories, and practices. This multiplicity of elements, some complementary and some in opposition, are not indicative of a working-class woman's idiosyncratic understanding of life. What this indicates is a reflection of what Karen Mary Davalos sees as our "ambiguous subjectivity." For Davalos, human agency is full of ambivalence and ambiguity; it is "fluid" and "porous" revealing "multiple perspectives and contradictory stories."[60]

●●●●●●●●●●●●●●●●●●●●●●
The Aesthetics of the Moment

Efforts to define new forms of aesthetics are, as bell hooks says, "to challenge the assumption that certain groups are not fully human, [that they are] uncivilized, and that the measure of this [is their] collective failure to create 'great art.'"[61] The purpose in this final section of the chapter is neither to challenge the meaning of "great art" nor to search for cracks within the classical Western definition of aesthetics in order to structure an argument on how quotidian cuisine does in fact enter within the prescribed parameters of such a formulation. This theoretical inquiry fosters the acceptance of *one* specific view of "greatness of art." Oftentimes women's expressive creativity does not fit preexisting formulas or forms. The classical Western definition of aesthetics is one area where the cooks-as-artists' art-in-process does not enter easily.

El arte culinario casero opens the door to developing theories about the aesthetics of the moment. These aesthetics are about being present in the moment. This presence, however, is not a momentary disconnection to or a transcendence of ordinary reality. As a matter of fact, the aesthetics of the moment as generated by culinary artistic creations are an engagement in a participatory relation "to the soil, to water, to plants and animal species, as well as to other humans."[62] Due to this sense of relationship to concrete everyday ordinary elements, the aesthetics of the moment are holistic, since food, the essential element for a culinary creation, is a sustenance that feeds the mind, body, and soul while connecting all three. Furthermore, the aesthetics of the moment created by *el arte culinario casero* are sensory-based and emotional.

The art-in-process of quotidian cuisine captures the aesthetics of being present in the moment. Being in the moment is a basic concept that for me comes from my recent introduction to Eastern philosophy, particularly Tibetan Buddhism. While the scope of this chapter does not permit an in-depth discussion of Buddhist principles, I feel that it is necessary to briefly explain how I came to explore this particular path of knowledge in relation to food. The catalyst for this intellectual probing was a shared meal at the home of yet another nonacademic theorist and most definitely a cook-as-artist, Lucy Fischer-West. Ever since she and I met, we have had an ongoing *charla culinaria*. In the process, we constantly discover our love, respect, and appreciation for food, for "the significance of making each meal matter," as she says. We also recognize that such love, respect, and appreciation extends to those we share meals with and offer meals to, and to those whom we rarely meet but whose labor contributes to the food in our kitchens.

In the process of sharing meals and sharing our life experiences, Lucy Fischer-West has introduced me to the world of Tibetan Buddhism. After the first meal I shared at her table, I discovered that for her every meal is an art-in-process where all the senses are stimulated. To this day, I can still remember the smell, taste, and presentation of what she served the first time I ate at her table on Easter Sunday, April 15, 2001. When she presented the main dish, "Long Simmered Chicken in Lots of Garlic," for a moment my senses were confused. I did not know by which of them I should be guided: should I just look at it and take in its colors; should I just smell it and let its aroma transport me to the serenity of an open field; should I taste it and let its flavors provide the pleasure of the moment? I did all three. Since then, on the few occasions a group of Tibetan monks has come through town, I have helped her feed them. Without speaking the same language, we do communicate in the moment of sharing a meal, making eye contact and smiling often. During these particular meals, I have experienced an unusual sense of tranquility. Fischer-West would say that what I have experienced is being present in the moment. For her, learning to "cultivate" the practices of "living in the moment" by "letting the senses" guide us to a full awareness of our surroundings allows us to "build a memory bank of moments that become strength-giving treasures." Due to these experiences borne of sharing a meal, I began to explore ways of understanding food's social influence and the aesthetic value of preparing a meal outside Western-based epistemologies.

In the book *In Buddha's Kitchen,* Kimberley Snow, co-founder of the Women's Studies Program at the University of California, Santa Barbara, describes how for her, the state of being in the moment happens in the kitchen: "The constant stream of intense taste sensations grounded me, providing a physical rather than mental reference for being. When I [am] working with food—slicing green peppers, mincing onions, paring zucchini—life [becomes] real. The color, smell, feel, taste of food provide[s] a link to the physical world."[63] Snow refers to being in the moment by what Tibetan's call "rol-pa." Through a series of metaphors such as "When you're writing on water, you can see the letters coming into being and going out of being simultaneously," or to "visualize silk flowing smoothly over the edge of a tabletop," Snow captures the powerful yet temporal presence of the moment, of "rol-pa." Snow indicates how Tibetans' "rol-pa is similar to descriptions of what we in the West call the timeless present, the flow, the ongoing moment of now."[64]

Philosophers Deane W. Curtin and Lisa M. Heldke, in their edited collection *Cooking, Eating, Thinking* (1992), suggest that being in the moment, in the state of *rol-pa,* is experienced through the simplicity of everyday cooking. "In the humble value of the kitchen," writes Curtin, "we can find deep meaning about the value of life. It is not 'somewhere else,' in some transcendental realm made secure by absolute knowledge. We find meaning in ordinary everydayness. . . . Had western philosophers begun their education in the kitchen, perhaps it would not have seemed so important to escape [from] the ordinariness of Plato's Cave to attain a glimpse of the meaning of life."[65] The value within the plainness of everyday cooking is not transcendental and abstract; therefore, it is not disconnected to a particular historical period or location. The aesthetic found within artistic culinary creations, whether they be fine cuisine (with a capital C) or ordinary cuisine (with a lowercase "c"), is always temporal. Food's "value is precisely that its 'moment' comes and goes."[66] The experiences of engaging in such a moment do not transcend its ordinary reality. As we have seen in the first two parts of this chapter, ordinary reality is full of knowledge, history, culture, and emotions.

The idea of temporality as it is connected within the realm of cuisine helps break down the hegemony that the theorization of aesthetics has had inside traditional Western philosophy. Simply stated, this tradition is based on an aesthetic form that transcends ordinary reality in order to represent it as universal and eternal; the aesthetics found in great art "remains stable and unobscure because the feelings that it awakens are independent of time and place."[67] While everyday meals generally are not considered within the field of study of philosophers or art critics who theorize about traditional (or nontraditional) forms of aesthetics, the concept that an "artifact" evokes feelings independent from time and place echoes what I have heard all the cooks-as-artists address. The range in age between these women is about thirty years; some are natives of Michoacán, Jalisco, Veracruz, Puebla, California, and Texas; most of the women who are native from Mexico are now residents of California. They all speak about a particular set of emotions generated by the aesthetics of the moment found in their own meals. I do not intend to suggest that these feelings are also independent of time and place, but I simply raise the question: why have traditional philosophers of aesthetics felt a necessity to separate feelings from time and place? Why must our emotions be addressed in the abstract?

Besides the gender and classist elitism that has prevented the consideration of everyday cuisine as artistic creations, another reason is the ideological assumption that aesthetics are a "contemplative engagement." The focus becomes the "individual artifacts" where sight, in the case of painting and literature, and hearing, in the case of music, are the only senses that allow a "contemplative engagement " to take place. Yet for philosopher Nicholas Wolterstorff, an artifact comes into its own not when it transcends ordinary reality and becomes a "contemplative engagement," but when "it is used for the purpose for which it was intended."[68] Such an intention is always in flux, depending on the artists and the occasion for an artistic creation.

Temporality, therefore, questions the very notion of universalism found in traditional theoretical constructions of aesthetic forms. One major critical tool offered by the aesthetics of the moment found in culinary arts is that such a moment is not absent of a localized history, meaning the history in which the artist (or art critic) situates her/himself.[69] Furthermore, universalism is achieved through a process of objective perceptions of reality, which are only obtainable through "the independence of the mind from the body."[70] Yet the very nature of culinary artistic creations rejects the separation of mind and body. Cooking requires the mind and body to work "together in union, engaged in thoughtful practice which ministers the whole person, an ordinary being, in an ordinary context."[71]

The aesthetic value in the artistic creation of a meal or a dish is experienced by being in the moment. While food is experienced briefly, such experience is always in connection to our sense of self, to others, to places, to specific times in rather concrete ways. Again, in the first two sections of this chapter and throughout *Voices,* we have seen many examples of such connections. Erika Morales offers one more connection when she speaks of her grandmother's connection to her Catholic faith in her process of making tortillas. Morales says, "My grandmother, the one who died, the mother of my father, made beautiful handmade tortillas. She would tell me, 'look, *mi'ja,* the cross of Christ gets marked on the tortilla, the crown with thorns. You can see some thorns marked in the middle [of the tortilla]' Yes, I noticed them. And she would say, 'look there is the cross; this is way the tortilla is sacred. People say that this is God's crown.' Yes, the cross would be marked [on the tortilla]. My grandmother's tortilla was very beautiful."[72] Morales's grandmother's *bonitas tortillas* offer a culinary process of conceptualizing history, as did Villicaña's *mole* mentioned above. Morales's grandmother's beautiful tortillas express a "sense of history"[73] connected to a people's religious faith. Esperanza Vélez also comments on the religious symbolism of tortillas. For Esperanza Vélez, the tortilla is sacred because its shape symbolizes the host and because the tortilla is for Mexicans "el pan de cada día" (our daily bread).[74] The religious faith connected with tortillas certainly goes beyond the shape. From pre-Colombian times to the present, corn has been sacred for many indigenous and *mestizo* people. A collection of writings by an indigenous group, *Mascualpakilstli,* describes corn as part of the cycle of life: "el maíz es igual de importante como el matrimonio, el bautizo, el entierro" (maize is equally as important as marriage, baptism, and burial).[75]

The way food connects us to the world has a long history and larger scope. Thirteenth-century Japanese philosopher, Dōgen extended this connection to the universe: "When one is identified with the food one eats, one is identified with the whole universe; when we are one with the whole universe we are one with the food we eat."[76] In the language of philosophical discourse, Curtin explains that these connections are achieved by experiencing what he calls "the authentic presence of food." Curtin suggests that "If we are to understand food in such a way [so] that its flavor [and meaning] is not lost in abstractions, we must be willing to acknowledge our relations with it [food] in such ways that they are not falsified by a theoretical bias for the abstract and the atemporal."[77] "The authentic presence of food" is one that grounds us in the ordinary, in the everyday aspects of life rather than pulls us away from it; it grounds us in the moment.

The appreciation for the aesthetics of the moment found within quotidian cuisine requires a social space where diverse forms of artistic expression coexist.[78] In *Nepantla,* Pat Mora calls for "a more egalitarian attitude toward creativity." She feels that arts need to be removed "from a pedestal," thus, making "them more a part of life" in order to capture "the vast capacity of the human spirit."[79] Nearly thirty years earlier in *In Search of Our Mothers' Gardens,* Alice Walker makes a similar remark by criticizing the nearsighted lenses that the *experts* use in assessing the aesthetics of an artistic creation. Walker writes, "[I]n the appreciation of art, or life what is always needed . . . is [a] larger perspective. . . . And yet, in our particular society, it is the narrowed and narrowing view of life that often wins."[80] The narrow view in society works to keep the status quo, which operates in multiple ways to silence working-class women's artistic creative experiences.[81]

Pomo basket weaver Susan Billy shares Mora's and Walker's belief. Billy feels that the "hermetic mode of museum display misleads the viewer into seeing the baskets as merely beautiful." Baskets in a museum display are baskets on a pedestal where their aesthetic value stays remote. The sense of touch, not simply sight, is needed to experience the aesthetics of the baskets. Billy says "that baskets are alive and need to be handled. They need your body oils, and your care."[82] To feel the aliveness of the baskets we need a connection between them and the human touch; in such a connection the beauty and liveness of the baskets has meaning.

Philosopher Sheridan Hough in her article, "Phenomenology, Pomo Baskets, and the Work of Mabel McKay," shows how the holistic approach to Pomo baskets surpasses the dichotomous split of art versus craft. The artistic creation of the Pomo baskets is a type of "spiritual path" that connects us to the universe at many levels. While Erika Morales does not speak using Hough's discourse, Morales's remembrance of her grandmother's tortillas, as mentioned above, overlaps with Hough's own theories. These are theories that Hough bases on her academic background, her interest in Pomo baskets, and personal interviews with basket weavers. In Hough's interview with weaver Susan Billy, Billy says, "'Weaving is not a craft, it is a spiritual path. It can't all be put into words, what it means every stitch has intention.' The standard question, 'How long does it take to make a basket?' must have a holistic answer: the reeds and rhizomes must grow; the seasons turn; the weaver must make her place with the materials she selects and cultivates."[83]

The holistic approach of quotidian culinary art is one expressed by Hilaria Cortés's discussion on how and why women from her town of San Miguel del Zapote, Jalisco, Mexico, make their own tortillas, as we saw in chapter 1. Another example of the holistic approach to an artistic expression is one experienced by Liduvina Vélez's understanding of the entire process of making tortillas. In chapter 2, we heard Liduvina Vélez describe the procedure of making masa for tortillas, including how to cultivate the *milpa* (corn), how to cook it, how to grind corn in the *metate,* and how to cook tortillas in *el comal.* This procedure connected her physically to the soil. The aesthetics of her tortillas at age sixteen reflected the spirit of a teenage-woman. At the age of twenty-six, while living with Aunt Dora, the aesthetics changed to reflect a history of class prejudices.

The *charla* held in June 2003 with Chef Norma Salazar, head instructor of the California Culinary Art Academy in South Pasadena, California, captures much of the art-in-process and the aesthetics of the moment of culinary artistic creations. She began her cooking career by baking cookies next to her mother.

Norma: *You have to love food and understand food in order to serve food. You have to have a passion for it. I teach my instructors to teach [the students] passion. You need to have a passion for whatever you do.*

Meredith: *To what degree have your mother's and grandmother's cooking talents influenced you?*

Norma: *I believe they gave me the foundation. Definitely to learn to love what you do. They love food so much that they would share that with others. Today I am that way. Giving is a part of me. [From the kitchen] you are giving substance. You are feeding the body, and the mind, the soul. Every part of your body is involved in experiencing food. All of your senses are being used. Eating something that you may not have had in years can bring back memories. Maybe a special peach, having this peach nice and warm might remind you of being at your aunt's ranch. Picking this peach and smelling it brings back those memories. This is what food is. I like to use my senses. My grandmother definitely taught me this. Smell is very, very important. They [my mother and grandmother] taught me to respect. Respect for people. Respect for food.*

The aesthetics of the moment offered by culinary art is expressed through the process of connecting, trusting, sharing, tasting, and opening our minds, and our mouth, to the universe presented in the meal being offered. For both the cooks-as-artists and the receiver, the aesthetics of the moment manifests itself in experiencing nourishment that feeds our intellect, our awareness of history, our appreciation of culture, and our souls as we, quite literally, take in the world created by the cooks-as-artists.

El arte culinario casero, therefore, reflects an artistic creation that does not fall under Western canonical definitions of aesthetics, but that also goes beyond the notion of minority oppositional art. For example, the aesthetics of the moment in *el arte culinario casero* go beyond the politics of "anti-aesthetic" art creation. "Anti-aesthetic," as defined by Hal Foster, "signals that the very notion of aesthetics, its network of ideas, is in question."[84] Questioning the network of ideas that inform the meaning of aesthetics, as I have done with both Jean-François Revel's hierarchical separation between "erudite

cuisine" versus "popular cuisine," and Linda Nochlin's social apparatus that create "great men artists," is a worthy intellectual pur-
suit. Yet while "'the anti-aesthetic' is useful for initiating a dialogue
concerning the limitations that are created by what we view as 'classical form,' [it] only recognizes minority cultural production in oppositional terms."[85] This particular view reduces the creative spirit
of working-class women's culinary art-in-process, which is informed
by their *sazón,* their senses, and inspired by their emotions, to forms
of *reacting against* rather than *acting toward* something.

The agency that some cooks-as-artists experienced through
their culinary art-in-process could be conceived only as acts of resistance, instead of underscoring their agency as acts of affirmation.
But Liduvina Vélez's *bonitas tortillas* were not simply an act of resistance to the matriarchal power governed by her mother-in-law at
the age of sixteen when she was first married. Those tortillas were
also an act of affirmation of her own sense of *self.* María Luisa Villicaña also affirms the method in her way of making *mole,* which asserts something about herself even if her *mole,* as her husband says,
is missing sesame seeds, an ingredient necessary for *mole* that is
"truly" from Puebla. While Villicaña's *mole* might be missing the
sesame seeds needed to be authentically from Puebla, it is not missing what for her are the most important elements. Villicaña says,
"Lo hice con tanto amor. Le puse todos mis ingredientes. Las ganas,
eso si, las ganas" (I did it with lots of love. I added all my ingredients. [And] enthusiasm, oh yes, enthusiasm). The love and enthusiasm invested in the preparation of *mole* is for Villicaña an act of
affirming her affection for her guests.

Resistance and affirmation are not necessarily mutually exclusive. Prolonged forms of oppression can, and do, lead to cultural and
personal acts of both resistance and affirmation. Affirmation, however, addresses a way of knowing based on lived experiences.
Affirmation is about a field of knowledge (of *saber*), as opposed to a
field of study (of *conocer*), where the experts of the art-in-process of
el arte culinario casero are the cooks-as-artists, where their quotidian culinary creations reveal the aesthetics of the moment. "El arte
culinario casero" is in fact, as Alma Welty says in the opening of this
chapter, "una maravilla."

CHAPTER 4

• •

Kitchen Talk

Cooks-as-Writers

When Alma Contreras, my sister, explains how she developed her recipe for making what in our family is known as Alma's *famosas enchiladas,* she expresses part of her identity, of her life: "Okay, one time I made a salsa with oregano using *el molcajete* [mortar and pestle], and I thought of putting it in the middle before putting in the cheese and folding the tortillas. One day, I thought of this, and it tasted good, and now this is how I do it. Which means, I have already changed my recipe. To some people I tell them, and they say, 'But those are not enchiladas.' I know how I like them, and this is how I make them."[1] In affirming her right to creative expression, Contreras asserts her agency. Her *chiste,* while it causes others to see her enchiladas as unauthentic, conveys a story of a woman who at moments sees cooking as more than a wife's duty and obligation. The authority she claims for her own style of making enchiladas, within the specific content of the *charlas,* tells the story of a woman who no longer feels apologetic about her supposed lack of culinary knowledge toward her academic sister, me, known in our family as the young gourmet cook. Our aunt, Esperanza Vélez, holds the title of the elder gourmet cook in the family. In a larger content of women's subjectivity, Contreras's culinary authority is an act of empowerment. While I do not wish to romanticize the culinary practices of women from the *charlas* or their lives for that matter, they are not void of moments of agency, of a voice, and of a strong sense of self. Contreras's style of making enchiladas and of normally eating when everyone else is done, for she prepares the enchiladas as people are eating them, could tempt some of us to argue that she is not "at *will* the taker and initiator, for her own right."[2] If this is all we hear, what happens to Contreras's last statement quoted above, "yo sé como a mí me gustan y es como yo las hago" (I know how I like them and that's how I make them)? Her moment of assertiveness would get lost.

The previous three chapters show a number of ways women from the *charlas* appropriate the kitchen to make it their own *space,* understand the *sazón's* sensual-logic, and express their creative talents. Chapter 4 further explores how women's kitchen talk represents a form of narrating life stories. While the previous three chapters speak to this fact, here I focus more broadly on the *charlas* to hear women's own voices as they articulate how they develop their recipes, their attitude about food, and some of the familial, cultural, and social stories that kitchen talk raises. Paule Marshall describes women's kitchen talk as "highly functional." Marshall remembers her mother and her mother's friends' kitchen gatherings serving "as therapy, the cheapest kind available to my mother and her friends . . . it restored them to a sense of themselves and reaffirmed their self-worth. . . . But more than therapy, the freewheeling, wide-ranging, exuberant talk functioned as an outlet for the tremendous creative energy they possess.[3] "Kitchen Talk: Cooks-as-Writers" reflects on how women from the *charlas* inscribe their everyday reality on cooking practices so that their knowledge, talent, wisdom— their very lives—do not "succumb to the alchemy of erasure."[4] Women, through their kitchen talk, the sharing of recipes, spoken or written, anecdotes, and food's sensual and emotive way of communication, seize subjectivity.

All conversations revolving around food include recipes, recipes that express part of a person's life story. In this chapter I explore the ways in which, through the process of sharing recipes, women from the *charlas* write parts of their lives' narratives. In describing the development of specific recipes, these women become cooks-as-writers. The idea of cooks-as-writers comes from literary critic Tey Diana Rebolledo, who refers to Chicana writers as "writers as cooks."[5] The distinctive forms of making a meal, seasoning a recipe, along with the anecdotes shared in the process, represent a spoken culinary genre, a form of culinary memoir, of the cooks-as-writers.

All culinary memoirs include recipes as will this chapter. The recipe description follows the manner in which they were given during the *charlas* to show how the cooks-as-writers speak to other cooks (Mexican cooks) who have the ability to fill in the "missing" steps from a recipe's procedure. I keep the recipes in this manner to underscore the theme of *Voices,* the recognition and validation of different fields of knowledge. The cooks-as-writers, as do academics, communicate with a technical language (at times referred to as "jargon" within the academy) understood by those within their community of reference.

Alma's *famosas enchiladas*

First you cook guajillo *chiles with a tomato, to avoid* las agruras, *okay. Then, you make a separate sauce. You cook some tomatoes with green chiles* jalapeños. *Then you mash them in the* molcajete, *or blend them in the blender, depending on how many enchiladas you are going to make. Transfer this salsa to a container and add a little bit of vinegar, chopped onion, and a bit of oregano. Of course, salt* al gusto. *Now returning to the* guajillo *sauce, you also mix it in the blender with salt, garlic, and a piece of onion. Then you sauté the sauce a little. Now make the enchiladas. First dip the tortillas in the chile sauce and then fry it in hot oil. Next place them on a plate, put some oregano salsa and* queso fresco *in the middle, and then roll them. The last step, place some lettuce, slices of tomato, slices of onion, and a little cheese on top. Finally, eat them. ¿Que rico, no?*[6]

Numerous feminist critics, first and third world alike, underscore the self-empowerment found within the act of expressing one's story. Mexican feminist critic María Elena de Valdés argues that narratives are "the prime source of our concept of the world and therefore also the basis for our belief systems and ideological determination."[7] In language, says de Valdés, the individual "constitutes" herself as "subject, because language alone establishes" what we know as reality.[8] In the last section of chapter 1, "A *Place* of Their Own: Appropriating the Kitchen *Space,*" the specific attention I direct to Liduvina Vélez's constant reference to "el marido" (the husband) shows a reality in Vélez's life as she knew it. *El marido* was a man Vélez never intended to marry. Since Vélez and I have had a total of seven recorded *charlas* (and numerous that have taken place without the recorder), she continues to refer to

Juan Abarca as "el marido" and more often than not to the six children of this marriage as "mis hijos." In a *charla* with María Luisa
Villicaña and Irma Vásquez, I shared this observation with them:

Meredith: *In the* charlas *mom and I have had, she always says "my
children" and "the husband." She rarely has said "our children"
or "the father of my children." In all the* charlas, *she refers to
Juan as "the husband," not even "my husband." In other* charlas
*with Alma, with my grandmother, with my aunts, they do say
"my husband" and "our children" or "the father of my children."*

Irma: *I sometimes also say "my children" and sometimes "our children." I am trying to be better at saying "our children." I like saying "our children." I think that it is our culture, our custom to
say "my children."*

Meredith: *But is it also the case with "the husband"?*

Irma: *I think that is because of her situation.*

Meredith: *That's what I think too, that many times it is the situation that [makes us say certain things].*

Irma: *Saying "the husband" I think it is because of her situation.
But I think that saying "my children," that's our culture. Because I might tell you "my children," when I know that Luis has
always been a responsible father and the children are his too. So
I should say, I am trying to say, "our children." I think we do this
because we had them.*

Duvi: *They are part of you. . . . We had two little grocery stores across
the street and he [Juan] would not let me ask for food on credit.
No, [I could not get food] until he sold a pair of sandals. If no
sandals were sold all day long, the children would be without
eating all day. That [attitude] would make me very angry since
my children were hungry. That's why later, I began selling food.[9]*

Vásquez and Vélez agree with de Valdés's argument that language
expresses our reality. I pointed out how Vélez in previous *charlas*
refers to *el marido;* she critically reflects on her habit of referring to
her children as *mis hijos* and to Juan Abarca as *el marido.* For
Vélez, who had a marriage that left much to be desired (it is in this
same *charla* that Vélez speaks of the abusive and negligent behavior of *el marido*), it makes sense that she would not want to share
her children.

Language does say much about who we are and how we see our
life, as does food. For anthropologist Mary Douglas, "Food always

has a social dimension of utmost importance in the system of communication" for it is a "medium through which a system of relationships within a family is expressed."[10] Furthermore, food and its preparations form one aspect of a nation's, a culture's, and a person's identity. Cooking and eating also express "the most deeply felt human experiences, and thus [express] things that are sometimes difficult to articulate in everyday language."[11] On the personal level, in the opening quote, Contreras speaks of food's ability to communicate strong emotions in regard to her creative agency, and the phrase *Alma's famosas enchiladas* captures, in words, the strong emotions evoked by her family when eating her enchiladas. In a recipe, a woman narrates parts of *her-stories* and, thus, she speaks as a subject.

In 2003, I taught a course, called Women Philosophers in the Kitchen, and when we reached the section of recipes as life narratives, one particular student expressed skepticism that recipes could offer more than just instructions on preparing a meal. Literary critic Cecilia Lawless makes clear the root of my student's reaction by explaining that because historically the chore of domestic cooking falls into women's hands, the process of cooking as a "gendered discourse" often loses its force of empowerment.[12] Yet this gendered discourse in cookbooks, for instance, offers themes of life and death, youth and age, faithfulness and betrayal, memory and forgetfulness, aesthetics, and on making a life's daily routine into meaningful physical and spiritual moments of substance. Cookbooks, argues Janet Theophano in *Eat My Words* (2002), are "records of women's social interaction and exchange," as they often include history, current events, folk wisdom, religious events, racial and class tension.[13] For cultural anthropologist Arjun Appadurai, cookbooks are "revealing artifacts of culture in the making."[14] For Anne Goldman, recipes are autobiographical assertions.[15] In *Encarnación's Kitchen: Mexican Recipes from Nineteenth-Century California* (2003), Encarnación Pinedo, with the title of one recipe, expresses the racial tension felt by Californios as Anglos descended on the golden state and eventually took economic and political control of it. The classic American breakfast of ham and eggs becomes in her cookbook, "Huevos hipócritos (con jamón)" ("Hypocritical Eggs [with Ham]." In the introduction to her cookbook, Pinedo describes her feelings more expressively: "The English have advanced the art [of cooking] a bit, enough that several of its writers have published on the subject: a Mr. Pegge in 1390, Sir J. Elliot in 1539, Abraham Veale in 1575, and Widover Treasure in 1625. Despite all this, there is not a single Englishman who can cook, as their food and style of seasoning are the most insipid and tasteless that one can imagine."[16] Pinedo certainly communicates strong emotions through her feelings about food.

The skepticism regarding women's discourses extends beyond the language of food since other women's linguistic codes are also undervalued and at times unrecognized. María Dolores Gonzales, in *Speaking Chicana: Voice, Power, and Identity* (1998), points out this lack of recognition by the little scholarship "women's linguistic behavior" receives even though women "have historically been the guardians of language and culture." More studies on "women's linguistic behavior," affirms Gonzales, would "reveal that women have at their disposal various linguistic codes that they deem appropriate to use across private and public domains and with select interlocutors."[17] Women's forms of communication extend beyond the literal spoken or written word. In the collection *Speaking Chicana*, art historian Charlene Villaseñor Black explores women's pictorial language: "a semantic extension of language beyond words to pictures."[18] The pictorial language reflects one form of women's self-expression. Native American, African American, Latina, and other scholarship focuses on minority ethnic women and brings to our attention women's nonverbal communicative codes expressed in the practices of basket weaving, quilt making, sewing, gardening, and cooking. In *Remedios* (1998), Aurora Levíns Morales speaks eloquently about women's ways of communication. Speaking about Puerto Rico's history, Levíns Morales says, "Let's get one thing straight. Puerto Rico was a woman's country.... We were never still, our hands were always busy. Making soup. Making candles. Holding children. Making bedding. Sewing clothing. Our stitches held sleeve to dress and soul to body. We stitched our families through the dead season of the cane, stitched them through lean times of bread and coffee. The seams we made kept us from freezing in the winters of New York and put beans on the table in the years of soup kitchens."[19] In Levíns Morales's description, women speak with their hands and a needle.

Another Puerto Rican writer and literary critic, Rosario Ferré, makes explicit the connection between the *sazón,* the sensory language spoken in the kitchen, and the written word. Ferré demystifies the dichotomy of superiority that juxtaposes male to female writing with its essentialist gender differences vis-à-vis women's cooking practices, particularly our mother's. She says, "What is important is not to determine if we as women have to write with an open or closed writing structure, with a poetic language or with an obscene language, with our heads or with our hearts. What is important is to apply that fundamental lesson that we learn from our mothers, the first ones, after all, who taught us to fight with fire: the secret of writing, like the secret of good cooking, has nothing to do with gender, but with the wisdom with which ingredients are combined."[20] Ferré sees the importance of the written word and the practice of our mothers' cooking as part of the same continuum, as part of the same process of writing stories.

Despite the increase in scholarship on modes of communication beyond the literal written and spoken word, these two remain privileged within the academy. If women's written or spoken linguistic codes are not among those which conventional sociolinguists generally deem worthy of study, much less so would be their nonverbal, sensory codes as those found in the practices of quotidian cooking. As a matter of fact, with the exception of Charlene Villaseñor Black, the linguistic concerns *Speaking Chicana* explores discuss largely Chicanas' spoken linguistic codes. Nonetheless, the sociolinguistic scholarship presented in this collection, serves to close the gaps created by neglecting "women's linguistic behavior." Scholarship on folklore such as the collection *Chicana Traditions: Continuity and Change* (2002) helps in increasing the visibility of women's way of communicating through their many creative talents.

Scholarship on nonwritten and nonspoken forms of women's communication continues such efforts. By nonwritten I refer to those forms of sharing a story, knowledge, history that are literally not written in a conventional way. In this chapter, and throughout *Voices,* I am the one writing about the cooks-as-writers recipes and the stories embedded in them. Most of these women, as mentioned in previous chapters, do not actually write down recipes. Perhaps if they did, and simply offered a copy of a written recipe, the *confianza* created between us by the *charlas,* where the stories unfold, might not have flourished, and they might not have shared as much about their lives. By nonspoken, I specifically refer to the communication of the *sazón,* the *chiste,* and the act of offering food, accepting it or rejecting it. All of these communicate social relations. The cooks-as-writers' narratives, therefore, create a somewhat unconventional genre that requires unconventional reading practices, a practice that involves the use of all the senses.

Food *is* a system of communication. In the words of anthropologist Carole M. Counihan, "food is a powerful voice, especially for women, who are often heavily involved with food acquisition, preparation, provisioning, and cleanup." Counihan's work on "food-centered life histories . . . give voice to traditionally muted people—people not part of the political, economic, or intellectual elite, especially women."[21] Anthropologist graduate student Ramona Lee Pérez's research on "kitchen table ethnography" is a "data collection method focusing on women's food narratives."[22] Methods such as these and the *charlas culinarias* help us learn from the experience and knowledge of those most often not heard, particularly women. In the case of the *charlas,* with food as a system of communication that uses the *sazón* to develop a lexicon with its subjective and fluid (as opposed to objective/universal) *al gusto,* the cooks-as-writers add their own personal *chistes* to their recipes so their narratives reflect the peculiarities of their stories.

Voices and *charlas culinarias* add one more title and concept to the growing areas of food as voice and feminist scholarship, as *Telling to Live* (2002), expressing and exploring how personal and collective forms of empowerment are gained through the process of sharing *her-stories.* With the research on food as voice, such acts of empowerment are not limited to the literal written expression. While writing *is* a vital form self-expression, what happens to a woman who, to echo Virginia Woolf, lacks not only a room of her own but paper of her own as well? The women from the *charlas,* and other women like them, are cooks-as-writers whose kitchen talk and *sazón* narrate the value of the mundane. The inflection in their voices, their facial gestures, the rhythms of their body speak of how they are able to create a culinary lexicon to express their own familial and extended social relations. Their food voice works as their *testimonios,* "a crucial means of bearing witness and inscribing into history those lived realities that would otherwise succumb to the alchemy of erasure."[23] Kitchen talk, written in cookbooks or memoirs, or spoken as in the case of ethnographic research on food as voice, offer moments of seizing subjectivity and narrative authority, which allows women to embrace the power of their own history—its pain, its suffering, its joy. Critical reflection on our own history is the first step in a process of *conscientización,* which leads to empowering moments of personal and collective acts of freedom.[24]

For Liduvina Vélez, kitchen talk offers her the opportunity to articulate the experiences and knowledge she gained through her years of farm life as a teenager. Once Vélez began to speak about her culinary knowledge, she realized the power embedded in telling a story and of her own *sazón.* Vélez's bashfulness disappeared as she expressed the excitement of what she knows.

> *With Aunt Celía, I learned all the process from milking a cow to making cheese. I know how to tie the legs of a cow so it will not kick you; I learned how to take the calf from the cow. The knots with which you tie the cow's legs have to be knots that you can easily remove. To milk the cow also has its own technique. If you squeeze tightly, the cow won't let out the flow of milk. You have to have a certain strength in your hands, and position them in a certain form so the cow will let the milk flow. Boy, I used to get some big buckets of milk. The milk was foamy! About agriculture, I think I learned lots with my aunt and uncle. I also learned to make cheese. From coagulating the milk—it is called curd . . . it is something you get from the cows when they are killed. The curd is dried with salt. I also learned to make cream. Over there it's called* jocoque. *But it does not have any chemicals.*[25]

What Vélez describes here goes beyond the physical and chemical aspect of all these procedures. Her last sentence discloses her awareness and concerns about preservatives added to foods. With one sentence she exemplifies Michel de Certeau's philosophical argument that consumers are not passive individuals at the mercy of progress disguised under scientific apparatus.[26] Vélez is fully aware of the implications of buying processed foods and relying on mass production. While it is time efficient, it is not always nutritionally efficient. The price for progress, with its multiple choices for the consumer, is that the stories (the realities) of many families with long histories of making cheese (as well as other dairy and agricultural products) are heard with less frequency.

The cooks-as-writers' narratives oftentimes express a form of a collective familial subjectivity. For a number of women from the *charlas,* these changes have begun by preparing food. For Susan García viuda de Melo, as mentioned in chapter 1, the transfer of her culinary practice into a business expresses her desire to offer her daughters the opportunity to make a living doing something other than physical labor. Hilaria Cortés, Ana María Ruvalcaba, Raquel Merlo, and Liduvina Vélez are motivated by the same factors. In the case of Liduvina Vélez, some thirty plus years since she and I bonded in the kitchens of the restaurants she worked in when I was a little girl, I follow in her footsteps. While I do not literally sell food, I earn a living theorizing and teaching the epistemologies embedded in everyday culinary practices, with the hopes of developing a food consciousness that would enable us to fully appreciate, value, and learn from the wealth of knowledge found in the ordinary practice of cooking. The cooks-as-writers' narratives show that seizing subjectivity helps to change the life path for their children due to their confidence in their *sazón* and their courage to face life's challenges.

Since recipes are individual authorities, the cooks-as-writers establish their narrative authority through the process of adding their own *chiste* to their culinary practices.[27] As they give their recipes, they establish a "community of practice" where they share concerns about what they are doing and about what that means in their lives and their communities. For Susan Leonardi, a recipe's narrative is "reproducible, and further, its hearers-readers-receivers are *encouraged* to reproduce it, and, in reproducing it, to revise it and make it their own."[28] Consequently, a new story is narrated. The ethnographic emphasis of *Voices* is not to write out recipes so the readers can appropriate them through a process of recreation. Such appropriation changes the meaning of the story. *Voices* encourages readers to *listen* to the cook-as-writer's own *chiste* in her cooking practices so that her story can be heard. If a reader wishes to recreate recipes throughout *Voices,* by all means, but the recipe recreated will be a version of the reader's own story, a story that involves reading this book.

In the act of piecing together recipes and creating new ones, women take authorship of their creation. Alma Contreras explains this process in the following way: "Nowadays I make a very good *pozole,* but I created it from a number of different recipes. I got the recipe from one person and I made it. And then I would get other people's comments, opinions. And then at the end, I did it in my own way. At the end, I fixed the recipe in my own style. Like a puzzle, you arrange each little piece you get from different people until you make your own menu. This is how make my *pozole.*"[29] An individual's authorship in developing her own menu is never just based on a person's independent creative talent. Since a recipe speaks to part of our identity, Contreras's description indicates how our sense of self comes through interactions with others. Yet such involvement serves to develop, as Contreras says, our "own menu"; thus close interaction with others does not take away our "autonomy, creativity, and capacity for self-definition."[30]

Alma's *pozole, a su gusto* (to her liking)

You cook some chile guajillo. In a different pot, cook the pork, pata de puerco, and chicken. (Well, I add chicken because my friend Cheryl does not eat pork, and she really likes pozole. So, I had to adjust the recipe a bit.) To the meat add garlic, salt, onion, and oregano. When the pork has cooked half way, then add the chicken; otherwise the chicken will come off the bones. Then you blend the chiles in the blender with salt, garlic, and onion. Before adding the chile sauce to the meat, you put it through a sieve. Then add the hominy (maíz), and you wait until it is done. This dish is served with chopped cabbage, chopped radishes, onion, lemon, and tostadas. Add the chicken when the pork is almost half way done cooking; otherwise you will over cook the chicken.[31]

Not long ago, I found out that *pozole* with pork and chicken is New Mexican style. Cheryl and Contreras's friendship goes back over twenty years, for this long I have eaten *pozole* Alma's style. Not until the *charla* took place and Contreras gave me her recipe did I learn her personal motives for adding chicken. "Yo quería que mi amiga disfrutara la comida, so la modifiqué" (I wanted my friend to enjoy the food, so I modified it). A bond of friendship influences the creation of "Alma's *pozole, a su gusto.*"

Ordinary people doing ordinary things (with critical social awareness) create change. When speaking of cultural imperialism, "the imposition of cultural practices by one economic or political power," and cultural colonialism, "the appropriation of such practices by such power," philosopher Lisa Heldke remarks how "cuisines are always a patchwork of borrowing and lending, undertaken at various conditions of liberty and bondage." The borrowing and lending helps her consider "the possibility that members of a culture may be responding to colonization as [people] who are deciding for themselves whether and how they will incorporate the strange foods that are making their way into [their] community."[32] I believe this to be the case because people stripped of economic and political power remain "active agents whose sense of self is projected on to and expressed in an expansive range of cultural practices."[33] Steven Flusty takes this argument one step further in *De-Coca-Colonization* (2004), by arguing that globalization happens "only because it is woven through the planet's social fabric from the ground up."[34] For Flusty, the influence of change from the ground up affects the nature of globalization. In *Voices,* the cooks-as-writers express changes at a micro level rather than at a macro one.

Since *Voices* speaks mainly of one cultural group, Mexican (or Mexican American), the specific forms of cultural imperialism and colonialism, as Heldke defines them above, might not always apply. But the efforts for cultural exclusiveness exist within a single ethnic group, even when referring to a group of a similar socioeconomic class. How else do we explain the remark Contreras at times gets that her own way of making enchiladas is not authentic? Just like Heldke, I agree and take seriously Joanna Kadi's issue "that 'many people of color are just as inattentive to these issues [of cultural appropriation] and thus act inappropriately toward each other,' and that focusing only on relations between whites and some other group(s) of color, 'support[s] the lie that we [people of color], can only be discussed in the relation to white people, that our only important relationships exist with white people.'"[35] Those who have suggested to Contreras that her enchiladas are something other than enchiladas are Mexican people. In conceptual and practical terms, therefore, I see cultural imperialism, cultural colonialism, and cultural exclusivism as carrying similar ideological forces that can silence the voices of others by denying them the right to express their own *chistes,* their right to narrate their life from their own culinary perspectives.

Changes in a recipe do not render them unauthentic, making a person cultureless. What, after all, does authenticity mean? Emiko Ohnuki-Tierney in *Rice as Self: Japanese Identities through Time* (1993) argues that authenticity is only an invented term, often used for marketing purposes. James Clifford's "On Collecting Art and Culture" sees the notion of authenticity in artifices as one imposed by the "I/eye" of economic power to the exotic other.[36] Lisa Heldke also sees the notion of authenticity in food as that which is exotic to *her,* yet for others this same food could be the most ordinary of meals. I see the claim of authenticity as a double-edged sword.

Those who award themselves the privilege of defining authenticity in any ethnic food, whether they are cultural outsiders or insiders, inflict wounds that either appropriate cultural and personal knowledge or essentialize it, causing a stifling of creative growth.

Mexican cuisine (all cuisines) is neither restricted to one symbolic interpretation, nor are its culinary products restricted to one never-changing notion of authentic cooking. For instance, corn as a central crop of Mexican cuisine, epitomizes change.[37] Corn for Gloria Anzaldúa represents a perfect social and political metaphor to articulate the *mestiza* consciousness. In *Borderlands/La Frontera* (1987), Anzaldúa says,

> *Indigenous like corn, like corn the mestiza is a product of cross-breeding, designed for preservation under a variety of conditions. Like an ear of corn—a female seed-bearing organ—the mestiza is tenacious, tightly wrapped in the husks of her culture. Like kernels she clings to the cob; with thick stalks and strong brace roots, she holds tight to the earth—she will survive the crossroads.*

> Lavando y remojando el maíz en agua de cal, despojando el pellejo. Moliendo, mixteando, amasando, haciendo tortillas de masa. *She steeps the corn in lime, it swells, softens. With stoneroller on metate, she grinds the corn, then grinds again. She kneads and molds the dough, pats the round balls into tortillas.*[38]

Anzaldúa uses corn and the process of making tortillas as a metaphor to represent the new *mestiza* consciousness, a consciousness that reflects change by the fact that a person is always at crossroads. For cook-as-writer Erika Morales, as mentioned in the previous chapter, her grandmother's handmade tortillas' religious implication with the cross forming the center also symbolizes a historical moment of two cultures meeting at crossroads, the Spanish and the indigenous.

The catalysts to a person's *chiste* in their way of cooking or their attitudes about food reflect how an individual's life is constantly at crossroads. *Chistes* range from adding an oregano salsa to the enchiladas, to eating tostadas with cabbage, to having polenta, *nopalitos,* and flan during the same meal. *Chistes,* within a family, can reflect different geographical and economic status between two or three generations. The following dialogue about Liduvina Vélez's

past and Alma Contreras's present exemplifies one aspect of geographical and economic changes in their lives:

Alma: Sopitos, *tamales,* uchepos, *and all those things I like. But
they are laborious [to make]. I'd rather buy them. That's the
good thing about this country, that I work and I can buy whatever I want without having the necessity of having to cook
[them]. Otherwise, you have to cook or don't eat.*

Duvi: *That's the best thing about this place. But over in the countryside from where I come—*

Alma: *But the good thing is that I was not raised in the countryside,
'amá.*

Duvi: *Over there in the countryside you don't have a choice. You
have to do everything. The good thing about this place, if you
don't cook or if you don't know [how to cook], you can go buy
[food], as long as you have a job. But over there in my countryside, from where I come, you learn and you find out a way of
[cooking].*

Alma: *Or you die of hunger.*

Duvi: *Or you die of hunger.*[39]

Does the fact that the *sopitos,* tamales, and *uchepos* Contreras
enjoys now are not homemade by our mother's hand, take away their
authenticity? No. Are Contreras's memories of eating these foods
cooked by our mother diminished because she now buys them made
by a stranger's hands? Are these foods then no longer authentic to
our family's history? No. For the people who cook authentic ethnic
foods, must their cultural practices and socioeconomic status remain unchanged throughout endless generations? No. Do changes
in cultural practices and socioeconomic status render people cultureless? No. Are my family and I less culturally Mexican because
we enjoy eating my invention of Mexican spaghetti: spaghetti with
a *chipotle* and cilantro-based sauce? No. Is eating tortillas spread
with peanut butter and jelly instead of refried beans a sign of being
cultureless? No. José A. Burciaga, whose children use a tortilla instead of a slice of bread for peanut butter and jelly sandwiches, sees
this culinary combination as an act of biculturalism.[40] Mexican cuisine, like all cuisines, develops by cultural encounters. Trinh T.
Minh-ha's speaks of cultural encounters by saying that "there is a
Third World in every First World, and vice-versa."[41]

• •

Guadalupe Flores

Guadalupe Flores's way of cooking resonates with Contreras, as it comes from observing others. Yet she does not cook like any of the people she has observed, particularly her mother and mother-in-law. She relates, "When I got married, maybe I incorporated into my cooking a little from what I saw here and there. You see others and then you arrange things your own way. Reading here, searching over there, you find out that a meal can come out better. Searching for [how] technology [can help], *mi'ja*. Searching for the modern things. I modified my style of cooking different from other people. I do not cook like my mother or my mother-in-law."[42] Flores cooks with her own *chiste*.

Avoiding fatty foods and spending too much time in the kitchen are central themes in Flores's culinary narrative.[43] The way she describes recipes reflect these major concerns of her life: "I always try to reduce the lard or oil in food. Yes, [my] food is not as good as your aunt Esperanza's, maybe because I do things differently. For example, they [Esperanza's family] eat enchiladas. I never make enchiladas. I make *entomatadas*."[44] Her *entomatadas* are made, as she says, with "una salsa de tomate," to which she adds "de esas Campbell soups . . . que *chicken mushroom* o bien sea *cream of chicken,* o *cream of mushroom.*" She adds one of these cream soups to make the *entomatadas* "un poquito más nutritivas, [a] que nomás estes traganado tortilla" (little more nutritious, instead of just eating tortillas). Eating what she feels is healthy food, particularly in order not to gain weight, comes up more in Flores's *charlas* than in any other. These attitudes explain her response regarding the idea of comfort food. I told her that when I feel somewhat sad, lonesome, and in need for comfort I crave *chilaquiles,* particularly my mother's *chilaquiles;* when she experiences similar emotions, she feels like eating fruit or nothing at all.

Because of Flores's general interest in weight and health issues and with her general disinterest in food, while she likes traditional Mexican food, she avoids eating it due to its lard or oil content. Yet on occasions she does have it and enjoy it. For instance, when discussing foods normally eaten during *cuaresma* (Lent), the period before the crucifixion and resurrection of Jesus Christ, we mentioned *tortas de papa.* "I want you to know that it had been years since I ate *tortas de papa,* and this last Lent I made them. They absorbed a lot of oil [when you fry them]. You should have seen how much we ate! Your uncle really liked them. Of all the things I fixed, I think what we all ate the most were the *tortas de papa.*"[45]

Another example of Mexican foods that Flores tries to avoid is tamales.

Lupita: Nowadays [my children] like tamales. Before they didn't like them. I didn't use to buy tamales. There were no tamales here. I am somewhat chocantoza because I don't like food with lard. And people who make tamales, they use a lot of lard that you eat a bit of tamal and feel the chunk of lard in your mouth. Guácala!

Meredith: I like my mother's tamales because a lot of people make them very thick, that you end up eating a lot of masa. Mom makes them thin. She does not use so much masa. Therefore, the masa works more like a thin layer covering the meat that goes in the center. This is how mom makes them. But it is a lot of work to make them. That's the problem.

Lupita: Yes, it is a tremendous amount of work. No, no. I try to avoid those [kinds of foods]. I feel in life there are more important things to do than spend so much time doing something so meticulous.[46]

While for (male) philosophers, architects, and politicians *home* is the place of rest, Flores does not share this view, as briefly mentioned in chapter 1. Other women from the *charlas* (most) do admit that keeping a house involves a lot of work and cooking demands time. Flores, however, is the most articulate in expressing the efforts of keeping a house and the most active in finding ways to minimize the time spent in the kitchen.

Throughout the *charla,* Flores makes clear her disinterest in cooking. Of all the *charlas,* the one with her contains fewer descriptions of recipes. Only in the context of discussing our large family gatherings for Thanksgiving at her house does she mention recipes: "I made turkey, salads. Mmmm, carrot salad. Mmmm, mashed potatoes were never missing. I made pies. Okay, I have never ever been able to make pie crust. So, I opted for the most practical, I buy them. You guys liked lemon pie a lot. I also made pumpkin pie. I made bread. I wasted a lot of food because things would not come out well."[47] On these occasions she would cook for twelve people, but such family gatherings only lasted for a few years since my immediate family, mother and siblings, moved to California. Flores says: "Your family's move to California affected me a lot. I would make a huge amount of food because I knew that nothing would be left. After you all left, everything felt sad, you know, having an empty table."[48] The family gathering on Thanksgiving provided more than an occasion for a feast; it provided recognition and appreciation of her work.

Lupita: *You tell me that my turkey is very tasty. Okay, I didn't learn it from anyone,* mi'ja. *Just—*

Meredith: *Well you have learned to make it by combining different things, no?*

Lupita: *Exactly. [Back then] Felix [your brother] was the last one to arrive. He used to say that he wanted all of us to be done eating so that he could have all the remaining food. Do you remember?*[49]

The appreciation Flores remembers from her nephews goes beyond the enjoyment and delight expressed around her dinner table. It was an appreciation for her. When I asked her if my mother would contribute food for the meals shared at her house in Laredo, Texas, Flores laughed and said no. While she does not remember anything specific that my mother contributed for Thanksgiving or Christmas dinners, she does say that my mother "always brought tortillas from Nuevo Laredo. She would bring me fruit. She always brought me something from the other side [of the bridge]. I remember that Hugo would come and go on his bicycle [across the bridge]. He would fly on his bicycle! He was just a kid, *mi'jo chulo*. I'll never forget how he would come and go on his bicycle to bring me this and that."[50] Remembering her nephew Hugo's trips of affection and appreciation for her, trips across the international bridge, brings up a moment of quiet pain for both of us. Hugo, one of my brothers, had passed away a few years earlier in a motorcycle accident that took place as he was on his way to Laredo to see her. He intended his trip to be a surprise.

In the 1996 *charla*, Flores mentions how her own children do not offer the same kind of recognition and appreciation for her culinary creations as she received from my siblings and me. While Flores cooks more for her family than herself, she says, "Actually, one cooks for them. I am going to tell you something. Just for me, considering how little I eat, a warm tortilla would be enough. But when I cook, I cook for them. So that we can all eat together. And you feel horrible when they complain about everything you have cooked."[51] Food rejected communicates as many strong emotions as food accepted and celebrated. Flores does not suggest that her family never appreciates her food, for they do and make requests for particular dishes, such as *sopitos*. When she makes them, this becomes a moment of great enjoyment for all. Flores recalls her daughter asking her, "¿Cúando haces sopitos, mami?" (When will you make *sopitos, mami?*). After her initial shock at the request, since *sopitos* are made with masa prepared with lard, she made them: "*Sopes* are the ones you put salsa, cream, cheese, and onion on top. You place them on the *comal* till the cream begins to [liquefy] and blend with the cheese. Then you take them out. Wow, you don't just eat them, you devour them."[52]

Now in 2004, Flores's family includes sons- and daughters-in-law and grandchildren. Once again she has "mesa llena" for the holidays. Just as her family has "evolved and grown," as she says, so has her menu and motives for cooking. She makes the turkey as she has always made it, but the side dishes have changed throughout the years. Now she includes more vegetables, green beans, spinach salad, two kinds of broccoli salad, and two kinds of carrot salad. Her son-in-law likes them. The most popular pie with her grandchildren is pumpkin pie rather than lemon—but she continues to buy the crust. When I asked her how she actually makes her turkey, she said, "Ay, mi'ja, no tiene nada de gracia, nada de chiste" (Ay, *mi'ja,* it does not have anything special; it does not have a *chiste*). But her turkey, the way she expresses her style of making it does have a *chiste* that reflects her main concerns, avoiding fatty foods and opting for practical modern things. She refers to her own way of fixing it as "pavo sin receta" (turkey without a recipe) because it is simple to make, without a *chiste,* so she says.

Lupita's *pavo sin receta*

I always try to buy a Butterball turkey with a thermometer. If I can't find a Butterball, then I do make sure it has a thermometer. When I get a Butterball one, I don't add more butter because it already has a lot. When I don't buy a Butterball turkey, then I cover it with smart soy margarine. It's a little bit more nutritious. I buy a turkey bag and I place a little flour in it. But of course, the first thing is to clean the turkey well and dry it well.

Then I bathe the turkey with a mixture of garlic, celery, and pepper salt. I put a lot of this. I chop some bell pepper, celery, onion, parsley, sometimes carrots and I add it to the turkey. I place the turkey inside the bag, and I follow the bag's instructions. When the thermometer pops up, it's done. I don't make stuffing and when I do, I don't put it inside the turkey because it comes out too greasy. The turkeys are very fat. Greasy. They are big due to all those chemicals they are fed. Poor animals. When I do make stuffing, only my daughter-in-law likes it a little. My stuffing is sweet and salty because I make it with apples, raisins, almonds, celery, and onion. To make the gravy, first I take as much fat out from the turkey's juice; then I cook some flour with salt in [a little margarine and add the juice]. That's it, pavo sin receta.[53]

• •
Verónica Abarca

Events in our lives offer the plot of the story surrounding a recipe. Verónica Abarca's recipe description of *chiles en nogada* (chiles in walnut sauce) narrates two aspects that were central to her life when she ate this dish: her university studies and her family life. As the university student she was, Abarca opens with the recipe's historical background more than the procedures, in part, because she has never made *chiles en nogada* herself. As a matter of fact, in our *charla*, Vélez and I contribute in describing the actual procedure to help her remember. What she says, however, is the following:

Verónica: *Well, they are made only during a certain time of the year, which is in August. August 19, supposedly, this is a day to honor Saint Augustine. This saint is celebrated in some small towns of Puebla. That's why we have the tradition that this day you eat* chiles en nogada *in Puebla.*
Meredith: *Oh, yeah. Really? I didn't know.*
Verónica: *Yes that's it. They venerate Saint Augustine with the chiles. . . . [You serve each person] a chile on their plate, add the walnut sauce. You also put pomegranate seeds, [which are] red, and parsley, which is green. It looks very pretty because it is red, white, and green. The flag.*[54]

Chiles en nogada are prepared from mid-July to mid-September since this is the season when all the ingredients for them are found.

Chiles en nogada, **a description without a recipe**

Verónica: *You need chiles* poblanos. *What do you call them?*
Duvi: *Chiles* pasilla.
María Luisa: *Fresh or dry?*
Verónica: *Fresh. You make a mixture* (picadillo) *of fruits that are only found during this season: peaches, pears, bananas* (macho). *You peel the fruit and fry each fruit separately. Then you make a* (picadillo) *of meat and with tomatoes. Well, I don't know the recipe that well. I am just remembering from when I helped my mother. You mixed the meat with the fruit. Then you fill the chiles with the meat-fruit mixture and dip them in egg whites* (se capean), *then you fry them. Later you make the walnut sauce. You peel the walnuts, which are a kind that you can only find during this season; you add brandy. This is the* nogada. *This is what makes them taste good. Once the chile is fried, you pour some* nogada *on top. It's delicious and white. Then you sprinkle some pomegranate seeds. This dish is rather laborious and expensive.*
María Luisa: *I know of a recipe just like what you have described, except for frying the chiles. The entire process is exactly as you have said. You just don't—how do you say it?*
Verónica: Capear *(dip in egg whites).*
Duvi: *Well if they are not* capeados, *you will have less oil on your plate. I am trying to remember if the last time we had them with your aunt Esperanza were they dipped in egg whites?*
Meredith: *Yes they were.*
Duvi: *It's a good thing for them not to be dipped in egg whites. That way you eat less grease.*[55]

This moment of the *charla* offers two versions of the *chiles en nogada* so that people can eat them to their liking, *a su gusto*. The 1994 film adaptation of Laura Esquivel's *Como agua para chocolate (Like Water for Chocolate)* offers a mouth-watering representation of this dish. The novel itself gives a version of recipe.

Making *chiles en nogada* for Verónica Abarca represents an occasion for family visits and socializing: "When the time to make chiles approaches, my mother always selects a day and invites all the family, my uncles. My mother makes a big event of this. It is a special occasion. Later you say, 'All those dishes!' But at the moment it is great."[56] For Abarca, recalling the recipe for *chiles en nogada* conveys the memory of an occasion for a family's socialization and a moment of recapturing a bit of Puebla's history.

• •

Hilaria Cortés

Kitchen talk unfolds narratives describing pressing concerns in a woman's life. Hilaria Cortés, who learned to cook and sell food at seven by helping her own mother, recalls her mother's motives for selling food as a necessity created by their poverty. For Cortés, her financial situation continues to be a pressing issue to the point that she hardly takes a day off from work. Born in *la pobreza*, Cortés from an early age worked helping her mother sell food and gathering crops from the fields.

> *There were days when it rained and nothing, nothing, nothing, was sold. And we felt this deep sadness that you cannot imagine. From an early age, in Mexico, I worked in the field planting and picking bean crops. I actually didn't have a childhood, because a time that would be for me to play with dolls, I never had. I didn't have that playtime, because I have been working hard from an early age. That is why when my youngest brother begins to complain, I tell him, "Look brother, don't complain because you came when the plate was already served." In our poverty when there is not much to eat, what do we eat? A taco with salt and chile. When there are no beans, just a tortilla with chile and salt. We ate that because there was a time when there was no work. The field didn't produce anything. Everything was really ugly. The field yielded no crops.*[57]

Due to the necessity of having to work at an early age, Cortés's childhood was nonexistent. Now in her fifties, while she still sells food on the weekends to supplement her income, Cortés explains what her life has taught her: "Well, I did suffer, but I learned. Because like it or not, I know how to do [a little of] everything. I know how to milk a cow. I know how to milk a goat. I know how to make cheese [from scratch]. I know of everything. Nobody is going to tell me, 'that's not the way to make this.' No, because I know how to do it. In the way of doing things, in my way of thinking, nobody teaches me how, because I know how [to make things and who I am]. And when I don't know how to do something, I clearly say, 'I don't know how to make this. Tell me how.'"[58]

Cortés's experience of poverty and deprivation has made her frugal with her cooking. Her frugality becomes evident when she gives me a recipe for making, or better for not making, lasagna. When Cortés's children complain about her culinary repertory, she says, "Well, what do you want me to cook? I cook what I know. What I don't know I don't cook. [Her children answer], 'Make lasagna.' I go and ask how to make lasagna. I asked how to make lasagna; I was told how to make the lasagna. I made it. Oh, no! I spent hours making the stupid lasagna. I said, no more because it took me longer preparing and cooking the lasagna, than what it took them to eat it."[59] Her children complain because she made a small lasagna: "Y, ¿por qué hiciste tan poquita? Cuando hagas, haz mucha. Esto tan poquito ni agusta" (Why did you make so little? When you make it, make a lot. This was just not enough). Cortés responds, "Y, ¿cuánto le puse de queso? Como siete dólares de queso. Nó, nó yo yá nó les hago lasagna" (And how much cheese I put in there? About seven dollars worth of cheese. No, no, I don't make them lasagna). When Cortés gives a recipe, she usually refers to the main ingredient not by the amount of weight but by the cost of it. She won't make lasagna again not only because it took a long time to make, but also because to make a larger lasagna would cost more.

Cortés, with her culinary gendered discourse, expresses her knowledge about culinary matters and also how such experiences have influenced her way of thinking, of seeing the world. Her culinary discourse connects her knowledge, her struggles, and her sense of self-assurance. Cortés's ability to stand her ground against unscrupulous customers becomes a form of family subjectivity as her children learn to defend their rights and dignity as they observe their mother. In this next section of Cortés's culinary story, she speaks of some of her defensive tactics. Her narrative technique involves different voice inflections to distinguish the customer's voice from her own. For purposes of clarity the following transcription reads as an exchange between Cortés, the customer, and the park manager.

Yaya: *My God! There are some occasions that you meet wicked customers.*
Customer: *Give me my change.*

Yaya: *What change?*

Customer: *I gave you a hundred dollar bill.*

Yaya: *What hundred dollar bill? That day I was on the verge of making the mistake of calling the police because the wicked (infeliz) man wanted me to give him the change from a hundred dollar bill. He had not given me a hundred dollar bill. How would I give him the change? But he was stubborn.*

Customer: *I gave you a hundred. Don't be abusive. Go take advantage of someone else, not me. If you don't give me the change I am going to call the police.*

Yaya: *Okay, how would I return the change if you did not give a hundred dollar bill. At that moment the park manager came over and I made a hand gesture to him to hurry up. The manager comes over and asks, "What is the problem?" Look, this man says that he gave me a hundred dollar bill, and I don't have any one hundred dollar bills. So I say that one of us should call the police. If I have the bill, they can arrest me. But if I don't have it, he should be arrested, and make him pay me for my time [that he has wasted] and the insult. Then the manager says to the man,*

Manager: *Look, if you didn't give her a hundred, you need to be careful with what you are saying because she is a woman and you are man. You are incriminating her. I can call the police and if she does not have the money that you say you gave her, and if you don't have any money on you, they will arrest you, not her.*

Customer: *You are in agreement with her.*

Manager: *No, but if you want, I am calling the police right now.*

Yaya: *Then when the manager got on his radio, since the customer didn't understand English, he took off running. He wanted to commit an injustice. He wanted change for a hundred! I had not yet sold twenty dollars worth of food that day. From where would I give him the change? Therefore, you always have to be very alert because sometimes you find really evil people.[60]*

Even though Cortés ran the risk of getting a citation for selling food without a license, she would rather take the risk than allow an act of injustice to take place.

When the *charla* took place, the state of California, concerned for the safety of its citizens, mandated a law that required car insurance and car seats for children. From Cortés's perspective, based on selling food in the parks on weekends, she sees the consequences of such laws as follows: "Now the police are very strict. Before it was not mandatory to have child's car seats. It was not mandatory to have insurance. Therefore, people who have a car and do not have insurance don't go to the park. People who don't have insurance prefer not to go out. People who have children and don't have insurance don't go out because [a cop] stops them and they are left *bailando* [with a ticket]."[61] California, in order to keep people safe, it keeps many in their homes and others with fewer resources to make ends meet, according to the perspective of a park food vender, Hilaria Cortés.

Cortés has taught her children not to go through life full of "vergüenza" (shame and with downcast eyes). She goes through her life without *vergüenza* because "para que tú puedas vender, nececitas no tener vergüenza" (in order to sell you need not to be embarrassed). The word *vergüenza* has different connotations depending on its context. In Cortés's case it ranges from shame to embarrassment to shyness. Her children have learned not to have *vergüenza* (shame) to such a degree that it causes her to be embarrassed at times because her children are not bashful about eating a lot. One of our *charlas* took place at our friends' Margie and Scott's house where they and I had invited Cortés and her children for dinner.

Meredith: *Listen, why did you bring food? We invited you to eat and you bought all the food.*

Yaya: *I know but I said, "I don't know if Magui has the rice ready." No. I'd rather take something everywhere I go.*

Meredith: *But you brought everything, meat, rice, tortillas, and drinks.*

Yaya: *It has happened to me, particularly with my husband's family, that they would invite me to eat and when I arrived there was no food. When my children were small, this was a terrible thing for me. I arrived with my small children and there was nothing to eat. From then on, I have developed the habit of taking something everywhere I go.*

Meredith: *But also here to Scott and Margie's house? There is always a lot of food here.*

Yaya: *I know, but we know how to eat.*

Meredith: *Don't you think we do too?*

Yaya: *No is not that. But look, Americans have limits on their food. Okay, it's the same thing with the time. Take a look at time. Americans have their exact hour—*
Meredith: *Exact hour for what?*
Yaya: *For everything, to eat, for everything. Mexicans don't. Mexicans don't have an exact hour. If you are working with Mexican time, you say "I will be there at three." But you arrive at four or four-thirty. That's Mexican time. American time is exact time. The same thing with food. American people ask, "How many people?" If they have a party, if they invite someone to eat, "How many people," [they ask]. They prepare food for just that amount of people. They don't over prepare food. Okay, here [with Scott and Magui] it's a little different. But the majority of Americans I have seen, they count five or six people, and they cook exactly for those people. Each one of my children eats what three people would eat. [Therefore] I'd rather take food.*[62]

Cortés's proactive approach to social gatherings is a result of her observations of social etiquette, not just based on national, cultural differences but also within the same family.

When Cortés and her children are invited to Margie and Scott's house for dinner, she usually brings marinated *carne ranchera* or chicken ready to grill.

Yaya's *carne ranchera*
Oh, it is delicious. I buy ranchera *meat that is not cut in a long strip, but cut steak style* (bistec a lo a travesado) *so that it is tender and good. Later to prepare it, I add beer. The one I brought today did not have beer since my children say that Scott does not drink. Therefore, I just squeezed in an orange; I added a little mustard and garlic salt. That was all. Don't over grill it. You have to leave it like a sirloin steak, so that it is juicy and delicious. If you grill some Mexican onions, and have some beans and* nopalitos! *The Mexican onions are large green onions. They are white with a big head. The American onions are the skinny ones; they don't even have a head. Don't wrap the onions in aluminum foil, just place them on the grill. They are very juicy.*[63]

Cooks-as-writers' culinary narratives express their life's concerns. Cooking is a universal practice, and food is symbolically charged with social messages. Food *is* a voice. The cooks-as-writers' food voice offers an alternative form of expression to avoid silencing women who speak, share, and assert themselves in ways other than writing. As we listen (and read, as in the case of the *charlas*) to these stories, we must ask ourselves these questions: What do women say in their kitchen talk, not so much about their food per se, but about their relationship to the social body as it is articulated through their cooking practices? How do these relations frame their awareness of their familial, social, cultural, and political identities? In order to understand the critical social awareness cooks-as-writers express through their everyday cooking practice, we must develop an acute reliance on all of our senses.

CHAPTER 5

• •

The Literary Kitchen

Writers-as-Cooks

Food is life. Food as knowledge feeds our hunger for understanding, for belonging, and our need for change. Literature explores the depth of our hunger. Food in literature pacifies such hunger. M. F. K. Fisher, food writer, cooks because she is hungry for love, for understanding, and for community.[1] Lorna Dee Cervantes, Chicana poet, writes with the muse of hunger as "the first sense" and "Imagination [as] the last."[2] Food and literature feed the hunger of our body and soul, but they also feed our intellect while nourishing our creative expression helping us claim our cultural, social, political, and personal *space*. This chapter focuses on analyzing culinary social symbols found in literary works by women writers, mainly Chicana and Mexican writers, though Harriet Beecher Stowe's *Uncle Tom's Cabin*, Toni Morrison's *The Bluest Eye*, and Marge Piercy's "What's That Smell in the Kitchen?" form part of the following literary analysis. The reason for including these three literary productions is twofold: food as a literary voice is not exclusive to Latina literary creations, and food as voice shows that despite all of our differences— age, ethnicity, class, religion, sexual orientation—we, women, do speak with our *sazón*. What we say differs, but we understand the sensory-logic of food's cognitive discourse.

Kitchen as *space, sazón* as knowledge, cooking as art, and kitchen talk as empowering stories discussed in the previous four chapters are now explored within the realm of literature. This literary kitchen analysis is a *salpicón,* a touch of this and a touch of that, to create a meal with an aromatic flavor that enriches the savoring taste of an empowered voice. While this chapter will not focus on the grassroots theorists of the *charlas,* their way of expressing themselves about their kitchen *space,* their *sazón,* their *arte culinario casero,* and general attitude about their culinary lives influence the approach and questions I ask about literature. In 1986, I read my first novel in college, Toni Morrison's *The Bluest Eye,* and in 1989 I took my first course on feminist theory. Since then, the literature and theory I have read is such that I cannot possibility remember it all. Yet every story and every theory expands my analytical approach to literature. Likewise, the *charlas culinarias* that began in 1996, and continue, inform my interpretation of literary culinary metaphors. Thus, the conceptual views on food and the world from working-class women shared in the *charlas,* and expressed in previous chapters, influence the inquiries of this literary analysis.

• •
Food as the Muse of Writing

Phyllis Stowell and Jeanne Foster in *Appetite: Food as Metaphor* (2002) describe food in poetic expression as the "organizing metaphor for life's imperatives."[3] In *A Feast of Words: For Lovers of Food and Fiction* (1996) Anna Shapiro describes literature as "brain food, food for character, [for] mood altering." Literature, she says, "feeds the starved soul as well as the merely bored one. It is the nitrogen that makes the imagination bloom."[4] Tey Diana Rebolledo seals the connection between food and literature with the term "writers as cooks" in *Women Singing in the Snow* (1995). Rebolledo develops this term because of the overwhelming presence of kitchens and food in the works of Chicana writers, and because the idea of "writers as cooks" emphasizes the activity of writing and cooking as icons of self-identity. Rebolledo argues that in "the process of formulating an identity, both ethnic and female, one area that is distinctly original is the concept of the writer as cook. It seems that one way to express individual subjectivity (while at the same time connecting to the collective community) is by reinforcing this female identity as someone who cooks. One of the spaces traditionally construed as female is the kitchen, and Chicana literature is filled with images of active women preparing food. These images are a far cry from the anorexic Victorian heroines of nineteenth-century Anglo-European novels, who sublimated their hunger as well as their sexuality."[5] The "writers as cooks" use food as symbolic representation of tradition, sexuality, gender, generational and class differences, and struggles for cultural, political, and social spaces.

While kitchens "epitomize women's work in terms of food preparation and production," write Rebolledo and Eliana S. Rivera in *Infinite Divisions* (1993), they "also delineate symbolically the nurturing aspect of many women." Rebolledo and Rivera explain how in "much Chicana literature, kitchens are closely associated with grandmothers and with cultural values related to the Spanish language and family traditions. Food is generally commented on in terms of Mexican staples—*tortillas, frijoles,* and *tamales*—not in terms of more Americanized food. And while the kitchen can enclose and enslave, generally speaking it is a nourishing and nurturing safe haven where the writers can return for emotional and psychological sustenance in terms of female support via their *abuelitas,* mothers, and sisters."[6] For many Chicanas the inspiration for writing often comes while in the kitchen. "[F]or some poets, words come between . . . the leaves of lettuce they are washing at the sink. This is not exclusive to the world of Chicanas; this 'poetry as household activity' comes from being female."[7]

Writers who engage in "poetry as a household activity" do not divorce themselves from ordinary activities of cooking and gatherings in the kitchen, for it is here where they find their source of creative knowledge, skill, and ingenuity. "We cannot, nor will we divorce ourselves from our families," writes Helena María Viramontes. Speaking as a writer, Viramontes cannot divorce herself from her family, particularly her mother. Viramontes's own power of invention, innovation, and imagination, crucial elements for the creation of fiction, comes from her mother's creative culinary talents: "We *mujeres* are inventive people. My mother, for example, faced the challenge of feeding eleven people every evening. Time and time again, I saw her cut four pork chops, add this and that and this, pour water, and miraculously feed all of us with a tasty *guiso*. Or the *nopales* she grew, cleaned, diced, scrambled with eggs, or meat, or chile, or really mixed with anything her budget could afford, and we had such a variety of tasty dishes!"[8] For Viramontes, domesticity does not stifle creativity. She finds her muse within her mother's culinary inventiveness.

María Claudia André in "Culinary Fictions" argues that cooking as language deconstructs the very notion of the speaking subject within traditional Western thought that conceives of it as male, rational, and logical. André argues that the deconstruction of the male speaking subject disrupts the idea of a fixed center, of universalities, of objectivity.[9] Furthermore, as illustrated in chapter 2, cooking with the sensory-logic of the *sazón* rejects the binary split between mind and body; thus it challenges binary thinking: male as speaking subject and female as muted object, male as the project of Becoming and female as simply Being (Doreen Massey), the masculinization of the "higher senses" and the feminization of the "lower senses" (Carolyn Korsmeyer). Kathleen Batstone in her analysis of Laura Esquivel's *Como agua para chocolate* expresses the importance of disrupting the idea of a fixed center as how "cooking . . . creates an environment in which rigid definitions are replaced by more fluid and hybrid conceptions of our relations to the world around us."[10] André's and Batstone's theoretical explanations of the importance of a fluidity that speaks to different concepts of our self-identity resonate with Alma Contreras's concept of *al gusto* and my own notion of the ability to add one's *chiste* to a recipe.

● ● ● ● ● ● ● ● ● ● ● ● ● ● ● ● ● ● ● ●
Kitchens of Their Own

Kitchens as women's *space,* as a feminist site, reject centralities, rigid order, and universal principles. When the kitchen becomes a feminists site, indicates André, "it can be a 'utopian' space of liberation, uncontaminated by the masculine rule, where women reclaim their bodies, identities and memories of a collective past, where gender is no longer a given image defined by the masculine" gaze.[11] While I share André's belief, I want to be careful not to idealize the conversion of a patriarchal kitchen into a feminist site and ignore that this ideological reconstruction is also fluid and not a complete or permanent block to the power of the male gaze, at times manifested in some of our own (women's) actions. Arlene Voski Avakian's introduction to her edited anthology *Through the Kitchen Window* illustrates the fluidity of meanings associated with the kitchen conceived as both a woman's social *place* and as a woman's own *space.* In 1997, Avakian experienced the contradictions found within the kitchen's site when it is both a woman's obligatory *place* and a woman's liberating *space*. When Avakian sent out a call for contributors to *Through the Kitchen Window,* an anthology on women's relationship to food, cooking, eating, and sharing, the response was overwhelming. "The stories, poems, and essays I received," says Avakian, "evoked both tears and laughter. They spoke of oppression and resistance. They told of individual and cultural transformation."[12] "Cooking," states Avakian, "is something that was and continues to be imposed on women, but it is also an activity that can be a creative part of our daily lives. As such the work of cooking is more complex than mere victimization. . . . Cooking becomes a vehicle for artistic expression, a source of sensual pleasure, an opportunity for resistance and even power."[13]

The kitchen and the preparation of food always evoke strong and contradictory feelings and meanings. As mentioned in chapter 1, many feminists advocating gender equality denounce the kitchen (i.e., the home) and cooking, for they see this site and practice as concrete manifestations of women's oppression by a dominant male culture. As argued in chapter 1, I do not deny this fact. When a kitchen *does* remain within the politicization of a masculine gaze, it can in fact represent a woman's vulnerability.

Violations to the female body do take place in the kitchen, and these violations need to be addressed. If we agree, with some caution, that the kitchen is a woman's *place*, then Toni Morrison's *The Bluest Eye* (1970) reveals the patriarchal control and invasion of a woman's (girl's) body. Morrison uses a third-person narrator, a character from the novel, to convey the story of Pecola Breedlove, a young black girl who wants to have the bluest eyes so that people, including her parents, can notice her existence. The only time her father does notice her, his touch is lethal: "He staggered home reeling drunk and saw his daughter in the kitchen. . . . Following the disintegration—the falling away—of sexual desire, he was conscious of her wet, soapy hands on his wrists, the fingers clenching, but whether her grip was from a hopeless but stubborn struggle to be free, or from some other emotion, he could not tell. Removing himself from her was so painful to him he cut it short and snatched his genitals out of the dry harbor of her vagina."[14] In this narrative, Pecola never gets an opportunity to speak, to narrate her own story. The readers simply view Pecola's ultimate escape from her life's circumstances as she retires into her own internal world of eventual insanity. Had the Breedlove's kitchen window been opened and had Pecola been given an opportunity, a *space,* not by Morrison but by society at large, to voice her needs and fears, in short, her life, would her life have had a different outcome?

Naomi Quiñonez's poem "Spousal Rape" exemplifies another moment where we view a woman's violation as we stand outside her kitchen window. Quiñonez symbolically represents a woman's body as the main course that must satisfy a husband's violent, sexual desire. For lunch, the husband, represented as a lion, will savor her thigh as "the main dish." While the frequency with which he devours her thigh remains unspoken, "only the teeth marks on her throat" and the "bay water" in her eyes will know the intensity of her pain.[15] In Quiñonez's poem, the kitchen as the place where a meal is prepared situates a woman's body within a violent and uncontrollable sexual patriarchal desire. Quiñonez's and Morrison's works show the kitchen as a woman's *place* operating under an exclusive patriarchal design can in fact represent for many women domestic enslavement.

The kitchen, however, does not automatically constitute a social inscription resembling a prisonlike state, even when other aspects of a woman's life might be. Harriet Beecher Stowe's *Uncle Tom's Cabin* offers a wonderful moment of a slave woman's act of claiming the kitchen as her *space.*[16] Since Dinah, from the kitchen, challenges dominant cultural ideology, I do not read the effect of this particular passage as one intended by Stowe. Dinah's kitchen illustrates a moment where a slave woman asserts her agency. Therefore, I read the exchange between Miss Ophelia, a white woman from the North, and Dinah, the slave cook, as a crack in Stowe's narrative, through which Dinah's voice filters through the walls of an early Victorian kitchen design. Such design located the kitchen in a separate building at the rear of the main house or "in the back of the house as far away as possible from the 'public' rooms used for entertaining."[17] Dinah's voice escapes from the hidden away place of a kitchen design ideologically informed by class and racial fears.[18]

Dinah is never meant to speak as a woman. In Gillian Brown's analysis of Dinah's kitchen, Dinah's character functions only as a symbol of the intrusion of the market economy into the privacy of the home. Dinah's "promiscuous housekeeping," says Brown, "is used by Stowe to show how" slavery disrupts and disempowers the cult of domesticity. Slavery, "according to *Uncle Tom's Cabin,*" states Brown, "undermines women's housework by bringing the confusion of the marketplace into the kitchen, the center of the family shelter."[19] Ain't Dinah a woman? As a slave, she has no right over her own body; she has no voice; she has no self. But ain't Dinah a woman? She is. She is, and she affirms her right to Become a speaking subject.

Dinah's kitchen, where she is the "principal of all rule and authority . . . generally looked as if it had been arranged by a hurricane blowing through it."[20] Dinah's cooking style, *a su gusto,* according to the novel's narrator, lacks a cultivated talent governed by scientific logic. Her *sazón,* her sensory-logic, instead is looked as simply an intuitive part of her nature, the nature of "a native and essential cook, . . . a self-taught genius, and like geniuses in general, was positive, opinionated, and erratic, to the last degree. Dinah perfectly scorned logic and reason in every shape, and always took refuge in intuitive creativity; and here she was perfectly impregnable. Dinah was mistress of the whole art and mystery of excuse making, in all its branches."[21] Dinah's kitchen organization and her cooking talent are not seen as positive, to say the least. Brown's analysis presents Dinah's character and kitchen as the "horror that slavery holds for the mothers of America . . . that the family life nurtured by women is not immune to the economic life outside it."[22] For Stowe, Dinah's character represents something similar. With Dinah's authority in the kitchen, "the Southern house mistress has lost her own moral authority to the unruly principles of the market economy." She has lost, her "character and capacity" to "subject to [her] will, and bring into harmonious and systematic order . . . the servants of [her] establishment." Marie St. Clare, Dinah's mistress, does not have the capacity "to regulate" the servants' "peculiarities, and so balance and compensate the deficiencies of one by the excess of another, as [to] produce a harmonious and orderly system."[23]

A careful reading of Dinah's *kitchen,* however, reveals *her* personal ingenuity and knowledge that the bonds of slavery do not strip away. What Dinah's kitchen arrangements illustrate is a cultural practice not subsumed by a dominant patriarchal or matriarchal economy. Before Miss Ophelia came to the South and tried to restore systematic, orderly household management, Augustine St. Clare, Dinah's master, had already failed in such an effort: "When St. Clare had first returned from the north, impressed with the system and order of his uncle's kitchen arrangements, he had largely provided his own with an array of cupboards, drawers, and various apparatus, to induce systematic regulation, under the sanguine illusion that it would be of any possible assistance to Dinah in her arrangements."[24] Yet, Dinah's actions undermine St. Clare's hopeful illusion of systematic regulation. Dinah recreates a new purpose and function for each drawer added to the kitchen. The more drawers in the kitchen, says the narrator, "the more hiding-holes" Dinah has "for the accommodation of old rags, hair-combs, old shoes, ribbons, cast-off artificial flowers, and other articles of *vertu,* wherein her soul delighted."[25] Rather than reading Dinah's character as representing an unruly market economy, I read Dinah's manner of using the kitchen's drawers as her resistance to the boundaries inscribed by her master. In her reinscription of the kitchen drawers' function Dinah constructs the kitchen into her *own* space.

Miss Ophelia's efforts to implement a white, middle-class, matriarchal and materialistic value system in Dinah's kitchen are met with a strong rejection. Miss Ophelia, appalled by Dinah's chaotic manners, points out how Dinah completely disregards "her mistress's best table cloths."[26] Kitchen rags and the finest tablecloths hold the same value for Dinah, who uses both in a rather practical manner. Since all the kitchen towels "was missin'," Dinah simply used a tablecloth to wrap up meat. Dinah subverts the importance of material value by making everything in her kitchen suit her needs, and she emphatically defends her *own* kitchen arrangement. When Miss Ophelia lifts "out the sifting papers of sweet herbs," Dinah says, "I wish Missis wouldn't touch dem ar. I likes to keep my things where I know whar to go to 'em."[27] Dinah certainly governs the logic of what has become her kitchen *space.*

Through the power of her gaze, Dinah further asserts the kitchen's *space* as her *own.* When Miss Ophelia enters the kitchen to establish order, Dinah "did not rise, but smoked on in sublime tranquility, regarding her movements obliquely out of the corner of her eye, but apparently intent only on the operations around her."[28] Dinah's gaze carries what bell hooks calls the "power of looking." In *Black Looks: Race and Representations,* hooks explains that the "politics of slavery, of racialized power relationships, were such that slaves were denied their right to gaze." Dinah claims the right to her gaze, "a rebellious desire, an oppositional gaze."[29] Hooks goes on to say that by "courageously looking, we defiantly declared: 'Not only will I stare, I want my look to change reality.' Even in the worse circumstances of domination, the ability to manipulate one's gaze in the face of structures of domination that would contain it, opens the possibility of agency."[30]

Dinah's gaze assists in making the kitchen the feminist site where she asserts her presence. I suggest that Dinah's logic of "disorganization" represents a different cultural arrangement, a different cultural practice. As Dinah says, "I has things as straight as anybody, when my clarin' up time comes, but I don't want ladies round, a henderin,' and getting my things all where I can't find 'em."[31] Dinah makes *her* kitchen a subversive *space* where she asserts a cultural subjectivity that refuses to be subsumed by dominant culture.

Graciela Limón's novel, *The Day of the Moon* (1999), offers another example of a woman who asserts her agency by not adhering solely to a dominant cultural system of belief. In *The Day of The Moon*, Limón politicizes and empowers women's roles in the domestic space, particularly for indigenous, working-class women. If degrees of oppression are placed within a continuum from lesser to greater, indigenous women occupy the "greater" marker in such a continuum. Limón subverts this historical pattern with the structure of her novel, as she uses a third-person narrator, except in one chapter entitled "Úrsula Santiago" situated close to the middle of the novel. This chapter belongs to Úrsula, the indigenous servant, who narrates her own story from the kitchen. Here, Úrsula takes central stage, and so do we, the readers. "*¡Buenos días!* I'm happy to see you. Please, come in. [I am Úrsula Santiago.] Sit here by me. I hope you don't mind sitting in the kitchen. It's where I'm comfortable and no one will disturb us here."[32] She invites us to sit with her in her kitchen, forming a community among us within its walls.

Úrsula lives in a society that marginalizes indigenous people because the color of their skin, their idiomatic expressions, and their religious beliefs are constant reminders of the painful heritage of *mestizaje*. To be a *mestiza/o*, says Limón, is "to dangle between being Spanish and indigenous . . . existing between gratitude and rage. It means choosing white or brown. It means accepting or denial of color."[33] Historically, in Mexico, what is most often denied within a *mestiza/o* identity is the indigenous heritage. Consequently, one effect of *mestizaje* is that it has led to an attempt to silence indigenous people, to see them as less than human. Limón presents the "painful heritage of *mestizaje*" by a *mestizo*'s refusal to

accept and reconcile his indigenous ancestry. Don Flavio, the symbol of patriarchy in *The Day of the Moon,* "always thought it strange
that . . . he came from a body that was so dark. . . . He did not want
an Indian woman for a mother. . . . Flavio often thought that the beginning of his story was when he chose to blot his mother out of his
memory."[34] What Don Flavio experiences, in the words of Guillermo
Bonfil Batalla, is the incomplete "decolonization of Mexico." While
"independence from Spain was achieved, . . . [the] internal colonial
structure was not eliminated."[35] For Bonfil Batalla the root of Mexico's painful *mestizaje* is the discrimination against that which is
indigenous, "an attempt to hide and ignore the Indian face of Mexico because no real connection with Mesoamerican civilization is
admitted."[36]

Úrsula does not allow us to forget that the indigenous heritage,
the indigenous part of *mestizaje,* has a human face. Úrsula uses the
kitchen *space* to advocate justice for indigenous people: "You would
think that our people should be used to these things by now, but we
are not. The *patrones* think that we're oxes, that we don't feel the
humiliations, nor the pain, but we do. They think that because generations of us have endured the burden placed on our backs, we
don't feel rage or the desire to take vengeance where we are
wronged, but they are deluding themselves."[37]

Úrsula speaks as "a subject with expressive power."[38] As the
guests in her kitchen, our most pressing interest is for Úrsula to
confirm the rumors that Don Flavio killed his own daughter,
Isadora, who had an affair with an indigenous Rarámuri. Úrsula's
narrative, however, deviates from readers' expectations: "There is
only one thing I cannot tell you: what happened to *Niña* Isadora.
Let's go step by step with what I do know. If you get hungry, tell me;
I'll make you some *quesadillas.* Bitterness slides down better with
a bit of tortilla and *chile.*"[39] The significance of this deviation allows
Úrsula to speak from her own perspective, which affords a validation to her indigenous cultural knowledge.

When Isadora is taken away by her father and no one knows
what has happened to her, Úrsula prays "*novenas* of rosaries to the
Virgin of Guadalupe" and burns "*copal* and peyote to Tata Hakuli,
but nothing brought her back."[40] The religious syncretism evoked by
the Virgin of Guadalupe and Tata Hakuli does not have the power to
ease Úrsula's anxiety, but an indigenous *torteadora* helps her find
answers to her prayers. Thanks to this *torteadora,* Úrsula knows

that Isadora is alive. Among her people, says the *torteadora,* they "believe in Xipe Totec, the goddess of healing and life. This is her story: One day an evil sprit of destruction skinned her alive. But Xipe Totec did not die. She put on her skin and was restored to life."[41] This passage contains two significant aspects. First, Limón makes a *torteadora,* a woman who only appears for a short moment in the novel, the one who holds the key to surviving the painful heritage of *mestizaje.* The story of Xipe Totec affirms that despite all the cruelties committed against indigenous people, they continue to restore themselves to life. The cultural contact between Spaniards and indigenous people did not obliterate the natives' cultural beliefs. The second significant implication of Xipe Totec's story is that Úrsula, by analogy, understands that Isadora "was like the goddess." Symbolically, Isadora puts on her skin and is restored to life as Alondra, Isadora's daughter. The story of Xipe Totec affirms a cultural belief in a life cycle that does not begin at birth and end at death. An indigenous *torteadora* shares a story expressing a non-Western belief.

The *torteadora's* profession of making both *tortas* and *tortillas,* within the context of the novel, is "the most difficult job of all because it never ends," Úrsula tells us, for no "sooner does the tortilla come off the *comal* before it's gobbled up."[42] A metaphorical symbol represented by the *torteadora's* difficult job suggests the struggle indigenous people face as they refuse to give up their cultural practices. This passage brings to mind the irony that while, on the one hand, tamales and tortillas are a symbol of Mexico's national foods, *tamaleras* or *torteadoras,* those actually making the tamales or tortillas, on the other hand, experience exclusion from that pride. Indigenous people are often portrayed as the lower classes unable to cultivate newer and refined cultural practices.

In the kitchen as their *space,* Úrsula Santiago and Dinah from *Uncle Tom's Cabin,* members of subordinated groups, claim their presence within the narratives. They also assert the presence of indigenous people in Mexican society, in the case of Úrsula, and African Americans, in the case of Dinah. In Limón's novel, unlike Stowe's, however, Úrsula's expressive power is not an accidental crack in the narrative but an intentional rupture to it. Limón's usage of first voice narrative offers three symbolic implications. Úrsula claims her subjectivity by the right to name herself: "I am Úrsula Santiago," she says.[43] She also speaks from her own position of knowledge, and third, Úrsula's right to speak brings oral culture and her indigenous beliefs to the forefront in a society dominated by the written word and the ideologies of modernism.

Mexican writer Elena Garro's "La culpa es de los Tlaxcaltecas" takes place in the kitchen. Laura, the middle-class lady of the house, learns to understand why modern Mexicans suffer from lack of memory, as she talks to Nacha, the cook. A central topic in most of Garro's work is how modern Mexicans have managed to negate their indigenous past.[44] In "La culpa es the los Tlaxcaltecas," Garro traces the life of an Aztec woman who could not endure the destruction of her people by the Spaniards. This woman transports herself to modern Mexico and becomes Laura. Laura, like modern Mexico and Mexicans, says Garro, is left without "destino" (destiny), without memory.[45]

In Garro's story, the kitchen, as well as Nacha and Laura's congregation in it, functions as the *space* for reconstructing Mexico's destiny and reconciling Mexico's dual heritage. The story begins and ends in a kitchen that is separated from the world by a wall of sadness caused by a perpetual state of waiting for a productive conciliation of Mexico's dual heritage. Nacha and Laura's kitchen talk demolishes the wall separating the kitchen's stillness from the modern world of constant change, which fails to recognize Mexico's indigenous cosmology where time is cyclical and not linear. With their kitchen talk, Nacha and Laura recognize that they share a belief on the cosmology where "the past and present co-exist on the same plane."[46] Thus, through the stories exchanged in the kitchen, they are able to capture Mexico's painful heritage. They share a mutual understanding that the Tlaxcaltecas are to blame for the loss of historical memory in modern Mexico. The Tlaxcaltecas were an indigenous group who had been subjugated by the Aztecs. When Cortés arrived, the Tlaxcaltecas joined him in the conquest of Mexico. Even today, the Tlaxcaltecas are considered traitors.

At the beginning of the story, Nacha is in the kitchen and hears a knock; Laura is standing outside. Laura enters the kitchen and looks at the cook with questioning eyes. Feeling confident, she sits down near the stove and looks at her kitchen as if she had never seen it before.[47] Once she is in the kitchen, we find out that Laura had left the house for days and that this is a recurrent event for her. In the kitchen with Nacha, Laura recognizes that despite their class and phenotype difference, they share a similar history and belief in a cosmology that is not linear. Laura tells Nacha that during her disappearances, she travels in time and returns to see the destruction of Tenochtitlán in 1521. Laura also shares with Nacha that she simultaneously has two husbands: Pablo, the modern man without memory who only mimics as do all modern men, and her first husband, an Aztec warrior, who carries the weight of history on his shoulders.

As Laura recounts to Nacha her travels and encounters with her first husband, Nacha becomes her sympathetic listener and confidant; their kitchen talk creates a space for *confianza*. Nacha's character, while saying little in the story, functions in a manner similar to "torteadora" in Limón's *The Day of the Moon*. Cynthia Duncan has argued that Nacha "is a key figure in the story's development, for she serves as a bridge between the white and the indigenous worlds. It is not stated explicitly in the text that she is Indian; however, her position as a domestic servant certainly carries that connotation, and her way of looking at the world bears all the earmarks of an indigenous heritage."[48] The similar heritage Laura and Nacha share is one that those like Pablo have obliterated from their memory. In Gloria Bautista Gutiérrez's reading of Pablo, he represents "a man without memory, with an uninhabited body. He is a new man without evolution; therefore, having no memory, he has no recollections, meaning, no history."[49] Thus, he cannot understand Laura's thirst for history. "Mamá," he says to his mother, "Laura asked the doctor to bring her Bernal Díaz del Castillo's History of the Conquest; she says that's all she cares about."[50] Unable to understand Laura, Pablo declares her insane.

Laura looking at her kitchen "como si no la hubiera visto nunca" (as if she had never seen it) echoes Edward Soja's theory of thirdspace epistemology where one recovers or remembers places of knowledge lost or never sought at all. Laura looks at her kitchen as if for the first time and decides to inscribe a new destiny, her new destiny in "los mosaicos blancos de la cocina" (the white tiles of the kitchen).[51] At the end of the story Laura leaves her modern husband, who has no memory, to join her Indian husband and bear with him the burden of history. Nacha also leaves the house where memory and history do not exist: "Ya no me hallo en la casa de los Aldama. Voy a buscar otro destino" (I don't feel good in the house of the Aldama. I am going to look for a new destiny).[52]

The passage where Laura connects culturally with Nacha, and where Laura looks at her kitchen with the power of the oppositional gaze is fundamentally pressing for unearthing conflicting histories. Laura, sitting in her kitchen with Nacha, begins to voice her own struggle with her cultural heritage. Yet in Alberto Manguel's translation of Garro's story this passage is omitted. Perhaps this is an innocent omission on the translator's part, but its effect could lead to yet another implication of the silencing of women's voices coming from the kitchen.

When women appropriate the kitchen as their *space,* they enter into what a number of cultural critics call a thirdspace epistemology, where women invent new savory sauces to conceptualize their lives as they add their own *chiste,* not only to their cooking but also to organization and meaning of their kitchen *space.* Thirdspace epistemology offers the opportunity to hear the stories of resistance and affirmation. It helps us move beyond the dualistic thinking found in many Western sociospatial and philosophical concepts that keep us under the grip of a reductionist scientific model, as argues philosopher Henri Lefebvre, which limits our perception of knowledge to the sense of vision, and, therefore, neglects other forms of sensory-logic such as touch, taste, and smell.[53]

• •

Food Symbols, the *sazón* in Literary Voices

"Writers as cooks" incorporate culinary imagery into their literary creations through metaphor and metonymy as they negotiate both their individual and their collective subjectivity. "The message [food] encodes," says Mary Douglas, "will be found in the pattern of social relations being expressed" at the moment of offering a particular food.[54] Louis Marin argues that one avenue for deciphering the social messages presented within food is through the praxis of transignificance, the process of food becoming a metamorphosis for social and cultural meaning. "An edible thing," says Marin, "becomes a signified term."[55] The social messages encoded in food range in meaning depending on the setting in which food is offered. The symbolic meaning of food carries a different message because food refuses absolute categorizations and absolute categories; not all people, for instance, have the same taboos about foods. Furthermore, culinary imagery as the *sazón* in literary voice finds its vocal power in food's transformative nature. The fluidity of meaning in both cooking and food makes them transformational cognitive devices. Cooking transforms raw material into edible food that "exerts a fundamental bodily transformation on those who engage in its consumption."[56] For Mervyn Nicholson, food helps us engage in a daily activity of self-creation, or, I would say, self-recreation by the process that leads us to add *chistes* to cooking and its meaning.[57]

Since the *sazón* reflects social understanding based on the knowledge of the senses, likewise in its literary manifestation it is through the senses that its meaning is understood. The sensual culture of gastronomy, therefore, moves beyond the discipline of culinary studies. Marge Piercy in "What's That Smell in the Kitchen?" uses the epistemology of smell to declare war against the indifferent behavior that leaves women feeling as leftover food in Tupperware. While women ought to offer food, which symbolically represents them, on silver platters and serve it with joy, the lack of appreciation for their talent metaphorically transforms them from the delicacy and succulence of "roasted duck" to "Spam." Thus to fight this transformation of their lives, "All over America women are burning/Food" not as ineptitude but as a declaration of "war."[58] The smell of burned food declares freedom, freedom to choose not to adhere to existing gender, marital paradigms. Burning food becomes in Piercy's poem the weapon women use to seize their own subjectivity.

Rosario Castellanos, in "Lección de cocina" ("Cooking Lesson," 1971), uses the unpleasant smell and the aesthetically unappealing aspect of a shrinking burned piece of meat as a way to articulate the effect societal demands have had on women. In Castellanos's story the cultural gender roles drive a woman to a state of personal invisibility. Castellanos uses the sense of smell, associated with women, as the epistemological device to expose the social myth that women's only life aspiration is for a blissful marriage. The memories evoked by the smell of burned meat serve as the protagonist's way of conceptualizing and admitting to herself the hollowness a chronically unfaithful husband creates in her life. Castellanos uses the sense of smell, one of the "lower senses" and a disgrace to reason's logic, to challenge the notion that such sense offers neither knowledge nor aesthetic enjoyment. The bad odor of the burned meat and its grotesque appearance do offer social knowledge. It shows how a woman forced to adhere to patriarchal behavior codes can potentially end up like a piece of burned meat, while it also forces women in such a predicament to face their life's circumstances and keep themselves from actually becoming just like the burned piece of meat.

The protagonist of "Lección de cocina," a middle-class house-wife, narrates her own story about her repeated failures in attempting to adhere to a married woman's traditional role. As the story unfolds, it becomes clear that for Castellanos the failures do not indicate the wife's incompetence.[59] The culinary failures symbolize a woman's search for possibilities of "another way to be human and free."[60] The emphasis on middle-class women in Castellanos's short story raises some poignant connections with working-class women's culinary experiences and appropriation of the kitchen's *space*. It is often argued within Latin American feminist circles that in a society like Mexico, class distinctions pose a serious hindrance to a development of a collective feminist consciousness. As social critic María Elena de Valdés says, "Any commentary that ignores class issues and addresses women in general will fail to reach all but a slim minority of upper-middle class women in Latin American."[61] Castellanos broaches the strong class distinction between women in Mexico by creating a dialectic between class privilege and institutionalized sexism. Castellanos implies that all women—upper class, middle class, or working class—can share the kitchen and its culinary language. Any woman carving out a space for herself from her mandatory social *placing* actively engages in a process of personal and social *conscientización*. The rearrangement of the kitchen's function as a female *space* provides the setting for reconstructing its preimposed ideological functions.

The protagonist in "Lección de cocina" embarks on a journey of self-reflection as she sits contemplating and reading the kitchen's social definition. The protagonist's journey leads her to discover and recognize her personal self as she struggles to redefine another way of reading the social function of her kitchen's purpose. She recognizes that society offers her only two means of self-identification: kitchen and wife. The kitchen, she points out, is synonymous to woman: "My place is here. Since the beginning of time, it has been here. Like the German proverb says, woman is synonymous to 'Küche, Kinder, Kirche.'"[62] The kitchen, therefore, *ought* to be her proper social place. If the kitchen *must* be her proper *place,* then, she ironically admits, she has been lost, wasting her time "in the classrooms, streets, offices, cafés—wasting myself on tasks I must now forget in order to take on others."[63] Once, perfectly placed in her so-called natural setting, she questions her identity. According to the registers of her social milieu, she concludes that the most sensible answer to her question of identity is that she is *a wife.* "But who am I? Your wife, of course. And the title is enough to distinguish me from all the memories of the past, and all the plans for the future." [64] A wife, as the narrator tells us, only has an identity in the present with no past or future. It only has a husband's present.

The kitchen within this story provides the setting for the narrator to unveil the social mask that she has been made to wear: the mask of a wife. The unveiling takes place as the narrator cooks a piece of frozen meat. As the meat cooks, it goes through a number of metamorphoses. The observation of these changes enables the narrator to engage in an examination of her own life. The meat symbolically personifies her entire existence. With it, she smells, sees, and touches her loveless marriage, empty life, and exposes a number of myths about a woman's natural and cultural identity.

The narrative structure of the story moves from the present, the actual moment of cooking, to the narrator's past and to her hypothetical future. In the present moment, the narrator attempts to prepare dinner. Cookbooks are of no assistance in preparing dinner since they use a language unfamiliar to her. She simply opens the freezer and withdraws the first thing she touches. "I open the meat compartment of the freezer and extract an unrecognizable package covered with crystals of ice. I plunge it into hot water, and the label, without which I would never have been able to identify its contents, reveals itself to me." [65] The correlation between the meat and the woman shows that just as the substance of the meat would not be recognizable without a proper, preimposed title, so a woman will also never be recognized without her proper societal titles, those of wife and mother. From this point on, the story moves back and forth, making a connection between the transformation of the meat and an episode of the narrator's life. The meat's metamorphosis recaptures the memory that marriage hopes to erase, the memory of her own life.

With the first connection the narrator makes between the meat and her life, she casts off another piece of her social mask. Once defrosted, the meat reveals a red that looks as if it would start bleeding at any moment. The meat's appearance reminds her of the sunburn her husband and she suffered during their honeymoon in Acapulco. Their burned backs prevented neither of them from "playing their" social roles. In bed he would lie face down to protect his throbbing skin. She, on the other hand, would lie on her back supporting not only her weight but his. In this way they would make love in the classic position that yielded for her moans of pain and pleasure: a woman's classic moan. For the narrator, a woman's natural moans and readiness to accommodate represent nothing else other than "a myth, myth."[66] The reference to a myth resonates with Theodor Reik's theory on the origin and function of myth: "According to Reik, myth is used to assuage the guilt feelings of mankind, which 'have their roots in aggression and violence.' Myth . . . allows a culture to explain itself in a more favorable light and to justify its behavior."[67]

The recollection of the narrator's honeymoon is short-lived as the meat in the frying pan brings her back to the present moment. The meat, paradoxically enough, keeps her in the kitchen as a woman's *place,* while at the same time it allows her the possibility of envisioning a different lifestyle that excludes living with a chronically unfaithful husband. When the meat in the frying pan ultimately burns on one side, she conceives of a number of possible solutions to deal with the meat's current state. First, she could air the kitchen and throw away the meat and never acknowledge the emptiness of her married life. Another possibility is not to air the kitchen and not to throw the meat away. Her husband's response to this would lead to a number of insults about her incompetence, but she would confront the nature of their relationship, which has destroyed every aspect of her sense of self. Metaphorically, this second option leads her to trace the trajectory of her life as she reconsiders what has happened to the meat: "Let us recapitulate. The piece of meat first appears with a color, a shape, and a size. Later it changes and becomes prettier and one feels very happy. Then it changes again and isn't pretty at all. And it keeps changing and changing and changing, and what one doesn't know is when to make it stop. Because if I leave the piece of meat indefinitely exposed to the fire, it will be consumed until there is nothing left of it. And the piece that once gave the impression of being something so solid, so real, no longer exists."[68] If she continues on her current social path, she, like the meat, will reach the point of being absolutely unrecognizable due to the fires of social conformity that will consume her "until there is nothing left of her." While Castellanos does not clearly define what if any path the nameless protagonist will take, the seed of transformation is planted in the consciousness of the protagonist, as she goes through a process of reinscribing the social function of the kitchen as she conceptualizes the symbolic connection between meat and women (between kitchen and women): "The meat has not ceased to exist. It has undergone a series of metamorphoses. And the fact that it is no longer perceptible to the senses does not mean that the cycle has concluded, but rather that it has simply taken the quantum leap. It will continue to function at other levels: in my conscience, in my memory, in my will, changing me, guiding me, establishing the direction of my future."[69] The narrator's conceptualization of another way of being and sharing her thoughts with her readers creates a community where she begins to restore her sense of self. In Castellanos's "Lección de cocina" a woman acknowledges her sexual, sensual, and personal being through a process of "remembrance-rethinking-recovery . . . spaces lost . . . or [spaces] never sighted at all."[70]

The outcome of a war fought in a culinary battlefield with the armory of burning food reveals how smells are not "simply biological and psychological phenomenon," but are "cultural, hence a social and historical phenomena."[71] It is through the smell of burned food in both Castellanos's story and Piercy's poem that the ideological (natural) roles of a woman in a marriage are contested. The kitchen and the burned food serve as catalysts in writers-as-cooks' works by illustrating the social contexts that have led some women to a point of personal invisibility.

The epistemology of the senses in Bárbara Brinson Curiel's poem, "Recipe: Chorizo con Huevo Made in the Microwave" (1989) marks a family's geographical, cultural, and generational changes.[72] The poem represents the life story of a generation that does not "feel the pangs of nostalgia for tradition."[73] The memories evoked through the sensory epistemology foreground familial and cultural practices at a crossroads: what place does the older generation, tradition, hold within the life of the younger, or modernity? The entire poem describes the efficiency of cooking and eating *chorizo con huevo* made with modern technology, the microwave, where *chorizo* cooks within only four minutes and eggs in two. *Chorizo* with eggs becomes a simple cooking process. In terms of family politics, there is nothing simple about simply cooking in the microwave. The consequence of modern technology dims "memories of abuelita / feeding wood into the stove." The narrator admits that the price for modern efficiency is an odorless tortilla, since it is no longer cooked in a *co-mal.* By eating a modernized version of this Mexican traditional breakfast, the grandchild should remember how the grandmother's appetite "aches" for the ways of the past.[74]

The gastronomic changes for the grandchild began at eight with the desire for "peanut butter and jelly" rather than "sopa de fideo" and later with the introduction of the microwave.[75] The introduction of these two changes encountered a mother's raised eyebrow and a grandmother's "hard stare."[76] The accusatory implication of these two gestures from a mother and grandmother who represent the voice of tradition runs the risk of silencing the voice of someone who has a "sense of contemporary, time-saving living."[77] The voice of the younger generation is obviously not mute since we see the grandchild eating "chorizo con huevo made in the microwave." Because of the grandchild's *chiste,* cooking with modern technology, the poem's persona seems to insist in placing an internalized guilt on the grandchild for altering tradition. "While your mouth is full,/recall that [grandmother's] appetite/ached/for a seasonless sky."[78] Blaming those who do change traditional patterns, I argue, is a misplaced blame because alterations to cultural practices are unavoidable, and as the poem says, "Ni modo, pues."[79] While not clearly stated in the poem whether the grandchild is a woman or a man, generally speaking, women are the keepers and teachers of traditions. How do women negotiate adding their own *chistes* to traditional dishes, like *chorizo con huevos* made in the microwave, so that their *sazón* speaks to an original moment in their particular life circumstance?

Regardless of the "major modifications of traditional foods" caused by globalization, Warren Belasco says, "romance of ethnicity can coexist with globalization."[80] But what is the cost, and who pays the price for holding on to the "romance of ethnicity"? In Brinson Curiel's poem, cooking on an "outdoor wood burning stove" expresses the idea of romance. The romance *for* ethnicity raises the thorny issue of who has the right (the power) to speak as the true voice of cultural representation. Which recipe for *chorizo con huevo* is the most culturally authentic: the grandmother's or the grandchild's? If we do assert one recipe as more authentic over the other, we run the risk of rendering someone's life experiences less relevant, less valid. Furthermore, does the new taste, smell, and appearance of *huevos con chorizo* cooked in the microwave mean a loss of a particular kind of memory, a particular kind of history? No. It reflects the daily process of making history.

For the protagonist in Silvia Molina's *El amor que me juraste* (1998), Marcela, the aroma coming from the kitchen of a restaurant transports her to her mother's own kitchen and to her early adulthood. I focus on a rather brief episode in *El amor que me juraste* that can easily be overlooked where the aroma of food transports Marcela to her mother's kitchen. Sitting in a restaurant, Marcela perceives the aromas flowing out from the kitchen: "I sat in a corner next to a window, and I ordered a cold Corona. The odors of the food they were preparing reminded me of my mother's kitchen, where I was happy. Most of the time the family could come together there."[81] As Marcela remembers her mother's cooking and a happier time of her life, for the first time she realizes that the differences between the culinary aroma of her house and other houses is the *pasión* she adds to her *sazón*. "It was not just the odors and flavors that made the kitchen of my house different: it was her, my mother. It was the passion in her cooking when she cooked for us, because she was not fulfilling a monotonous obligation; she was performing a ceremony of which she felt proud, therefore, she didn't mind doing it. Cooking, sewing, and being afraid of my father were the only things she did naturally."[82] One central theme of the novel is the journey in quest of self-discovery and self-acceptance of one's complicated and contradictory nature. Marcela's mother's acceptance of herself and her life—a life that involves having a husband who has another family on the side—is expressed by her passion for life through her cooking. While Marcela finds her mother's attitude unacceptable, she is also in search of discovering and learning to accept the levels of her own passionate nature.

Marcela is a married woman with two children. Her husband Rafael, unlike her father, is a faithful man. Life with Rafael offers security but lacks in passion; Marcela finds passion in the arms of her lover, Eduardo. The novel, however, begins at the end of her affair with Eduardo. The pain of losing her lover and the shame of cheating on her husband drives Marcela to embark on an exploratory journey for her paternal origins. Marcela's valuable discovery takes place only when she is invited to accept herself as she is: a woman who has been fortunate to feel passion in her life by her courage to have an affair. A history professor helping her unveil the saga of her paternal origins tells her:

> "Not every woman has the good fortune to experience what you have."
> "You call it good fortune?"
> "Indeed."
> "To suffer as I do?"
> "I told you, another Eduardo will come to your life."
> "God help me!
> "Accept yourself."[83]

After having this conversation with the professor, Marcela acknowledges that she has never thought about accepting herself, about exploring the deepest of her passions. She realizes that the nature of her own passion is borne from the remembrance of her mother's cooking: "To her I owe my joy for cooking. . . . It is fun for me to select the ingredients of the dishes, combining them. I like to play in that laboratory where one invents formulas, where one experiments, where one practices, where one calculates."[84]

The sensory perception memories evoked by the aroma of food as Marcela sits in a restaurant project the end of the novel when she will learn to accept her passions. By the end of the novel, Marcela connects her culinary passion with the rest of her life by accepting and allowing herself to experiment in the laboratory of love. One can say that Marcela transfers her culinary *sazón* that frees her to endless possibilities of inventing, experimenting, practicing, tasting, and touching new passions.

Cristina Pacheco, a Mexican journalist/writer who often writes in the genre of testimonial literature, uses the culinary metaphor of soup to illustrate a social discourse that contradicts the comfort most of us associate with the sight, the smell, and taste of a hot savory soup. In a vignette entitled "Sopita de fideo" (1988), Pacheco disrupts the associations of comfort suggested by a bowl of soup to show the destitute, of those living on the economic margins of society. The vignette opens with Luz, a wife and mother, moving about in her small kitchen making *fideo* and cooking beans. Luz's main concern is to take the soup to Santos's work for his dinner. Since Luz's youngest child is barely two months old and she must stay home waiting for the man who will come and fix the leaking gas tank, her daughter Josefina must take the soup to her father.

On the Metro, on her way to her father's work, with the multitudes entering and leaving the Metro, Josefina drops the soup. The pride she felt as the carrier of nurturing substance for her father becomes sadness, fear, and pain. Josefina returns home without reaching her father's work: "Josefina goes sadly. The sound of the empty food container suffocates her. As she decides to climb the stairs to enter the Metro and return home, she thinks of her younger sister Lety, of her brothers anxiously waiting to have dinner, of her mother who had to push them away from the kitchen table so that they would not devour the father's soup. She feels fear as she knows that a severe punishment waits her at home; but what pains her the most is to think that today, her father will not eat."[85] The message encoded in Pacheco's vignette exposes this family's level of poverty as such that they are not even able to eat and take comfort in *sopita de fideo.*

Pacheco uses the symbol of soup to highlight the hopelessness many poor people face in Mexico City. When the soup spreads on the train's floor, people's commentaries reflect the degree of hopelessness. Now, not even a dog will savor that wonderful smelling soup. As Josefina steps over the puddle of soup to leave the Metro, Pacheco describes the soup as repulsive. For people like Josefina and her family, not even soup remains a sign of hope.

Chicana writer-as-cook Edna Escamill, in "The Pan Birote" (1993), uses the symbol of bread as a young girl's struggle for justice in a society of double standards. "The Pan Birote" presents an *abuelita* (grandmother) who accepts the gender double standard as the way of life, and through her attitudes teaches this social behavior to her three grandchildren: two boys, el Güero (the White/Light) y el Prieto (the Dark), and a girl, Chiltepín, the youngest. The two boys, who for the *abuelita* epitomize how men are and thus the way of the world, are rude, aggressive, and above all, imposing. While in church during High Mass, el Güero and el Prieto "wriggled and sat on Chiltepín until they pushed her out and got the aisle space, where there was a little more room for themselves."[86] Abuelita does not say a word.

"The whole world" is at High Mass on this particular Sunday because of the free "pan para los pobres" (bread for the poor) the congregation will receive. On their way home, Abuelita gives the boys the "responsibility of carrying the pan birote home safely." The boys soon drift behind Abuelita and Chiltepín, and "El Güero, with the authority of the oldest, pinched and twisted off one end of the pan

birote, along with the surrounding area, and popped it into
his mouth. El Prieto followed with his loaf."[87] Chiltepín sees her
brothers eating the *pan birote* and asks Abuelita to stop them. To
her dismay, Abuelita replies that they are just doing what men have
always done. Chiltepín, however, knows in "spite of being younger
and a girl, deep in her blood she [knows] the meaning of equality.
She [is] hungry and she [has] a right to eat too. And this [has] nothing to do with who [is] bigger or better."[88] She pulls away from
Abuelita, walks up to her brothers, and plants herself in front of
them; she screams: "'I want it! I want it! Give it to me!' demanding
more from the world than just bread."[89]

Escamill's choice of bread as the symbol of Chiltepín's struggle
for justice carries a strong ideological significance. The bread holds
a religious implication of self-sacrifice, and according to Catholic
teaching, it is a woman's virtue. Abuelita seems to accept self-
sacrifice as her virtue. In a subtle way, however, she rejects the very
principle in the act of self-sacrifice. Abuelita is willing to sacrifice
her portion of *pan birote,* but not with a generous heart. She feels
anger toward the boys since with "an angry voice," she says to
Chiltepín, "'Ande cabrones! No les pongas atención!' Those jerks!
Don't look at them!"[90] Chiltepín, however, neither pretends to accept nor believes in gender double standards as the way of the
world. Chiltepín literally claims her right to fight for her own well-
being and prosperity. The symbol of the *pan birote* for Chiltepín represents her struggle for changing familial patterns.

• • • • • • • • • • • • • • • • • • • •
Kitchen Talk

The appropriation of the kitchen as a woman's *space* and culinary
symbols as the *sazón* in literary voices permits women's subtle, stra-
tegic, and tactful resourcefulness to overcome a number of socially
imposed limitations. When a woman uses the kitchen to cast off societal demands, she crosses over into the realm where her actions
inscribe her kitchen's function. With kitchen talk in a woman's *space,*
a woman gives voice to her life stories, affirms her right to be, and
claims her right to become what she imagines.

While the women from the *charlas culinarias* broached the subject of sexuality in subtle ways or as a result of my bringing this topic
into the conversation, the writers-as-cooks use culinary metaphors

to place women's bodies and their sexuality on center stage. Women claiming the right over their bodies and sexual desire is a topic much explored in the literary voices of kitchen talk. Within a Mexican context, male discourse has conceptualized women as an embodiment of sexual passivity. Intellectual critic and poet Octavio Paz expresses women's passivity in a rather contemptuous manner: "Woman awaits disdainfully as the male cavorts around her. She is the center of his universe, a magnetic passive polar force. She attracts and passively receives; she does not seek and at [the] center of her magnetic force is her hidden passive sexuality. 'It is a secret and immobile sun.'"[91] Within a Catholic, patriarchal society, a woman's passive body belongs to God, to the nation, to the husband, or to a combination of the three, but never to herself.

Mexican or Mexican American women reject the idea of their sexual passivity and celebrate sexuality for their own pleasure. For instance, writer-as-cook Beverly Silvia in "Sin tí no soy nada / Without You I Am Nothing" (1998) celebrates herself, her love, and her desire for her lover through a number of culinary metaphors. The persona in this poem humorously expresses her sexual desire by connecting food and sex. The persona indicates that the lover is like "The salsa in my enchilada/ . . . the olive in my tamal/ . . . the chile in my beans."[92]

The lover in the poem, as Rebolledo says, adds "that 'extra spice' that enhances the food—such as the salsa—as well as being the essential ingredient, one without which the dish could not be itself— the meat in the burrito, the chocolate in the mole." "The part that belongs" to the speaker of the poem, states Rebolledo, "is the substance that wraps itself around the ingredients."[93] In Silva's poem, the social message encoded in food is the celebration of a woman's sensual and sexual desires.

In the one-act play *How Else Am I Supposed to Know I'm Still Alive* (1996), Evelina Fernandez uses the kitchen as the *space* to present two middle-aged women who are full of life, love, hope, and courage, thus demystifying woman's passivity. Nellie, a Chicana of fifty-two, and Angie, a Chicana of forty-eight, are two "grandmother" figures who talk about and have sex. In the kitchen opening scene, Nellie speaks to herself: "Well, Nellie, you still got it. Fifty years old and you still drive them crazy. So what if he was fat, bald, and toothless. He's still got an . . . imagination." At this moment, Nellie pricks her finger on a rose thorn, and addressing God, rather than herself,

she says: "I guess you think an old bag like me has no feelings any-
more. Hey, I need my thrills too. You think cuz I'm old I don't need a
little wink, a little smile, a little pinch on the butt? How else am I
supposed to know I'm still alive."[94] Angie's visit interrupts Nellie's
soliloquy.

As Angie and Nellie talk in the kitchen, Nellie discovers how
Angie too needs to know she "is still alive." Sitting in Nellie's
kitchen, Angie says that at forty-eight she still gets her period and
that this particular month she is late.

Nellie: *After so many years. I knew you would take Joe back sooner
or later, but I didn't think you'd go as far as having sex with him.*
Angie: *(Quietly.) It's not Joe's.*
Nellie: *(Laughs her big laugh.)* ¡Cochina!
Angie: *Ay Nellie,* cállate. *It's not funny. I'm a pregnant grand-
mother.*[95]

Of course, at this point Nellie wants to know how it happened, with
whom, and when. Angie and Nellie are devoted Bingo players and
always go together, but during Lent, as a penance, they decide to ab-
stain from playing Bingo. One Friday night, however, the jackpot
was four thousand dollars and Angie did not resist, so she went
without Nellie. There she met Henry who walked her home; during
their walk, they found out they went to the same high school. Angie
invited Henry to her house to look at their high school yearbook. At
her place, Angie says: "We smiled and laughed and smiled and
laughed again. Like we were 16. Then you know me . . . I started
thinking about Joe and how he hurt me and I started to cry. . . . Then
he pulled me into him and I don't know what he was thinking but he
started crying too. . . . Then when we were through crying . . ."

Nellie: *You screwed.*
Angie: *No. We talked about life and how we can't give up cuz we're
older and we kind of gave each other courage.*[96]

While all this is interesting to Nellie, what she really wants to know
is the "juicy part."

Angie: *He kissed me and I kissed him back. And I don't think he
thought we were gonna go all the way, but I uh . . .*
Nellie: *You what?*
Angie: *I touched him.*
Nellie: *My God! Angie, not you!*

Angie: *I just did it without thinking.*
Nellie: *And was it hard?*
Angie: *(Nods. Quietly.) And big.*[97]

After telling Nellie how it happened, Angie also confides her solution to have an abortion, which she calls a "you know what," unable to say the word.[98] In part, Angie decides on this solution due to her age and the shame of revealing to her granddaughters, old enough to have children of their own, "Your Nana had a one-night fling and now she's *panzona.*"[99]

Nellie's kitchen table provides the setting for Angie to reveal her one-night adventure and, thus, her pregnancy: her period is late and she is having morning sickness. As the play goes on we find out that in fact Angie is not pregnant but simply "three hours late!"[100] The real consequence of Angie's one-night fling, though, is that Angie does reclaim the right over her own body. After years of marriage and nine children, it is during her one-night fling that Angie experiences her first orgasm. Angie happily declares, "I'm glad I didn't die without knowing what it feels like."[101]

Fernandez in *How Else Am I Supposed to Know I'm Still Alive* contests the patriarchal myths that women are sexually passive, and after reaching a certain age they become asexual. In these myths, mothers and grandmothers do not have sex. The kitchen as a woman's *place* to serve the needs of the family is contested in Fernandez's play since Nellie's kitchen is the site where two middle-aged women in their late forties and early fifties celebrate their sexuality, their desire to still be alive. In this celebration of love and sexual desire, Nellie engages in a pseudo act of homemade tortilla making to "seduce Menny."[102] She lures Menny to breakfast with her ability in making handmade tortillas, but she says this while opening a store-bought package of tortillas and putting them in the oven. She throws some flour on her apron to convince Menny that she actually cooked them.

Alicia Gaspar de Alba's poem, "Making Tortillas" (1993), relates the production of handmade tortillas using the *metate* to women's sexuality.[103] In Gaspar de Alba's poem, *tortilleras,* the maker of tortillas, are not simply reclaiming their sexuality, but they are reclaiming a lesbian female subjectivity:

> *Tortilleras, we are called,*
> *grinders of maíz, makers, bakers,*
> *slow lovers of women.*

The process of tortilla making becomes for the speaker an expression of love and of making love as her body remembers the meaning of loving slowly. The catalyst for this recollection is the "smell of wet corn" as it soaks through the night.

In Gaspar de Alba's poem, *tortilleras* are women who emotionally and sexually love and desire each other; thus, *tortilleras* express their female sexuality and sexual desire in the process of making tortillas. The emphasis in the poem on starting from scratch is for a creation of a social *space* for the Chicana lesbian subjectivity. The cultural value in "Making Tortillas" represents the desire for a larger social and cultural sensitivity toward same-sex love, especially within the Chicana/o community.

"Mexicans have long associated the act of grinding corn on the metate with female sexuality" and one hidden agenda in the "tortilla discourse," mentioned in chapter 1, was an effort by the elite class to control "the lustful [sexual] excess they attributed to lower-class women." [104] The classical image of a woman's posture as she grinds corn, or anything else, kneeling in front of the *metate,* which is always placed on the floor, creates the sexualization of the *metate.* During the height of the tortilla discourse, some in the elite class saw the sensual and sexual image created by the use of the *metate* as a "threat to the nation's morality." [105] The elite class viewed women from the lower economic class as over-sexed because of the bodily movements involved while grinding on the *metate.* Yet, the creation of this image is in the eyes of the beholder, not necessarily a conscious effort on the part of the woman actually doing the grinding. Certainly, this is the way women from the *charlas culinarias* conceived the sexualization involved in the practice of using the *metate.*

The sensualization and sexualization of the *metate* does not appear in the *charlas culinarias.* First of all, when women speak of their *metates* or their mother's or grandmother's (referring to a woman who used it close to a hundred years ago), the *metate* is never placed on the ground. When I ask them what they think of the prevailing sensual and sexual image of a woman using a *metate,* their responses suggest that such a claim is a created fantasy. Irma Vásquez's resounding "No, para mí no tiene nada de sexual lo del metate" (No, not for me there is nothing sexual about the *metate*), epitomizes the initial response of the women in the *charlas.* After more consideration on the topic, some women acknowledge the sexual implications suggested with the use of the *metate* (and the sexual innuendoes associated with certain foods) are deliberate on the part of the women, if and only if, sex is on their minds. In other words, they express that the most effective aphrodisiac is our mind. Hilaria Cortés explains this with a rather colorful and energetic performance: "Sensual yes. Sexual no. It depends on how you think about it. People say that it is sexual because when you work on the *metate,* you have to move your entire *colera.*"[106] As Cortés says this, she begins rhythmically to sway her hips, increasing the paces of her movement at different intervals. Cortés continues, "It depends on how you take it. Because if you take having to grind on the *metate* as a job you have to do, that's it. But if you take the *mano* of the *metate* and start moving your hips."[107] Cortés rhythmically sways her hips and goes on: "If you move the *chilique* and dance as you grind on the *metate,* well that is something else. It depends on how people take it, of how they think about it. It depends on each person's mentality."[108] The "chilique" comes from chile, as in a big chile. A chile is a vernacular sexual metaphor that refers to a man's penis. In this case, Cortés refers to the "mano" as the chile. While the cooks-as-writers of the *charlas* are not always intentional with their associations of food and the celebrations of sexuality, as are writers-as-cooks, Silvia, Fernandez, and Gaspar de Alba, the association of food and sex does not escape their critical analysis.

Life happens and is understood in the kitchen. Eating is life. As we cook and eat, we actively engage in the transformation of personal histories by voicing our stories. Evangelina Vigil-Piñón's poem "kitchen talk," for instance, speaks of women's pragmatic philosophies developed from dealing with life's unexpected journeys. Responding to a granddaughter's realization that we never know what life brings us from one moment to the next, the grandmother says, feeling in one instant all that she had felt in her life, "no, pues, no" (no, we don't). With life's unexpected events and "with routine rising of coffee cups and spoons," the grandmother formulates a "thought perfectly balanced."[109] Writers-as-cooks and cooks-as-writers make life happen in their kitchen *space,* nourish it with their *sazón,* and balance it with their stories.

CONCLUSION

• •

Maybe Dessert First?

Charlas Culinarias

Often when I go out to dinner, especially to a new restaurant, my inclination is to look first at the desserts. Knowing what I want to have for dessert determines what the main course will be. Following this logic, that dessert determines the meal, I want to close with one more taste of the *charla culinarias*. They have, in fact, become the dessert around which this book revolves. The *charlas* represent spoken personal narratives, testimonial autobiography, and a form of culinary memoir, one created by the cooks-as-writers who speak from their kitchen *space* as they give voice to their *sazón*.

In personal narratives, testimonies, and autobiographies, women find ways to inscribe their experiences so that their very lives, as the Latina Feminist Group says, do not "succumb to the alchemy of erasure."[1] These three forms of telling stories validate personal experiences. They all share a similar urgency for women, the need to express their own sense of identity, often denied by patriarchal, capitalist, religious, racial, heterosexual ideologies. According to Sidonie Smith in *The Poetics of Women's Autobiography* (1987), women do not have an "autobiographical self." Smith writes, that "the ideology of gender makes of women's life script a nonstory, a silent space, a gap . . . [I]n patriarchal culture, the ideal woman is self-effacing rather than self-promoting, . . . From that point of view women have no 'autobiographical self' in the same way man does. From [that] point of view, she has no 'public' story to tell."[2]

I hold a different view from Smith: Women do have an "autobiographical self." Some inscribe it in oral narratives, others in their sewing, basket-weaving, gardening, or cooking. All of these activities form part of *testimonios*. I am defining *testimonio* as a process "in which the personal and private become profoundly political."[3] Aurora Levíns Morales sees *testimonios* as "genealogies of empowerment: How did ancestors, parents and especially the women in our lives validate our right to think and trust ourselves?"[4] Personal narratives, as do *testimonios,* also "provide a unique perspective on the intersection of the individual, the collectivity, the cultural, and the social. As an analytic technique and source, . . . [personal narratives] can access motivations, emotions, imagination, subjectivity, and action in ways less available from other sources."[5] What women in the *charlas* say about their lives resonates with these arguments. The *charlas,* with their casual talk, do lead women to explore the ways in which their own character has developed. For example, María Luisa Villicaña captures the power of assertiveness in validating her life as she says, "Taking into account the poverty in which I grew up, the ignorance, I feel that I have come very far, maybe not as far as I had hoped, but yes I have come far."[6]

Conceptually, then, the *charlas culinarias* as a form of a genre share similar characteristics to those found in personal narratives and *testimonios*. The recipes throughout the *charlas* closely relate them to a culinary memoir. The distinction remains that the actors in this form of kitchen talk are not writing down their own stories; they are telling them through their *sazón,* and I am the one transcribing. This specific dimension approximates the *charlas* to what María de Valdés calls the "testimonial literature" or "testimonial biography." Testimonial literature, as de Valdés defines it, "involves direct use of a subject's experience and the narrative structuring of the subject's story. [It is a] major source of breaking the silence in which women, especially illiterate women, have lived for centuries in Latin America."[7] Yet the *charlas* as the text of the cooks-as-writers break the *notion* of silences in which ordinary women are assumed to live under. The stories in these conversations are about ordinary working-class women doing an extraordinary thing: asserting themselves, not an easy task considering the circumstance in which some women were raised. For some, it has been a world of poverty and ignorance, robbing some of their childhood, others of their childhood innocence.

Stories expressed in *charlas* require that we develop a new set
of reading devices. Law professor Margaret E. Montoya argues "stories told from different cultural [or linguistic] perspectives require
that we suspend our notions of temporal and spatial continuity,
plot, climax, and the interplay of narrator and protagonists."[8] In
the case of analyzing stories found in the *charlas* and their distinctive quality, the *sazón,* the quintessential interpreting skill is willingness to learn from the field of knowledge found in the mundane
practices of daily cooking performed by ordinary women who *do*
speak out to change the circumstances of their lives, who define
their own subjectivity and acts of agency.

I close (but do not conclude) by giving the podium to one woman
from the *charlas.* María Luisa Cárdenas's kitchen talk presents her
perspective on regional culinary differences as well as regional politics and more. I will not include the entire *charla,* but only a few selected sections. The words in brackets are added for clarity of particular sentences. The conversation with María Luisa Cárdenas
took place in Nuevo Laredo, Tamaulipas, Mexico, where Guadalupe
Flores, her daughter Itzel Flores, my grandmother, Aurora Larios
Cárdenas, and I participated. I will focus mainly on things Cárdenas
said. Cárdenas, known in my family as Licha, often claims to be
"casi, casi mi papá" (almost my father). When my mother was ex-
pecting me, already separated from *el marido,* Cárdenas lived with
her. The two of them and my five siblings all lived in a single room;
thus Cárdenas shared the only bed in the room with my mother. My
mother and aunts see Cárdenas as their fourth sister. She has three
children and has lived most of her adult life in Nuevo Laredo, but,
like all of my family, she was born in Michoacán, Mexico. I will not
attempt to analyze any of Cárdenas's words. I simply leave you with
her voice, the voice of a working-class Mexican woman theorizing
about life from the ground up.

Licha: *We were kids when we met, [Lupita and I]. Then we started
growing, in age not in height. In age. Now, I have to tell you that
I had a mom, who thanks to, as I remember my childhood, we
didn't suffer from hunger. We didn't have a lot of things, but we
were not hungry. My mother was very resourceful to figure out
what to cook. I remember seeing people with more money to whom
my mother would offer their kids a taco, and the kids would take
the taco. And people would come to my mother to offer her food,*

*"hey, Marianita, I will give you some of my food, you give me some
of yours." She would make very simple tacos, what nowadays are
called flautas filled with* requesón *[cottage cheese]. My mother
was one of those people whose salsas are always delicious. What
did she put in it? I think all the love in the world, so that she could
feed so many. Yes there were a lot of us. Look, there were eight
children; I am the oldest of the eight. But my mother also raised
two of her sister's daughters. That would make ten of us. Then,
both my parents, that makes twelve.*

Lupita: *Plus all the guests that would come over.*

Licha: *There were always people in my house. But my mother had
faith that when you shared the food that God gives you with
someone, you would never be without food. You would always
have food, as long as you were not greedy.*

Meredith: *By sharing, somehow you get more. To give makes it possible for you to have more to continue giving.*

Licha: *Yes. She would say that as long as she was not without corn
in the house, there would always be food to share and bring to
the table. Our table, well nowadays I have seen tables scraped
that back then I thought ugly, but now they are expensive.*

Meredith: *Now they are in fashion. The country, rustic look.*

Licha: *Yes. We didn't have chairs. We used a bench. Everything was
rustic back then, and we didn't appreciate those things, right?
But now I would want to have those benches and table. Really.
[Ah] those tablecloths [hand embroidered], I am telling you, were
so beautiful. But understand that my mother did not go to school.
She was born and died illiterate. But she never let anyone to
come to the table naked; they had to at least have a tee shirt. She
would say that food was blessed. She would ask, "What do you
ask God when you pray a Holy Father?" She would answer, "to
give us our daily bread." So she would say that we needed to come
to the table with respect. Thanks to God, we were never hungry
because my mother was* muy luchona *[a fighter] to make food.*

Meredith: *What kinds of food would she make?*

Licha: *Well, back then we had* quelites *for breakfast.*

Meredith: *What are* quelites?

Licha: *Some weeds that used to grow in the fields. That now, as my
mother said, "everything ended with the concrete." Also, now
with so much insecticide used for other things, to some degree it
has ruined the vegetation in Apatzingán.*

Aurora: *[Licha's mother] was a woman, as Licha says, without schooling but intelligent. Very intelligent.*

Licha: *A waste, a waste of brains as my son says. Ha, ha, ha. She would say, my mother, that she didn't know of any schools until she became a mother. She didn't even know what was a school. But, nonetheless, she had a sharp mind. . . . Listen, it's a myth to say that at home you don't work. Because, my God, how she worked! Back then there was no laundry machine,* ni que ojo de acha. *No laundry machine. Ironing? We didn't have electricity. We would place the irons on the hot* comal *to be able to iron. We had to carry water [in buckets]. The garden that my mother had [wow]! And we had to carry [in buckets] to water the garden. We also carried water to clean the street. But we were not the only ones to do this. The neighbors would clean their side of their street. That street looked like it had rained. No one would stay behind [and not clean].*

You can never imagine, coming from so far, that life brings you so many changes. Back then, even though we were poor, we didn't think as people do now who get easily traumatized with anything. We didn't have that way of thinking. What we wanted was to finish with our chores fast so that we could go out and do childlike things. I have never felt emotionally affected [by my childhood]. Personally, I had a good childhood. I can't complain. I don't have bitter memories of my childhood, like other people who blame their parents because they suffered for this or that. No, because my mother did what was humanly possible for us. If she did it right or not, it was what she could do. Okay, my mother thought as long as she fed us and taught us how to work, that was enough. We accepted. She didn't do more because she could not. But it is very difficult to raise a family in an environment without the things we have nowadays. As we were growing, in years not height, my mother would assign each one the chores we need to do.

Meredith: *Did your mother teach you to cook?*

Licha: *Yes, first by helping her. Later, I decided to leave the house. I went to Mexico City. You always learn. Some things you learn by the adults around you. People say that we parents teach our children. I believe the opposite is true, we, the parents, learn from our children. I almost can assure you that we, the parents learn more from our children, than they from us.*

• • • • • • • • • • • • • • • • • • •

Licha: *Here [in Nuevo Laredo] I turned twenty-one years old. I am now fifty-three. What is this telling you, that I have spent more than half of my life here, obviously I feel that I belong here.*

Lupita: *At first [in Nuevo Laredo], remember that we could not find a job, mi'ja?*

Licha: *No, because they asked us to "pickinglish" [speak English] and we did not.*

Lupita: *And that we were supposed to belong to, what was it? S.O.—*

Licha: *S.M.O.P., which means, we needed to belong to a syndicate.*

Lupita: *We had to belong to the syndicate in order to find a job.*

Meredith: *That was the case in Nuevo Laredo or Laredo?*

Lupita: *Here, here [in Nuevo Laredo].*

Licha: *Now that's no longer the case. Now Nuevo Laredo, well, look before only the capital [Mexico D.F.] was [the city], everything else was [just] the country. Okay.*

Meredith: *Yes, especially the north of Mexico, all of northern Mexico has always felt very isolated, very far from the center [in terms of culture and politics].*

Licha: *Yes, like Porfirio Díaz said, "poor México so far from God and so close to the United States." [Here in Nuevo Laredo], the mayor is still fighting the bridge tolls, which generate a lot of revenue. All the money from the bridges is taken for benefits to other areas of the republic.*

Meredith: *To the politicians' pockets.*

Licha: *Yes. Here [federal politicians] don't even leave enough to the mayor to even clean the street. I tell you [we in Nuevo Laredo] are no longer a ranch. I say, "we are," because I have lived here for so many years, I have raised my family here that I really feel that I am from here.*

Licha: *Mi'ja, making enchiladas is a pain, because you have to put a lot of effort for them to come out truly well. I have heard a lot of people say, "Ay las enchiladas"! I say, the famous enchiladas that I know are the ones from Apatzingán. They are very different from other enchiladas I have eaten. One of Fausto's aunts sold food in Apatzingán. Teresa, Fausto's sister, would go help her, and I would see how they made the enchiladas. They are very, very different, because you even use radishes. You cook a tomato* *in chicken broth. You blend it, without hot chiles, without onion, without garlic. Without anything. Beforehand, you would have already pickled an onion, a tu gusto, with either lemon or vinegar; you do this way in advance so the onion is no longer strong (picosa). You add garlic salt and oregano to the onion. And you cover it. You mix it from time to time so it gets all fermented or pickled. Whichever word you use. Then, using a little bit of that vinegar, already with oregano and the flavor of the onion, you can mix it with the cooked tomato. Beforehand, you would also cook a few carrots. I prefer them cooked than fried.*

Meredith: *So that they are not so greasy.*

Licha: *Chop the cooked carrot and add to the tomato [sauce] with some radish. Now the chile. You fry it a little bit, as well as garlic and tomato. Then you blend it all, and you put it back in the frying pan, but first put it through a sieve. You cook it; then dip the tortillas in the chile sauce and then in the oil. The chile has to be thick so the tortilla won't be all pale, like the first one I did. Then you fold the tortilla, put some onion, the one you had prepared in vinegar, and cheese.*

Itzel: *And inside, you don't put anything?*

Licha: *Yes, onion and cheese.*[9]

Notes

Introduction

1. Hauck-Lawson, "Hearing the Food Voice," 6.
2. Smith, *Decolonizing Methodologies*, 15.
3. Pérez, *Decolonial Imaginary*, 127.
4. Quoted in Abu-Lughod, *Writing Women's Worlds*, 5.
5. Hurtado, "Sitios y lenguas," 140.
6. Pratt, *Native Pragmatism*, 27.
7. Quoted in Hurtado, "Sitios y lenguas," 138.
8. Long, "Culinary Tourism," 182.
9. Alarcón, "Theoretical Subject(s) of *This Bridge Called My Back* and Anglo-American Feminism," 356.
10. Smith, *Decolonizing Methodologies*, 5.
11. Winchester, *Aesthetics across the Color Line*, 7.
12. McDowell, "Spatializing Feminism," 31.
13. Katrak, "Food and Belonging," 267.
14. Quoted in Rebolledo, *Women Singing in the Snow*, 144.

Chapter 1

1. By chimney she means a type of wood burning stove made of adobe bricks. It was a rectangular structure with one side open to put in the wood, and it did not have a chimney for the smoke since the kitchen was out in the open; a roof and two walls made up the structure of the kitchen.
2. Después de dos años de casada, tu papá ya había comprado un terrenito y mandó hacer una casita. Ahí yo ya tenía mi propia cocina. Era una chimenea, pura de barro, pura de tierra. Pero yo enjarré todo mi cuartito. Es algo que se hace de adobe—no sabes [tú] ni qué es adobe. Yo

enjarré todas las paredes y el piso también, a mano. Todos los días porque como al caminar se suelta la tierra, entonces todos los días tienes que volver a enjarrar. Cuando ya tenía mi casita, mi cocina, ya me sentía independiente. Con algo mío.

3. Realmente fué de casada, por compromiso, porque tenía que hacerlo. No me quedó de otra. No estaba mi mamá para que me cocinara allí. Tuve que ponerme a cocinar yo. Pero de soltera, que yo me acuerde, cocinar, nunca.

4 McDowell, *Gender, Identity and Place,* 5.

5. Ahrentzen, "Space between the Studs," 189.

6. Un "hot tub" con agua calientita y el vino, estar allí nomás. Si yo tuviera la servidumbre, y fuera [yo] rica, ¡Ay qué rico! Quien cocinara, quien planchara.

7. Massey, *Space, Place, and Gender,* 120.

8. While the term *place* now holds a more complex meaning, particularly for geographers, in the everyday use of such word, the idea of unchanging location still remains. See McDowell's *Gender, Identity and Place.*

9. Massey, *Space, Place, and Gender,* 120.

10. McDowell, *Gender, Identity and Place,* 4.

11. Te voy a decir una cosa, cuando estás haciendo, y haciendo y haciendo, y nadie te toma en cuenta nada . . . como que te sientes como que nomás eres usada, ¿verdad? Como un robot. Que nomás haces, haces, haces. Pero nadie te toma en cuenta lo que estás haciendo. Y como que llega un momento en que te fastidia eso. Que dices, "vale madre estar levantando zapatos, calzones, de todo."

12. Ahrentzen, "Space between the Studs," 193–94.

13. Doña Virgina, tu abuela, tenía un hermano que se ponía enfermo en ciertas temporadas. Se ponía loco. Una de sus obsesiones era que me quería matar a Felix. Felix tenía como seis meses. Yo siempre tenía mucho miedo de que me fuera a matar a mi chiquillo. Un día que Juan, tu papá, no estaba, yo agarré a mi chiquillo y me fuí a la casa de mi papá porque él estaba en los Estados Unidos y yo tenía llaves de su casa. Cuando tú papá regresó, quería llevarme de regreso a la casa de su mamá. Y yo ya no me quise ir. Le dije que no me iba. Yo necesitaba que me tuviera en donde vivir. Yo ya no me iba a la casa de su mamá. Para este entonces, él ya tenía un terrenito junto al deposito de agua. Luego ya fue y empezó a construir un cuartito en ese terrenito. Hizo un cuartito, como un tejabancito, como una alita de la casa. Al final del tejabancito se hizo la cocina. Primero estaba la mesita y luego la chimenea. Dure dos años en esa casita. En ese lugar fue donde nació Chava. Pero después de dos años me volvío a llevar a vivir con su mamá. Me quitó mi independencia, porque volví a estar de arrimada!

14. McDowell, *Gender, Identity and Place,* 93.

15. Es una forma de apapachar. Yo al menos así lo siento. Y siento que tú también lo ves desde ese punto de vista. Y a tí te gusta la cocina. Y yo creo que tú me comprendes porque a tí también—yo he visto que cuando yo llego te pones a cocinar o llega alguien que tú quieres, tú cocinas. Porque a ti también te gusta la cocina . . . Lo disfrutamos.
16. Ardener, *Women and Space*, 3.
17. Quoted in Avakian, ed., *Through the Kitchen Window*, 5.
18. Narayan, *Dislocating Cultures*, 102.
19. Domosh and Seager, *Putting Women in Place*, 34.
20. For further reference on this issue see Engels's treatise on *The Origin of the Family*. Here he argues that a woman's condition is nothing more than a superstructure of the economic system and the way wealth is distributed.
21. Sí me casé . . . porque la soledad es muy fea. Yo andaba rodando de aquí pa' allá y de allá pa' ca . . . parecía bola de billar. Pun pa' allá, pun pa' acá. Y dije me voy a casar. Tal vez así se compone mi destino. Y me fué peor. Me fué peor.
22. Joseph, "Searching for Baba," 144.
23. Avakian, *Through the Kitchen Window*, 7.
24. Massey, *Space, Place, and Gender*, 180.
25. Boydston, *Home and Work*, xv.
26. Brown, *Domestic Individualism*, 3.
27. Domosh and Seager, *Putting Women in Place*, 5.
28. Some of the most celebrated women in the deconstruction of a female's natural limitations toward progress, toward Becoming, are Christine de Pizan (fifteenth-century, France), Sor Juana Inés de la Cruz (seventeenth-century, Mexico), Mary Wollstonecraft (eighteenth-century, England), and Charlotte Perkins Gilman (nineteenth-century, United States). Simone de Beauvoir's renowned phrase—one is not born a woman but made a woman—epitomizes such struggles.
29. The needs of a capitalist society, the collaboration among industry for capital gain, with the help of government policies, are instrumental to the form and function architects give to the design of a kitchen, from its location within the house to its equipment and decorative elements. For a description of how corporate America influences the designs of kitchens and their social function, see the work of Plante, *Women at Home in Victorian America* (1997) and *The American Kitchen 1700 to the Present* (1995), also Domosh and Seagar, *Putting Women in Place* (2001).
30. Es que en realidad lo haces más que para uno, por ellos. Yo te voy a decir una cosa. Yo con lo que yo como, con una tortilla que me caliente tengo. Pero cuando haces de comer, lo haces por ellos. Para que todos comamos juntos, sí. Y te sientes pa' la madre cuando te ponen peros.

31. Boydston, *Home and Work*, xi.
32. Domosh and Seager indicate how "the consolidation of capitalism as the dominant economic system, and the increase in local and long-distance trading during [the fifteenth, sixteenth, and seventeenth-century] led to the removal of jobs from the home. Making beer, for example, went from being a job that was done in the farmyard by women, to a job that was done in the cities by men. Brewing developed into a commercial enterprise that was located away from the home and funded with capital," in *Putting Women in Place*, 3–4.
33. Pilcher, *¡Que vivan los tamales!*, 103.
34. Kreitlow, "Culture of Maize."
35. **Yaya:** *Porque toda la gente está acostumbrada a hacer su nixtamal, a moler su masa, y hacer sus tortillas. Porque las tortillas de tortillería, te las comes calientitas y son sabrosas, pero para otro día no sirven porque están tiesas, paludas. Y en cambio las que uno hace te duran dos o tres días. Las calientas y están blanditas, sabrosas. Las de la tortillería no. Salen muy tiesas.*
    Meredith: *¿Por qué cree que salen así?*
    Yaya: *Porque dicen que al nixtamal le revuelven mucho olote.*
    Meredith: *¿Qué es olote?*
    Yaya: *Olote es de donde desgranan el maíz. El centro de donde desgranan el maíz.*
    Meredith: *Y, ¿por qué cree usted que hacen eso?*
    Yaya: *Nomás para ahorrar dinero. Para que rinda más. Porque tú sabes que la maseca está tan reseca. Porque del maíz sacan muchos derivados. Sacan el aceite de Mazola, diferentes clases de aceite. Entonces ya cuando vienen haciendo la maseca, ¡ya que le quedó al maíz! Ya toda la gracita, todo el juguito ya se salió. Ya no tiene sabor. Entonces la maseca ya no tiene nada de sabor.*
36. Paz, *Labyrinth of Solitude.*
37. Ahrentzen, "Space between the Studs," 180.
38. Agrest, *Architecture from Without*, 7.
39. Ibid., 8.
40. The theoretical model of place, according to Agrest, "presupposes a natural linkage between function and form, the latter determined by the former." She goes on to say how "this preconception obstructs the development of the notion of codes" which create the relationships between function and form. Agrest offers two ways of understanding architectural codes; one explicitly suggests the notion of *place* as static, "codes as static structures . . . are to be understood as different sets of rules combined in a particular way, underlying the built environment." The other codes "have not always existed and are by no means immutable." The second type of architectural codes speaks to the notion

of the kitchen as a *space,* a process of constant change. *Architecture from Without,* 15.

41. Ahrentzen, "Space between the Studs," 189.
42. Lefebvre, *Production of Space,* 33.
43. Ibid., 47, 48, 164.
44. Quoted in Bell and Valentine, eds., *Consuming Geographies,* 72.
45. Fausch, "Knowledge of the Body and the Presence of History—Toward a Feminist Architecture," 40.
46. Ibid., 42.
47. Agrest, *Architecture from Without,* 174.
48. Ibid., 188.
49. McDowell, *Gender, Identity, and Place,* 39.
50. Hermanuz, "Housing for a Postmodern World," 234.
51. Ahrentzen, "Space between the Studs," 189.
52. McDowell, *Gender, Identity, and Place,* 30.
53. Ong, "Colonialism and Modernity," 86.
54. These theoretical concepts come form the works of Edward Soja (1996), Emma Pérez (1999), Linda T. Smith (1999), and Chela Sandoval (2000).
55. Ockman, *Pragmatist Imagination,* 8.
56. Debra Castillo, *Talking Back,* xiii.
57. Mi profesión no era realmente lo de la cocina. Si no que yo al quedar viuda, pues tuve [que cambiar] mi trabajo que era lo de la leche a lo de la comida. Porque yo tenía hijas que sacar adelante. Lo de la leche ya no me sirvió. . . . Yo vendía leche, hacía queso y todo. Pero éste, desgraciadamente, la camioneta en que yo transportaba la leche y todo, se la robaron a mi'ja. . . . Y pues yo ya me quedé totalmente manca. Entonces yo me dediqué a lo de la comida. Para sacar a [mis hijas]—para que siguieran estudiando. Entonces, pues yo de qué otra forma, más que guisar y guisar. ¡Pero hay, es un trabajo tremendo! . . . Y entonces, así, así empecé, empecé, empecé poco a poco, poco a poco. Y pues ahorita, bendito sea Dios, es con lo que yo vivo. Porque yo nó estoy ni pensionada. Yo no tenía dinero en el banco para salir adelante.
58. Y digo, por eso siempre dije . . . aún . . . al quedar viuda, 'no, mis hijas . . . tienen que salir, y tiene que salir mi'jas. Y tienen que terminar su carrera, porque el día de mañana que yo les falte, ¿qué van a hacer? Lo mismo que yo ando para acá y para allá. A mí no me importa estar de lavandera, a mí no me importa, no me importaría planchar lo ajeno, a mí no. Con tal de que ellas salieran [con sus carreras].
59. Si yo no hubiera emprendido de esta forma, no sé que hubiera sido de mi vida. Porque . . . yo no estoy estudiada. Yo terminé la primaria y nada más . . . porque mis padres desgraciadamente fueron muy pobres y no nos dieron para seguir estudiando.

60. Lo que mi mamá hacía para vivir era coser ajeno. Cosía vestidos muy bien. Y ella también no estaba preparada. No era de las que hubiera ido a una academia a aprender corte. Ella hacía los vestidos lírico.

61. Michel de Certeau defines institutions of power as constructed with the principle of strategy—given power a place (i.e., university, religion, marriage, police, prisons). Many scholars of color have articulated for the last couple of decades the different levels of oppression women of color faced daily. Gloria Anzaldúa speaks of a quadruple oppression facing many Chicana/Latina women: racism, classism, sexism, and homophobia. Angie Chabram-Dernersesian addresses the academic institutional oppression faced by Chicana scholars. Vicki Ruiz addresses the economic factors of oppression.

62. Cuando mi abuela se murió, papá ya había comprado una casita. Yo no quería que metiera mi papá a una mujer ahí. Porque se sabía que tenía muchas mujeres en las cantinas y al morirse la abuela pues iba a llevarse una mujer de planta. Y por eso yo quería aprender a lavar, aprender a planchar, aprender a cocinar. Según yo, para yo hacer el quehacer y papá no se llevara a nadie a la casa. Pero como quiera se llevó a una de la cantina, una tal Carmelilla a la casa. Y nos peleabamos mucho [Carmelilla y yo]. Por eso digo que no me metía yo mucho a la cocina porque ella nos escondia la comida, a Lupita y a mi, para que no comieramos. Y por eso yo me iba con el tío Mayolo, porque la tía Celia era bien buena y el tío también.

63. Ah, bueno. A la hora del [matrimonio] civil no, no se alcanzó a pensar nada porque fueron en los mismos días de que yo me enojé. Pero para la iglesia sí se tomó más tiempo porque se tenían que leer que las amonestaciones. Se tienen que leer, no sé, tres o cuatro domingos. Por si hay algún impedimento seguramente. Y, ajá. Entonces fué cuando yo si dije "nó, ¿pues que voy a hacer? yo soy tonta ¿cómo me voy a casar?" Pero ya estaba casada al civil. Y entonces yo planié salirme antes de casarme a la iglesia. Salirme de la casa. Pos nomás así de un de repente dije, "no me caso, y no me caso, y no me quiero casar porque no lo quiero." Y, y, y, y pensé irme una noche antes de la boda. Me pensé fugar. Pero me quedé dormida. Y fué un—me, me casé. Colorín colorado, ahí se acabo el cuento. Ahí estuvo la casada.

64. Yo enjarré todas las paredes y el piso también. Es igual que como si barrieras y trapearas pero se hace con la mano. Y tanto la chimenea, porque con la masa—¡imagínate el cochinero que se hace! Y luego se tiene que lavar el metate con una escobetilla, y se hace un salpicadero que parece que se cagaron los zopilotes. Así que tienes que limpiar todo para que todo quede en orden.

65. Yo siento que cuando me casé—no sé, como que me interesó ser una buena ama de casa. Porque—¡nombre! Con las vecinas, ¡ay! La que

saliera primero a sentarse a coser afuera de la casa era porque ya había terminado de sus quehaceres de la casa. Me iba yo, no sé, a las cinco de la mañana, yo creo, con mi nixtamal al molino. Me venía; hacía mi lumbre; hacía mis tortillas; limpiaba mi chimenea. Hacía el almuerzo, le daba de almorzar a los chiquillos, los limpiaba. Luego ellos se iban a jugar y yo a coser.

66. Siempre había un cierto orgullo en saber que es uno limpio, trabajador. Pero más que eso, pienso que es esa idea de compartir. Salía uno a coser y compartía uno sus patrones de costura. Aprendíamos una de la otra. Allá compartía mi costura, aquí mis libros.

67. Este, me acuerdo que nos convidábamos con la güera. . . . Ajá, de lo que ella hacía me mandaba y de lo [que yo] hacía le mandaba. . . . Pues yo creo que todos los días, según lo que hicera cada quien.

68. Hardy-Fanta, *Latina Politics, Latino Politics,* 46.

69. [En Aguililla] todas las tardes ponía una mesita ahí en la calle, en la puerta de la casa, sin sillas ni nada. Ahí la gente comía parada o se llevaba la comida pa' sus casas.

70. Cuando ya tenía muchos chiquillos, ya cuando tenía muchas criaturas, tú sabes que se necesita para comprarles ropita, calzoncitos, y empecé yo a sacar mi puestecito allí en la puerta de la casa. Hacía que morisqueta: arroz blanco y carne con chile. ¿Qué otra cosa vendía yo? Tostadas. Hacía pozole. Se me ocurrió vender cosas ahí en la casa, pos, porque quería ganar un cinco, quería tener dinerito para comprarles algo a mis chiquillos. Y de la única manera era eso. Empezar a vender ahí en la puerta. Sí tenía clientela. . . . Sí, pues sí le sacaba dinero de ganancia porque como quiera, ya de allí volvía a surtir y me quedaba para comprarles cositas a los chiquillos, comida o ropita.

71. Después de que yo ya tenía mi vendimia en Aguililla, [el] papá de mis hijos que quería que nos fuéramos a Apatzingán. Le decía yo que se fuera, que al cabo yo de allí yo estaba sacando para darles de comer a los niños. Y como quiera me quizo llevar. Pero luego cuando ya nos fuimos a Apatzingán, también él [el marido] empezó a decirles en el trabajo que si querían—allá les dicen "asistirse" en una casa para que les den la alimentación. Así que me empezó a llevar gente de los trabajadores. Y me daban creo que diez pesos por día pa' la comida. Pero creo que eran seis o siete, así que eran como sesenta pesos por día pero yo con veinte hacía la comida. Les daba de comer y me quedaban cincuenta y es más, la comida alcanzaba pa' mis hijos también.

72. Yo no tenía para el pasaje [y] le mandé pedir a mi mamá. Ajá, pero ella no quería que dejara al marido. Ella no quería que quebrara mi matrimonio. Pero me mandó un dinero pa' que les comprara ropa a mis hijos o juguetes. . . . Con ese dinero yo saqué el boleto. Él se había ido, a pues, estaba vendiendo sus huaraches en el mercado. . . . Yo me fuí a

esperar el camión no a la terminal, sino a un lugar que se llaman las glorietas. . . . Con todos mis muchachitos me fuí. . . . Nos fuimos a esperar el camión. Con mucho miedo porque pensé que toda la gente que me veía sabía lo que iba a hacer y que le iban a ir a decir a él. Pero no, el esposo me había dicho que le llevara de cenar en la tarde, y se quedó esperando su comida porque nunca llegó.

73. This particular part of her life story does not come from the *charlas culinarias* but from a *charla matrimonial* (marriage chat) we had in 1995.

74. Allí lo que pidieran, allí ordenaban los niños a la carta. No se les podía servir de lo que hacía [de] comidas corridas. Ah no, uno quería una cosa y otro quería otra. Gracias a mi mamá comian como reyes.

75. Le gustaba mucho tomar. . . . Ajá, y era macho, macho mexicano. Tomador y golpeador y mujeriego. Y de todo. Y pienso que todo tiene su límite. Llega un momento donde dices, "yo ya nó puedo más."

76. Ardener, *Women and Space,* 10.

77. **Duvi:** *Me acuerdo una vez fuí con mi madrina Felipa y me dió maíz, me dió no sé cuántas cosas. Pues no has de creer que se te renojó tanto éste santo hombre . . . y me hizo que regresara las cosas. ¡Cómo crean que me daba tanta vergüenza irle a decir a mi madrina, "pues no quiso las cosas"!*

    Irma: *¿Y si las regresó, Duvi?*

    Duvi: *No, sí [las regresé]. Me metió de fregadasos, entre quijada y oreja.*

    Irma: *¿Y así todavía le dice santo, Duvi? Se le puede llamar humano a ese tipo de persona?*

    Duvi: *Me daba mucho coraje, pues mis chiquillos tenían hambre.*

78. Massey, *Space, Place, and Gender,* 130.

79. **Duvi:** *A mí me gusta mucho mi cocina pero que esté limpia. Y verla. Y pasar por aquí y que esté limpio todo. Es como me gusta.*

    Alma: *Mamá cocinaba muchas cosas ricas cuando estábamos chiquillos, y ahora ya casi no cocina.*

    Duvi: *Pues sí, entonces tenía que, tenía a mis hijos chiquitos.*

    Alma: *Allí está, "tenía que." Allí estoy yo también. . . . Nunca me ha gustado la cocina. . . . Realmente fue de casada . . . tuve que ponerme a cocinar yo. . . . No me quedó de otra.*

    Duvi: *Si estoy en la casa, porque no [cocinar]. Lo que no me gusta es llegar ahorita cansada y ponerme a hacer de comer. Pero si estoy en la casa, me gusta lavar, planchar, limpiar mi casa, hacer la comida. . . . Hey, le digo a Panqui "sácame de trabajar y a ver si no vuelvo a hacer [de comer]." Yo siento que me siento que puedo ser ama de casa y que me gusta. Lo que no me gusta es que llego cansada . . . pa' hacer de comer. Si tengo tanto quehacer, tanto mugrero por todos lados. ¡Tú crees que quiero irme a estar metida en la cocina!*

80. McDowell, *Gender, Identity, and Place,* 93.

81. hooks, *Yearning*, 43.
82. Ibid., 42.

Chapter 2

1. **Irma:** *El arroz se dora, que vaya apenas medio poniéndose cafecito. Entonces cuando yá está [a] ese tiempo el arroz, entonces nada más le vacías la salsa [de jitomate] y le pones el agua. Y pues tienes que saber cuanta agua le tienes que poner. Porque si le pones mucha te va a quedar aguado y si le pones poquita va a quedar crudo.*
   María Luisa: *Y, ¿cómo sabes qué tanta agua?*
   Irma: *Pues yo pienso que eso se aprende. Porque yo nunca la mido. Yo la pongo y me queda a la perfección. Yo creo que aprendí bien. Yo la siento. Yo le hago así [le muevo] a la [olla].*
   Meredith: *En la vista, yo creo, ¿no?*
   Irma: *Nó, pienso que en la mano. Porque yo le muevo al arroz y yo sé cuando le falta agua o cuando yá está bien. Al ponerle el agua yo le muevo. Yo sé. No sé como sé. Eso sí no te puedo explicar.*

2. Y ya mi prima me enseñó que hacer jamón con piña. Ensalada de macaróne. Costillas en barbecue. Cositas que yo no hubiera aprendido porque uno no las come allá [en el pueblo].

3. Pues [es saber] hacer algo mi'ja, ¿no? Digo yo, a pesar que yo no era de allí del pueblo, de que yo era según de donde no se hacen esas cosas, ¿no? Tú sabes se va y se compran las tortillas. Y pues se sorprendieron [las hermanas de tu papá] porque no creían que yo fuera a saber echar tortillas.

4. Al poner la sal, la agarro con mis dedos y allí le calculo perfectamente bien la sal, en el nombre de Dios. Siempre digo, en le nombre de Dios. Sin querer por inercia lo hago, ¿no? Digo, es una costumbre mía, no. Yo siempre evoco a Dios. O me está bendiciendo los alimentos o el tantéo. Soy tan bruta que digo, "a ver en el nombre de Dios." Es algo que yo hago, nadie me lo enseñó. A lo mejor como yo estaba tan chiquilla cuando empecé a guisar con mi tía. Cuando me dejó mí mamá allí [con la tía] tenía yo como siete años. Así que me tenía que subir a un banco, una sillita de esas de madera chiquitas, para alcanzar la estufa y la olla. Porque la estufa y la olla, ya no alcanzaba yo la cazerola. Y en el metate, molía yo el jitomate, o lo que fuera para la sopa o para el guisado, ¿no? Y yo creo que quizás eso fue el orígen de la cruz. Porque a lo mejor era tanto mi miedo a que no me quedaran bien las cosas, y me fueran a zumbar. Entonces inconcientemente yo decía, "ay Diosito Santo, qué me quede bien." Con el miedo aquel. Sólo Dios me podía ayudar para que no le fallara yo a lo que tenía que hacer, verdad. A la receta que me había dado mi tía.

5. A mí me han dicho "tú tienes buen sazón. ¿Por qué no pones un negocio de comida" Nó. Yo nó. Yo guisar para un restaruante, para gente que no conozco, no me llama la atención.
6. Yo pongo a cocer mis frijoles nada más le pongo un chorrito de aceite, y un pedazo de cebolla, y la suficente agua. Para no echarle agua. ¡Para nada! Porque el chiste es que el agua [que le pones al prinicpio] te alcance para cocerlos. Entonces le pongo la suficente agua, y los tapo y ya a que se cuezan. Cuando yá están cocidos, los checo de vez en cuando. Cuando yá están cocidos así reventaditos, reventaditos, reventaditos, agarro mi salecita y en forma de cruz se la pongo. Le pruebo. Le faltó, otra cruzecita. Y yá los pruebo, y ya están bien, los dejo hervir otro ratito y les apago. Tú te comes un plato así de la olla y te salen riquísimos. Y si tú los coces en la otra olla exprés no tienen el mismo sabor.
7. De la Cruz, *The Answer/La Respuesta*, 74. "Pues ¿que os pudiera contar, Señora, de los secretos naturales que he descubierto estando guisando? Veo que un huevo se une y fríe en la manteca o aceite y, por contrario, se despedaza en el almíbar; ver que para que el azúcar se conserve fluida basta echarle una muy mínima parte de agua en que haya estado membrillo u otra fruta agria; ver que la yema y clara de un mismo huevo son tan contrarias, que en los unos, que sirven para el azúcar, sirve cada una de por sí y juntos nó. Por no cansaros con tales frialdades, que sólo refiero por daros entera noticia de mi natural y creo que os causará risa; pero, señora, ¿qué podemos saber las mujeres sino filosofías de cocina? Bien dijo Lupercio Leonardo, que bien se puede filosofar y aderezar la cena. Y yo suelo decir viendo estas cosillas: Si Aristóteles hubiera guisado, mucho más hubiera escrito."
8. De la Cruz, *The Answer/La Respuesta*, 35–36.
9. Heldke, "Foodmaking as a Thoughful Practice," 206.
10. Pratt, *Native Pragmatism*, 18.
11. Stoller, *Taste of Ethnographic Things*, 8.
12. Korsemeyer, *Making Sense of Taste*, 11.
13. Ibid., 19.
14. Ibid., 28.
15. Stoller, *Taste of Ethnographic Things*, 8.
16. Quoted in Lefebvre, *Production of Space*, 139.
17. Ibid.
18. Korsemeyer, *Making Sense of Taste*, 85.
19. Quoted in Stoller, *Taste of Ethnographic Things*, 8.
20. Classen, Howes, and Synnott, *Aroma*, 5.
21. Ibid., 5.
22. See Stoller, *Embodying Colonial Memories* (1995) and *Tastes of Ethnographic Things* (1989).

23. Classen, Howes, Synnott, *Aroma,* 4.
24. Korsemeyer, *Making Sense of Taste,* 31.
25. Ibid., 31.
26. Grosz, *Space, Time, and Perversion,* 26.
27. The *sazón* adds to the ways cross-cultural perspectives illustrate how all theories come out of their specific location and that some are not necessarily universal while others are specific to a particular group. Carole M. Counihan's *The Anthropology of Food and Body: Gender, Meaning, and Power* (1999) and James J. Winchester's *Aesthetics across the Color Line* (2002) talk about this particular benefit of cross-cultural research.
28. Stoller, *Taste of Ethnographic Things,* 9.
29. *Distinction: A Social Critique of the Judgement of Taste* (1984) Bourdieu illustrates this point by indicating how the faculty of taste to judge aesthetic value is connected to economic factors and education.
30. Since Greek times, two manifestations in efforts to control the body, the vessel of moral decline, have been fasting or chastity. Carole M. Counihan, in *Anthropology of Food and Body,* speaks of such control, as it has related to women, as the "Western Women's Prodigious Fasting." In an effort to save their souls, medieval women engaged in a "holiness" fasting; Victorian women fasted for "daintiness"; the modern women fast for "thinness," 111.
31. Curtin and Heldke, *Cooking, Eating, Thinking,* xiii.
32. De Certeau, *Practice of Everyday Life.*
33. Narayan, "Eating Cultures," 64.
34. Lupton, *Food, the Body, and the Self,* 13.
35. Es que es según la costumbre. Aquí los americanos son gente más civilizada, es lo correcto, ¿no? La medida. Pero cuando uno no tiene tiempo de medir, o cuando uno no tiene esa curiosidad de medir, no importa. Porque tú la tanteada la tienes en la mano y en el ojo. Donde pones el ojo o pones el tantéo, ya estuvo. Pero si tú no tienes el tantéo, pues necesitas medir. Pero si tienes el tanteo, no necesitas medir.
36. Massey, *Space, Place, and Gender,* 6.
37. Para dejar que el elote se haga maíz lo tienes que dejar en la milpa, en la planta, hasta que se ponga amarillo, hasta que se seca la hoja y luego se cortan las mazorcas. Y luego se desgrana, se coce y luego se hace el nixtamal. Se cose con agua y cal. Y tienes que saber cuanta cantidad de cal, que tan fuerte tiene que estar porque si te pasas de cal te queda amarillo y entonces sabe feo. Este, tienes que saber que tanta cal se le pone al agua y tienes que saber el punto de la cocida también. Para saber si ya están los granitos del maíz cocidos, agarras un granito y si ya se le quita el pellejito, ya está cocido. Y ya lo quitas de la

lumbre. Allí se queda para otro día. Otro día lo sacas, lo enjuagas y lo mueles.

38. **Meredith:** *Y de cantidades, ¿cómo sabes? Dices, "le echo estó y le echo el otro." ¿Pero cuánto? ¿Cómo sabes qué tanta cantidad?*
 Alma: *No sé decir yo de cantidades porque es algo que yo le calculo.*
 Meredith: *¿Cómo le calculas? ¿Cómo sabes más o menos?*
 Alma: *Pos' la porción que voy a hacer. Cebolla. Le pongo una cebolla si voy a hacer la olla grande. Le pongo sal, y eso es al gusto. Cualquiera le puede calcular al gusto la sal. A muchos les gusta salado, a muchos les gusta no salado. Chile. Usualmente la bolsa de chile. Si lo quieres muy picoso, dos bolsas.*
39. **Meredith:** *Y, ¿por qué se amargan? ¿Le pasa lo que al ajo?*
 Esperanza: *Ándale, le pasa lo que al ajo. A la hora de pasarse [de dorado], se amarga, se quema. Y entonces ya el pipián tiene otro color y otro sabor. No le pones la gran cosa. [Pero] es tan sabroso que yo a donde voy de visita que me toca llevar un platillo, "Ay señora, a usted el toca le pipián verde." "Esperanza a tí te toca el pipián verde." ¿Por qué? Porque a todo el mundo le gusta el pipián verde.*
 Meredith: *¿Tú lo has comido de otras personas?*
 Esperanza: *Sí.*
 Meredith: *Y, ¿Cómo les queda?*
 Esperanza: *Pues no es igual.*
40. Farb and Armelagos, *Consuming Passions,* 12.
41. Bauer, "Millers and Grinders," 6.
42. Gabaccia, *We Are What We Eat,* 222. Other food literature that deals with the practices of eating the "Other" range from discussion of culinary tourism, see the works of Lucy Long, to culinary colonialism. Also see Helkde (2003) and Narayan (1997).
43. **Alma:** *Nunca le he medido el agua. Pero la receta para que no te queden prietos es que al hervir le tienes que bajar [al fuego] y taparlos. Y solitos se cocen y no [hay que] agregarles más agua. O sea se tarda más en cocerse pero quedan güeritos. O sea cuando tengo ganas de frijoles americanos los hago así. Cuando tengo ganas de frijoles mexicanos los hago a la carrera. Les estoy eche y eche agua para que se cocan rapido y salen prietos.*
 Meredith: *¿Pero por qué unos son a la americana y otros a la mexicana?*
 Alma: *Los americanos son güeritos y los mexicanos son prietitos. . . . O sea depende del tiempo que tengas.*
44. **Meredith:** *Oiga, ¿cómo le iba cuándo vendía hot dogs?*
 Yaya: *A veces bien, a veces mal. Bueno al hot dog se le gana nomás necesita uno un buen lugar. Tu encuentras un buen lugar donde haya gente hispana, pero por lo regular mexicana porque si es salvadoreña no vendes nada.*

Meredith: *¿Por qué cree usted que ese es el caso?*
Yaya: *Porque los salvadoreños, ellos sólo compran lo tradicional de su tierra. Las pupusas, los platános fritos con frijoles. Todo eso. Pero el hotdog no se vende. Pero donde hay raza mexicana, eso es bien vendible.*
Meredith: *¿Por qué si los hot dogs no se producto de nosotros?*
Yaya: *No, pero son perros calientes de nuestro país. Nomás volteas el nombre y son perros calientes de nuestro país. . . . Antes vendía hot dogs. Ahora ya tengo mucho tiempo que no vendo. Con eso que me cambie de donde vivía. Ahorita hay puro salvadoreño donde vivo.*

45. Grosz, *Space, Time, and Perversion*, 30.
46. Bordo, *Unbearable Weight*, 38.
47. Lupton, *Food, the Body, and the Self*, 13.
48. Stoller, *Taste of Ethnographic Things*, 29.
49. De Certeau, Giard, and Mayol, *Practice of Everyday Life: Volume Two: Living and Cooking*, 156.
50. **Alma:** *Hacen muchas enchiladas [y] las meten al horno y luego ponen todo y todos se sirven. A mí no me gusta.*
   Duvi: *Pues nomás porque es más trabajo estar haciéndolas. Pero el saborcito, el saborcito calientito.*
   Meredith: *Pero de la otra manera se sientan todos a comer al mismo tiempo.*
   Alma: *Sí, [pero] a mí no me gustan así. A mí me gusta que estén casi bien doraditas.*
   Meredith: *¿Y a qué horas comes tú?*
   Duvi: *Al final.*
   Alma: *Al final. Cuando terminan todos, preparo las mías. O trato [de hacerlas] rápido para que quede una de las personas a comer conmigo—*
   Duvi: *Y en el micro, mi'ja. A lo mejor en el micro, sí.*
   Alma: *No, donde funcionaría muy bien es en los hornitos chiquitos. Quizás en el hornito sí, porque quedarían igual. Los tamales los he calentado en el hornito y quedan muy ricos. Mejor que en el microwave.*
51. O sea, es algo que disfruta hacer [mi mamá], cocinar. Algo que a mí no. O sea cuando yo estaba en la casa que me decía, "tienes que venir a ver para cuando te cases." Yo odiaba estar en la cocina. Nunca, nunca me ha gustado.
52. De Certeau, Giard, and Mayol, *Practice of Everyday Life: Volume Two: Living and Cooking*, 151.
53. Ibid., 157.
54. Ibid., 202.
55. Ibid., 201.

56. El metate que mi tía tiene es un metate que usó su abuelita. Mi bisabuelita. Tiene como ciento treinta años—¡más! Si mi tía tiene noventa y se lo regalaron a su abuelita. ¡Imagínate!

57. The specific image of transmitting a part of one's self through the use of a *metate* is by no means only operative in the hands of the women I am mentioning. We only need to recall Laura Esquivel's *Como agua para chocolate (Like Water for Chocolate)*. Audre Lorde in *Zami* uses the mortar and pestle as a way of feeling the presence of her own body and as a way of transmitting an essential part of the person into the food being prepared.

58. Mi mamá . . . sabe hacer un mole tan rico. Y todo lo muele en el metate. Yo le traté de ayudar en el noventa, cuando fuimos todos. Hizo mole pa' todos, pues. Le traté de ayudar a moler. Yo nomás veía que le molía tan fácil en el metate. Y le dije, "a ver amacita, deje ayudarle." Y me salía todo el chile pa' fuera. . . . Le empujaba, le tallaba pero salían los pedazos de chile. ¡Chilote! Y ella le molía [e] iba saliendo así remolidito, remolidito.

59. Carne con chile. Este, doraba la carne, y luego ella siempre molía los chiles guajillos y le ponía un chile pasilla . . . ella los molía en el metate. Yo pienso que eso es lo que le daba el sabor, que ella lo hacía siempre en el metate. Aunque hubiera licuadora, . . . ella de todas maneras molía sus chiles, y, este, el nixtamal en el metate. Yo pienso que eso era lo que le daba el sabor porque de otra manera es la misma cosa que nosotras hacemos. Lavas la carne, este, pones los chiles a cocer. Pero la única diferencia es que los pones en la licuadora. Y ella no. Ella siempre los hacía en el metate.

60. Lefebvre, *Production of Space*, 215.

61. Mauss, *The Gift*, 10.

62. Cuando vamos, . . . le encanta hacernos mole. Y usa el metate. Ahorita ella tiene su licuadora, porque también ya está grande. Pero a ella le gusta molerlo en el metate.

63. De Certeau, Giard, and Mayol, *Practice of Everyday Life: Volume Two: Living and Cooking*, 212.

64. Yo nunca apunto medidas. Tú también haces las cosas al tanteo. ¿O tú sí usas medidas? No creo que vayas a la receta. [Yo] no me baso al libro y estar viendo lo que va [en la receta].

65. **Alma:** *Los ingredientes. Pos' se prepara la harina, el huevo, el este para la elevadura. Y, este, se raspa la zanahoría y naranja, la cascarita de la naranja raspada. Y se mete al horno. Y quedaba bien rico.*

   Meredith: *Y ¿dónde aprendiste a hacer éste pastel?*

   Alma: *Por una receta de un libro. Pero pregúntame que lo vuelva a hacer ya no me acuerdo muy bien. Pero allá lo hacía mucho.*

66. See Elizabeth Grosz's distinction between corporal knowledge and inscribed knowledge in *Space, Time, and Perversion* (1995).

67. **Meredith:** *Oye, ¿y todas estas recetas, las [tienes] en un libro o [te] las [sabes] de memoria?*

    Esperanza: *Nó, de memoria. Yo no las tengo en recetas. Yo me las sé de memoria.*

68. Yo vine a ver libros de cocina hasta acá contigo, yo creo. Y aquí en las casas donde ando trabajando. Y allá en el restaruante donde entré [a trabajar] el Bay Window.

69. **Meredith:** *¿Platíqueme un poquito, bueno, no sé si le gusta platicar de sus recetas?*

    Susana: *De mis recetas, sí como no.*

    Meredith: *¿Tiene alguna receta que uste ha inventado? Que diga, "esto es mío."*

70. **Vero:** *¡Inventa todo!*

    Meredith: *¿Inventa todo?*

    Susana: *Dile.*

    Vero: *Te puede inventar todo. El otro día se puso hacer que costillitas al barbecue. Y le pone veinte mil cosas. . . . lo que tenga a la mano le pone y le complementa. Ahora sí, de lo que tenga y haya comprado.*

71. De Certeau, Giard, and Mayol, *Practice of Everyday Life: Volume Two: Living and Cooking*, 213.

72. Stoller, *Embodying Colonial Memories*, 25.

73. See for example Stoller's *Embodying Colonial Memories*, Lefebvre's *Production of Space*, and De Certeau, Giard, and Mayols, *Practice of Everyday Life: Volume Two: Living and Cooking*.

Chapter 3

1. Yo siempre he dicho que el arte de cocina es una maravilla. Que maravilla cuando uno ve como lo que uno cocina se lo comen con tanto gusto. . . . Y la verdad que es fácil. Todo esta en que a uno le agrade, le guste. . . . Pero sí, yo lo veo [el cocinar] como un rito. . . . Un rito como van las cosas. . . . Cuando te dan un chile en nogada, ya fue [por] un proceso fabuloso, fantástico. . . . Tu puedes hacer una salsa, la salsa que hace cual quier gente, pero te sale mejor si está echa con gusto y con amor. . . . La comida es un arte. El arte culinario casero.

2. The notion of an "invitation" expresses my desire to carry on dialogues that exchange intellectual ideas, creative expressions, and forms of claiming/creating spaces to exercise female acts of agency between nonacademic women and feminist academics. *Chicana Traditions: Continuity and Change* (2002) edited by Norma E. Cantú and Olga

Nájera-Ramírez is an excellent example of the richness such a dialogue can produce.

3. As the literary critic I am by professional academic training, I must pause and make a comment in relation to a statement made by Harold Bloom in *The Western Canon: The Books and School of the Ages*. There are two issues Bloom mentions in regard to aesthetic value that I want to address. Bloom writes, "'Aesthetic value' is something regarded as a suggestion of Immanuel Kant's rather than an actuality, but that has not been my experience during a lifetime of reading. Things have however fallen apart, the center has not held, and mere anarchy is in the process of being unleashed upon what used to be called 'the learned world,'" (1). In the conclusion of his work, Bloom states, "the aesthetic in America always exists as a lonely, idiosyncratic, isolated stance. . . . What are now called 'Departments of English' will be renamed departments of 'Cultural Studies' where *Batman* comics, Mormon theme parks, television, movies, and rock will replace Chaucer, Shakespeare, Milton, Wordsworth, and Wallace Stevens. [T]he artifacts of popular culture replace the difficult artifacts of great writers as the material for instruction" (519–20). I will present the two issues of critical importance that I wish to highlight about Bloom's remarks in the form of two questions. First, is there only one form of a "learned world"? What *Voices* argues for, as do many feminists and other scholars who work in the areas of postcolonial, decolonial studies, is to open up the spaces that the ideologies behind the criteria aesthetics within the Western Canon has failed to consider. Second, if we learn to conceptualize cultural artifacts within their historical time, might they have not been considered then by the same conceptual terminology popular culture is constructed today? The point raised with these questions is to explore what the root is that separates "popular culture" from "difficult artifacts." The hierarchical implications in Bloom's position reflects our western heritage of thinking in binary oppositions: light versus dark, good versus evil, popular versus erudite.

4. Jones, "A Feeling for Form," 291.

5. See the work of Pérez, 1997; Hollis, Pershing, and Young, eds., 1993; Smith, 1999; Narayan 1997.

6. Cuando me casé, las hermanas de tu papá y su mamá hacían las tortillas bien feas. Y cuando vi que ellas hacían unas tortillas feas, ya nó me dío vergüenza. Yo me acuerdo que quise demostrarles que yo sabía hacer las tortillas mejor que ellas. [Ellas] hacían las tortillas bien feas, feas. ¡Uy me lucía yo haciendo mis tortillas, las ponía así en un canastito! ¡Uy—y mis tortillas me quedaban bien delgaditas y se inflaban bieeeen bonito! Las que yo hacía. Este, sí, sí les ganaba yo pa' hacer tortillas allí. Sí, ellas hacían unas tortillas feas, panzonas, agujeradas.

7. hooks, *Yearning,* 111.
8. Quoted in Pollock, "Feminist Interventions in the Histories of Art," 302.
9. Some art critics have addressed this factor in their analysis of what have been the social obstacles preventing the recognition of women's artistic production. See the works of bell hooks, *Art on My Mind: Visual Politics* (1995), and Howard S. Becker's *Art Worlds* (1982), particularly in chapters 5, "Aesthetics, Aestheticians, and Critics," and chapter 9, "Arts and Crafts," also outlines how an elitist ideology defines the value of art objects.
10. Quoted in hooks, *Yearning,* 117.
11. Quoted in Gaspar de Alba, *Chicano Art,* 40.
12. De Certeau, *Practice of Everyday Life,* xv.
13. The notion of creating and conceptualizing knowledge by the act of actively doing something with our hands is one expressed by Chicana scholars in the production of theory and analysis that reflects the complexities of Chicanas' cross-cultural and cross-class lives. We see such notion in the titles of Chicana scholarly books as *Building with Our Hands: New Directions of Chicana/o Studies* (1993), *Women Singing in the Snow* (1995), *Chicana Voices* (1993), *Living Chicana Theory* (1998), *Telling to Live: Latina Feminist Testimonies* (2001). These titles symbolically reflect an active process of building theories with our daily lives.
14. Pollock, "Feminist Interventions in the Histories of Art," 303.
15. Levíns Morales, *Medicine Stories,* 129.
16. Quoted in De Certeau, Giard, and Mayol, *Practice of Everyday Life: Volume Two: Living and Cooking,* 217.
17. To explore a range of feminist approaches addressing the knowledge in everyday life, see the following works: *Situated Lives: Gender and Culture in Everyday Life* (1997), *Decolonial Voices: Chicana and Chicano Cultural Studies* (2002), *Home and Work: Housework, Wages and the Ideology of Labor* (1990), *Eat My Words* (2002), *Feminist Theory and the Study of Folklore* (1993).
18. Quoted in Curtin and Heldke, *Cooking, Eating, Thinking,* 122.
19. Quoted in Pilcher, *¡Que vivan los tamales¡,* 5.
20. Quoted in Curtin and Heldke, *Cooking, Eating, Thinking,* 249.
21. Ibid., 150.
22. Ibid., 151.
23. In the above accounts, cooking locally was not valued, yet in our present historical moment *slow* food (which involves eating locally grown products) food is something one aspires to. While theoretical, political, and economic debates rotate priorities, working-class women know how to rely on locally grown foods and how to make art out of it too.
24. Cooper, *"A Woman's Place Is in the Kitchen,"* 86.

25. De Certeau, Giard, and Mayol, *Practice of Everyday Life: Volume Two: Living and Cooking,* 217.
26. Cooper, "A Woman's Place Is in the Kitchen," 22.
27. Quoted in ibid., 86.
28. Cooper, "A Woman's Place Is in the Kitchen," 22. In Cooper's book we find out that according to French chef André Soltner, "the CIA saved the culinary profession in America. He believed that the CIA would help to perpetuate the profession by teaching the young culinarians, who would eventually take the places of those French chefs no longer residing in this country," 22.
29. Thomas Heyd, "Rock Art Aesthetics and Culture Appropriation," succinctly describes the general views on cultural appropriation within the domain of art.
30. Smith, *Decolonizing Methodologies.*
31. Particular examples that come to mind are the astounding success chefs Mary Sue Milliken and Susan Feniger, owners of the Border Grill in Pasadena, California, and the hostesses of "Too Hot Tamales," a TV Food Network cooking show, enjoy. Or one can also think of Diana Kennedy's fame. While Kennedy has been called "the utmost authority of Mexican cuisine," many of her recipes come from the women who worked for her, yet we do not know anything about these women. See Goldman, "'I Yam What I Yam.'"
32. Calvo, book review of *Decolonizing Methodologies,* 255.
33. Young and Turner, "Challenging the Canon," 10–11.
34. Ibid., 35.
35. Nochlin, "Why Have There Been No Great Women Artists?"
36. Quotidian cuisine as an art-in-process is a creative expression that goes against the grain of social norms. Read Alvina Quintana, Alicia Gaspar de Alba, and Tey Diana Robolledo on this particular issue.
37. "Ay que buena [comida], ¿comó la hiciste?" . . . Tenía un prima que para mí era muy buena cocinera. . . . Ya se murió. Se llamaba Alicia. Para mí era muy buena cocinera. Ella sabía hacer cosas diferentes. Porque mira, cuando tú eres de un pueblo, y eres una muchacha pobre, nomás sabes hacer caldo de res, carne con chile, morisqueta, que dice uno. Cositas asi. Que tu mole.
38. Mi mamá hacía tamales. Me ponía a veces a que le ayudara a batir la masa para los tamales, para que me enseñara como hacer los tamales. Todavía yo estaba chica. Me ponía yo arriba de un banquito, con una cuchara para que aprendiera a voltear las tortillas. Y había veces que me quemaba y le decía, "mejor yo las hago." Y mejor yo ponía la bolita de masa en la máquina y la aplastaba. Y salía la tortilla.
39. Yo me acuerdo que . . . me puse a hacer tortillas—yo sola cuando vivía con la tía Celia. Yo siento que fué cuando aprendí. En el transcurso de un año. Me fuí a los quince y me casé a los dieciseis. Pero la tía ni sabía

cocinar, y nos enseñábamos las dos, la tía y yo. Desde poner el nixtamal, moler en el molino, moler bien la masa. Hacíamos las tortillas con moldes, pero luego yo comencé a hacer [las] más [bien] con la mano, pininos a mano.

40. Esquivel's *Como agua para chocolate (Like Water for Chocolate)* also demonstrates how Tita, the protagonist, has the essential requirements from which she creates art. The ranch's kitchen is her social institute; her teacher is a knowledgeable indigenous woman who has mastered the art of cooking. Nacha, Tita's instructor who could not read or write, "pero eso sí sobre la cocina [tenía] tan profundos conocimientos como el que más" (when it came to cooking, she knew everything there is to know), 14.

41. Le pones suficiente aciete al sartén y le pones sal para que no te brinque [la pepita] tanto. Porque te brinca, es un brincadero tremendo. Y fríes las pepitas a un punto bonito, que no se te doren porque sino se te amargan, ¿verdad? Que te queden bien ricas. . . . Tiene un chiste el pipián verde. Por ejemplo, yo estoy guisando, tú nó puedes meterle la mano. Porque se corta.

42. Me encanta la tortilla de a mano. [Me quedan] redonditas y delgaditas. A ver [cuando] quieras vienes y nos ponemos a hacer tortillas de a mano. Mi mamá las echaba gordas, y le salían como estrellitas, no le salían redondas. . . . Salen super más bonitas las tortillas y se pueden hacer mejor y se esponjan [mejor] cuando se pasa la masa en el metate.

43. Smith, *Decolonizing Methodologies*, 127.

44. *Imelda: Mira, si yo no voy a trabajar, si es mi día de descanso, y por decir me dice mi'jo, "voy a ir a cenar." Sí, me gusta mucho cocinar. Pero si yo voy a cocinar nada más para Enrique y para mi, me da flojera.*

   Meredith: ¿Y, eso?

   Imelda: Se me hace como mucho entretenerme para dos comidas, para dos personas. Y si van a venir ellos [los hijos], me da ilusión de estar todos juntos. Y si hago mucha comida, yo se que todos no la vamos a comer. . . . A mi'jo le gusta mucho el mole. Y le hago mole de gallina, y [si] sobra, siempre me anda pidiendo que se quiere llevar tantito. [El mole] es entretenido y laborioso de hacerse. Y luego, como para hacerse nomás pa' dos personas como que es muy tardado. Esa es la única cosa. Pero si yo voy a tener gente, van a venir mis hijos, no, sí me gusta. Ni me canso. . . . Es como una fiesta, como reunión más bien. Yo siento que también a tu mamá le ha de pasar lo mismo. . . . Yo pienso que a todas las mamás cuando nos vamos quedando solas, así nos pasa.

   Meredith: Yo si cocino para mi sola. No todos los días pero por lo menos tres o cuatro veces por semana.

Imelda: Pero fíjate que como tú todavía no has tenido familia, no sientes la diferencia de estar sola y guisar. Pero nosotras sí.

45. I agree with Uma Narayan who argues that "members of ethnic immigrant communities, though they may wish to retain some aspects of their 'ethnic roots' also often wish to be seen as legitimate members of the cultural context they inhabit in the West, and not as mere 'representatives of a foreign culture somewhere else,'" *Dislocating Cultures,* 183. Smith also illustrates this point.

46. *Duvi:* Wow, que bonitia mesa.
    Meredith: Wow, que rica ensalada.
    Duvi: Wow, mira que chulada, la mesa puesta.

47. *Meredith:* Wow, de haber sabido que iba a hacer así, una fotografía, una cámara me hubiera traído.
    María Luisa: ¿Sí? Para que véan que es comida mexicana. Para que véan que hice comida mexicana.
    Irma: Ponga el mantelito, comadre. Para la foto.
    Meredith: ¿Cuál cámara, no pense?
    María Luisa: ¿Quieres una? . . . Déjame buscarla—
    Meredith: Eso aquí para que se vea que aquí están las tortillas. Uy, hasta puedo usar la fotografía para la cubierta de [el] libro.
    María Luisa: ¡Uy! Sí.

48. There is a conceptual parallel in this type of action as those suggested by Chicana scholars, e.i., Norma Alarcón, Ana Sandoval, Chela Sandoval, Sarah Ramirez, to mention a few, who argue that the cultural production of Chicana artists carries a political impact that challenges the historical ways by which women have been systematically silenced by patriarchy.

49. My reference to "true aesthetic value" is a deliberate one. G. Luckas has argued that an artifact, in his case the historical novel, in order to have a true aesthetic value, must contain historical reality. I accept that basic notion in Luckas' theory. However, I am inviting us to extend his concept of historical reality, to conceive of historical realities beyond grand master narratives of political, judicial, and economic ideologies written by the elite. The art-in-process of tortilla making does reveal socio-ideological issues, but from the ground up. The working-class does affect and shape significant historical events, as in the case of "tortilla discourse." See Pilcher, *¡Que vivan los tamales!,* 1998.

50. Valle and Valle, *Recipe of Memory,* 143.

51. Bulnes, *El provenir,* 6.

52. Ibid., 19.

53. En Atlisco [Puebla], llegamos a la casa de la tía Dora. Allí la tía Dora me ponía a hacer quehaceres para ganarme la comida. Como sabía [la

tía] que yo iba, de acá del pueblo, dijo, "No ésta mensa está buena para que trabaje afuera." . . . Y como sabía que venía del pueblo y ella también tenía maíz, se le ocurrió que me pusiera a hacerles tortillas. Así que también me puse a hacer el nixtamal y a llevarlo al molino, y a echarles tortillas. Según ella eso era fácil para mí. No te creas que era tan poquito que hacer.

54. Aunt Dora sees Vélez and her children inferior to her to the point that even during winter, while Vélez is living with Aunt Dora, Vélez is made to bathe her children outside the house in a tin tub.

55. See Bernardino de Sahagún's *Florentine Codex: General History of the Things of New Spain*, 12 vols. Salt Lake City and Santa Fe: University Press of Utah and School of American Research, 1950–82; Francisco Hernández's *Antigüedades de la Nueva España*, Madrid: *Historia* 16 (1986). Cronicas de América; Martín González de la Vera's "Origen y Virtudes del Chocolate" y Rosalva Loreto López's "Practicas alimenticias en los conventos de Nueva España," in *Conquista y Comida: Consecuencias del encuentro de dos mundos*. Coordinación de Janet Long, 1997.

56. Lambert Ortiz, *Encyclopedia of Herbs, Spices & Flavorings*.

57. Bonfil Batalla, *México profundo*, 17–18.

58. **María Luisa:** *Te fijas Vicente que no más a ti te gusta el pan. A Vicente, el pan.*
Meredith: *¿Con el mole?*
Vicente: *Con el mole me gusta el pan.*
Meredith: *¿Pero con otras comidas, la tortilla?*
Vicente: *Con otras comidas las tortillas, pero con el mole a mi gusta el pan.*

59. Montes offers a succinct definition of these two forms of *mestizaje* in "See How I Am Received."

60. Davalos, *Exhibiting Mestizaje*, 21.

61. hooks, *Yearning*, 105.

62. Heldke, "Food, Politics, Political Food," 315.

63. Snow, *In Buddha's Kitchen*, 151.

64. Ibid., 150.

65. Curtin and Heldke, *Cooking, Eating, Thinking*, 8 and 20.

66. Curtin, "Recipes for Values," 126.

67. Wolterstorff, "Why Philosophy of Art Cannot Handle Kissing, Touching, and Crying," 24.

68. Ibid., 27.

69. Norma Alarcón in "Anzaldúa's *Frontera:* Inscribing Gynetics," argues that women's voices (their life experiences) have faced multiple social, political, and cultural exclusions in the "Name of the Father and the Place of the Law," 114. The exclusion results from the seemingly

natural (thus ahistorical) and transcending ideologies that sustain patriarchy. Yet when women of color write as "located historical . . . subjects" or as a "speaking subject in process," their voice "emerges into conflictive discourses generated by theories of representation, whether it be juridical or textual/symbolic," and here I would add aesthetics, 116. The "conflictive discourses" result from the fact that women of color and working-class women's practices do not fit into preexisting theories. Yet as women become a "speaking subject in process" or create art-in-process, they enact in the development of theories that pose questions about how they are constructing their own lives, about how they are taking social spaces to affirm themselves as active agents of their lives. The emphasis on "process" needs to be underscored for its suggestion of an ongoing expansion of theories. Theories should not be about giving "final, for-all-time answers" but rather they should contribute to posing "interesting questions" as Rayna Green says in *Feminist Theory* (3).

70. Dabney Townsend offers a critique of this form of thinking in his article "Thomas Reid and the Theory of Taste," 341–51.

71. Curtin, "Food/Body/Person," 10.

72. Mi abuelita, la que se murió, la mamá de mi papá, tenía muy bonita tortilla ella cuando [las] estaba haciendo a mano. Entonces ella me decía, "Mira mi'ja como se me pinta la cruz de Cristo, las espinas, la coronita, se ven pintadas unas espinas en medio." Sí, les puse cuidado. Y hay veces que [algunas] personas se les pintan más que a otras. [A mi abuelita] se le pintaba esa coronita, pero bien pintada en medio. Y según dice ella, "Mira allí está [la cruz] por eso es muy sagrada la tortilla. Porque dicen que aquí está la corona de Dios." Sí se le pintaba. Bien bonita que le quedaban las tortillas a mi abuelita.

73. Hooks, *Yearning*, 104.

74. José Antonio Burciaga gives us another example of the spiritual aspect of tortillas. During the "height of the Chicano movement," writes Burciaga, "a priest in Arizona got into trouble with the Church after he was discovered celebrating mass using a tortilla as the host," 100.

75. Quoted in Guerrero, *Toneucáyotl*, 158.

76. Quoted in Curtin, "Recipes for Values," 127.

77. Ibid., 126.

78. Wolterstorff suggests that for such coexistence of diverse forms of art and their aesthetic value be recognized, what philosophers of art need to develop is "social practices of art, which include—practices of composition, practices of performance and display, practices of engagement," 27.

79. Mora, *Nepantla*, 181.

80. Walker, *In Search of Our Mothers' Gardens*, 5.

81. For those of us in academia interested in finding spaces where the voices of all women can be heard, we must resist giving in to our own

disciplinary pressures that often limit the multifaceted aspects of our research. See Córdova's "Power and Knowledge."
82. In Hough, "Phenomenology, Pomo Baskets, and the Work of Mabel McKay," 107.
83. Ibid.
84. Quoted in Quintana, "Beyond the Anti-Aesthetic," 248.
85. Ibid., 250.

Chapter 4

1. Okay, yo una vez hice una salsa de molcajete con orégano [y] se me ocurrió ponerla en medio antes de ponerle el queso y envolverla. Una vez se me occurrió y supo rico, y es como le hago. O sea yo ya cambié mi receta. A unas personas yo les digo y dicen, "Ay, eso no son enchiladas." Yo sé como a mi me gustan y es como yo las hago.
2. Hélène Cixous, "The Laugh of the Medusa," 880.
3. Marshall, "The Making of a Writer: From the Poets in the Kitchen," 6.
4. Latina Feminist Group, *Telling to Live,* 2.
5. Rebolledo, *Women Singing in the Snow,* 130. Rebolledo describes Chicana writers as "writers as cooks" since they often season their work with spices in the form of cooking memories of grandmothers, mothers, and daughters, a topic of discussion for chapter 5, "The Literary Kitchen: Writers-as-Cooks."
6. Primero se pone a hervir el chile guajillo con un tomate, para evitar las agruras okay. Luego por separado se hace una salsa. Se ponen a asar unos tomates y chiles verdes. Luego los mueles en el molcajete, o en la licuadora dependiendo que tantas enchiladas vayas a hacer. Pasas la salsa a un recipiente y le agregas un poquito de vinagre; le picas cebolla, y le pones orégano. Por supuesto, sal al gusto. Luego regresando al chile guajillo, también lo mueles en la licuadora con sal, ajo, un trozo de cebolla. Luego la pones a freir un poquito. Luego, hacer las enchiladas. Primero pones la tortilla en el chile y luego en el aceite. Luego en un plato y le pones la salsa [de orégano] y queso fresco en medio y la enrollas. Al final le pones lechuga, unas rebanadas de tomate, unas rebanaditas de cebolla, y quesito ariba. Y luego, a comertelas. Que rico, ¿no?
7. De Valdés, *Shattered Mirror,* 2.
8. Ibid., 195.
9. **Meredith:** *En las charlas que he tenido con mamá, siempre ha dicho "mis hijos" y "el marido." Pero casi no ha dicho "nuestros hijos" o "el padre de mis hijos." Y en todas las charlas siempre se refiere a Juan como "el marido," ni siquiera fue "mi marido." En otras charlas con Alma, mi abuelita, mis tías ellas si dicen mi esposo y nuestros hijos o el padre de mis hijos.*

Irma: Yo a veces digo mis hijos y a veces nuestros hijos. Pero estoy
tratando de decir nuestros hijos. A mi me gusta más decir nuestros
hijos. Yo pienso que es por cultura eso de decir mis hijos.
Meredith: ¿Pero decir el marido, también?
Irma: Yo pienso que esó es por la situación de ella.
Meredith: Eso es lo que yo siento, que es la situación mucha veces—
Irma: Lo del marido si yo pienso que es por la situación de ella. Pero
yo creo que eso de decir "mis hijos," eso sí va de cultura. Porque
quizá yo te diría "mis hijos" cuando yo sé que Luis ha sido todo el
tiempo un padre responsable y que son hijos de él. Yo debo de decir, estoy tratando de decir "nuestros hijos." Yo pienso que es porque
uno [la mujer] los tuvo—
Duvi: Es parte tuya. Son parte tuya [los hijos]. . . . Teníamos dos
tiendillas en frente de la casa y no quería [el marido] que [pidiera
fiado]. No, que hasta que se vendiera un par de huaraches. Si no se
vendía un par de huaraches [que él hacía], no iban a tragar los
chiquillos en todo el día. Y eso a mí me daba mucho coraje, pues
mis chiquillos tenían hambre. Y por eso ya después yo me puse a
vender comida.

10. Douglas, *Active Voice*, 82 and 86.
11. Farb and Armelagos, *Consuming Passions*, 111.
12. Lawless, "Experimental Cooking in *Como agua para chocolate*," 261.
13. Theophano, *Eat My Words*, 13.
14. Appadurai, "How to Make a National Cuisine," 5.
15. Goldman, "'I Yam What I Yam,'" 172.
16. Pineda, *Encarnacion's Kitchen*, 48.
17. Gonzales, "Crossing Social and Cultural Borders," 3.
18. Villaseñor Black, "Sacred Cults, Subversive Icons," 135.
19. Levíns Morales, *Remedios*, 32.
20. Ferré, "La cocina de la escritura," 154. "Lo importante no es determi-
    nar si las mujeres debemos escribir con una estructura abierta o con
    una estructura cerrada, con un lenguaje poético o con un lenguaje ob-
    sceno, con la cabeza o con el corazón. Lo importante es aplicar esa lec-
    ción fundamental que aprendimos de nuestras madres, las primeras,
    después de todo, en enseñarnos a bregar con fuego: el secreto de la es-
    critura, como el de la buena cocina, no tiene nada que ver con el sexo,
    sino con la sabiduría con la que se combinan los ingredientes."
21. Counihan, *Around the Tuscan Table*, 1–2.
22. Pérez, "Kitchen Table Ethnography and Feminist Anthropology."
23. Latina Feminist Group, *Telling to Live*, 2.
24. The Latina Feminist Group, of *Telling to Live*, when speaking of their
    position as academics recognize their relative privilege, socially and
    financially, (this would allow certain freedoms that a working-class

woman would not have), but they also speak of the marginalization they experience due to their research interest. "Our professional privilege comes from our locations in institutions of higher education, with good salaries and benefits, the luxury of pursuing our passions through our work, and for some of us, tenure and sabbaticals. However, because of our professional choices—to research, think, and write about Latinas in ways that take the subject seriously—we become marginalized by institutional cultures that reproduce hegemonic relations of power," 7–8.

25. Yo con la tía Celía aprendí todo el proceso de sacarle la leche a una vaca, hasta hacer el queso. Yo sabía amarrale las patas a la vaca para que no te vaya a patear, a quitar al becerro de la vaca. Los nudos con que se amarra a la vaca tienen que ser nudos que uno puede quitar fácil. Ordeñar una vaca también tiene su chiste. Si les aprietas feo no te sueltan la leche. Tienes que tener cierta fuerza y forma [en la mano] para que te suelte la leche. ¡No hombre! Me echaba yo unas cubetonotas de leche bien espumada. ¡No hombre! De agricultura yo pienso que aprendí mucho allí con los tíos. Aprendí a hacer el queso. Desde para cuajar la leche, se llama cuajo, es algo que le sacan a las vacas cuando las matan. Y lo secan con sal. También aprendí a hacer la crema. Allá le dicen jocoque. Pero no tiene ningún químico.

26. De Certeau, *Practice of Everyday Life*.

27. Goldman, "'I Yam What I Yam,'" 188.

28. Leonardi, "Recipes for Reading," 344.

29. El pozole me queda muy rico ahora, pero lo agarré por medio de puras recetas de diferentes personas. La agarré de una persona y lo hice. Y luego agarraba comentarios, opiniones de otras personas. Y luego ya al final lo hice a mi modo. Al final acomodé yo la receta a mi estilo. Como un rompecabezas vas agarrando pedacitos de cada lado y hasta que haces tu propio—tu propio menú. El pozole así es como lo hago.

30. Heldke, *Exotic Appetites*, 186.

31. Pones a hervir chiles guajillo. Aparte pones a cocer la carne de puerco, pata de puerco, y pollo (bueno el pollo se lo pongo porque mi amiga Cheryl no come carne de puerco y a ella le gusta mucho el pozole, *so* tuve que hacerle un pequeno ajuste). Le pones ajos, sal, cebolla y orégano. Luego mueles los chiles en la licuadora con sal, ajo, cebolla y lo cuelas antes de echarselo al caldo. Le pones el maíz, y te esperas a que esté listo. Este plato se come con repollo picado, rabanitos picados, limón, cebolla, y con tostadas. El pollo se lo pones a la carne cuando ya esta a medio cocer, porque si no se desbarata.

32. Heldke, *Exotic Appetites*, 186.

33. McRobbie, *Postmodernism and Popular Culture*, 58.

34. Flusty, *De-Coca-Colonization*, 4.

35. Heldke, *Exotic Appetites*, xxi–xxii.
36. Clifford, "On Collecting Art and Culture."
37. Maize is a grain that responds well to a variety of natural and laboratory hybridizations. Maize's hybridization has yielded a multitude of grains changing color, size, weight, and flavor. Maize comes in over three hundred variations.
38. Anzaldúa, *Borderlands/La Frontera*, 81.
39. **Alma:** *Sopitos, tamales, uchepos y todas esas cosas, me gustan pero son laboriosas. Yo mejor las compro. O sea, es lo bueno de este país que trabajo y me puedo comprar lo que yo quiera sin necesidad de ponerme a cocinarlo. Si nó, lo cocinas o nó comes.*
    Duvi: *Eso es lo mejor de aquí. Pero allá en el cerro de donde uno viene—*
    Alma: *Pero lo bueno es que yo no me crié en el cerro 'amá.*
    Duvi: *Allá en el cerro tienes que a fuerzas hacer las cosas. Lo bueno de aquí, si no cocinas o si no sabes, vas y compras. Nomás con que tengas trabajo. Pero allá en mi cerro, de allá de donde yo vengo, o te enseñas y le buscas la forma de hacerle—*
    Alma: *O te mueres de hambre.*
    Duvi: *O te mueres de hambre.*
40. Burciaga, "I Remember Masa,"98.
41. Minh-ha, *Woman, Native, Other*, 98.
42. Cuando me casé, quizás incorporé un poquito que veía aquí y un poquito que veía allá. Pero no porque yo cociné con mamá, o cociné con mi suegra o como aquí, o como allá. Uno vé y uno agarra lo que le gusta, ¿verdad? Leyendo aquí, buscanco allá, te das cuenta que puede salir mejor. Buscando la tecnología, mi'ja, las cosas modernas. Yo modifiqué [mi] forma [de cocinar] diferente a como ellas lo hacen.
43. Mexican food often gets critized as unhealty, by non-Mexicans and some Mexicans, due the lard contents in it. Yet this rejection does not speak about Mexican food but rather the rejection of some aspects of the legacy of the Spanish colonization of the "New World." *Manteca* (lard) is not indigenous to the Americas.
44. Yo siempre he tratado de rebajar [la grasa a la comida], no me quedará así sabroso, ¿verdad? Probablemente, porque no hago en la misma forma las cosas. Por ejemplo, con Esperanza acostumbran mucho las enchiladas. Yo nunca hago enchiladas. Yo hago entomatadas.
45. Pues yo quiero que sepas que tenía años que no comía tortas de papa, y ahora ésta cuaresma hice. Agarran mucha grasa. Vieras que tragadón dimos. Vieras tu tío que bien que les entró. Quiero que sepas que de todo lo que hice de comer, yo creo que fue a lo que más le entramos, a las tortas de papa.
46. **Lupita:** *Pues ahora a [mis hijos] les gustan. Antés no les gustaban. No compraba tamales yo. Aquí no había tamales. Yo soy medio chocantoza porque no me gustan las mantecas. Y a los tamales la*

gente les echa [mucha] manteca, que le muerdes al tamal y sientes
el pedazo de grasa en la boca. ¡Guácala!
Meredith: *A mi los tamales de mamá me gustán porque mucha gente*
los hacen bien gruesos, que comes muchísima masa. Mamá los
hace delgaditos. Ella no les pone tanta masa, entonces es más bien
como una capa que esta tapando la carnita del centro. Así es como
los hace mamá. Pero es una friega hacerlos. Ése es el problema.
Lupita: *No. Es una friega tremenda. Nó, nó. Yo trato de esquivar esas*
cosas. Como que siento que la vida tiene más cosas importantes
como para ponerte a hacer algo así tan meticuloso.

47. Hacía pavo, ensaladas. Mmmm, ensalada de zanahoria. Mmmm, el pure de papa nunca faltó. Hacía pies. Okay, nunca, nunca, nunca he podído hacer el *crust*. Así que opté por lo más practico, comprar los *crust*. Les gustaba mucho el pie de limón. Les hacía pie de pumpkin. Hacía panecitos. Echaba un montón de cosas a perder porque a veces no me salía.

48. Yo lo sentí mucho cuando se fueron para California. Porque yo hacía el montanal de comida porque sabía que no iba a quedar nada. Después cuando se fueron como que ya se sintió más triste porque yá se acabó, tú sabes, la mesa llena.

49. **Lupita:** *Como me dijiste tú que hago el pavo muy sabroso. Okay, no es*
que haya aprendido, mi'ja, de nadie. Simplemente—
Meredith: *Bueno lo has aprendido en base de hacer combinaciones de*
diferentes cosas, ¿no?
Lupita: *Exactamente. [En aquel entonces] Felix [tú hermano] era el úl-*
timo que llegaba porque decía que ya quería que hubiaramos co-
mido todos para todo lo que quedara comerselo él. ¿Te acuerdas?

50. Siempre me traían tortillas del otro lado [Nuevo Laredo]. Me traían fruta. Siempre me traían cosas del otro lado. Me acuerdo [que] Hugo, ¡cómo iba y venía en esa bicicletilla que tenía! [Él] me traía tortillas. Cuando me sentía mal, me traía pastillas; me traía inyecciones. Volaba él en su bicicleta! Tu sabes, chiquillo mi'jo chulo. Sí, tengo muy presente como iba y venía él en su bicicleta a traerme ésto, a traere el otro, a traerme aquello.

51. Es que en realidad lo haces más que para uno, por ellos. Yo te voy a decir una cosa. Yo con lo que yo como, con una tortilla que me caliente tengo. Pero cuando haces de comer, lo haces por ellos. Para que todos comamos juntos, ¿sí? Y te sientes pa' la madre cuando te ponen peros.

52. Sopes son esos que les picas encima y les pones salsa, le pones crema, le pones queso, le pones cebollita encima y los vuelves a poner en el sartén y cuando empieza a hervir la cremita asi arriba en el quesito, ya los quitas del comal. Y ¡wow, no comes, tragas!

53. Casi siempre trato de comprar un Butterball turkey con termómetro. Si no es Butterball, nada más trato de que tenga termometro. Si

consigo un Butterball no le pongo mantequilla porque ya tiene mucha. Compro la bolsa donde se mete el pavo y le pongo un poco de harina. O, cuando no compro el Butterball trurkey, entonces lo embarro todo de smart soya margarine. Es un poco más nutritiva. Pero primero, por supesto lo lavo bien y lo seco bien. Entonces ya después baño todo el pavo con el mixture de sal de ajo, celery y pimienta. Le pongo bastante. Pico *bell pepper,* apio, cebolla, perejil, *sometimes* zanahoria y se lo pongo al pavo. No hago relleno y cuando hago no se lo pongo adentro del pavo porque sale muy grasoso. Son muy gordos los pavos. Mantecosos. Son grandes a base de pura química que les dan para que engorden. Pobrecitos los animales. Cuando hago relleno, nomás a mi nuera le gusta poquito. Mi relleno es dulce-salado porque lo hago con manzanas, pasas, almendras, apio, cebolla. Pongo el pavo en la bolsa que compré y sigo las instrucciones. Cuando el termómero *pops-up,* ya está. Para el *gravy,* desgraso el jugo del pavo antes de usarlo. Pongo a cocer harina con sal en [tantita mantequilla]. Eso es todo, el pavo sin receta.

54. **Veronica:** *Bueno, se hace en cierta temporada del año que es Agosto. Agosto 19 cuando es que se supone se honora San Agustín. Es un Santo que se celebra en algunos pueblitos de Puebla. Por eso viene la tradición de comer chiles en nogada ese día en Puebla.*

    Meredith: *O, sí. ¿En serio? Yo no sabía.*

    Verónica: *Ajá, es eso. Haz de cuenta que según, que lo veneraban con los chiles. . . . Ya que se van a sentar en la mesa, entonces [a cada persona] se le pone su chile y se le echa la nogada. Se le echa granada, roja, y perejil que es verde. Se ve bien bonito porque es rojo, blanco y verde. La bandera.*

55. **Verónica:** *Son chiles poblanos. ¿Cómo se les llaman aquí?*

    Duvi: *Chiles pasilla.*

    María Luisa: *¿Verde o seco?*

    Verónica: *Verde. Se hace un picadillo de fruta que soló en esa temporada se da: duraznos, peras, plátano macho, el grande. Bueno, cada fruta se fríe por separado, y va pelada la fruta. Después se hace un picadillo con carne que se sazona con jitomate. Bueno, no me se bien la receta, me acuerdo de lo que le ayudé a mi mamá. Después se rellenan los chiles de ese picadillo y se capean y se fríen. Después se hace una salsa que es de nuez, también de esa temporda. Se pelan, se les quita toda la cascarita. Y se le pone brandy. Esto se llama nogada. Es lo que le da el sabor bien rico. Ya que esta frito el chile se le pone encima la nogada. Es rica y es blanca. Después se le pone granada. Es un platillo muy laborioso y por eso es muy caro.*

    María Luisa: *Yo se de una receta igúal que esa pero no se fríen. Se hace todo el proceso igúal como dijistes tú, pero no van—¿cómo dices?*

    Verónica: *Capeados.*

Duvi: *Si no los capeas, vas a tener menos grasa en tu platillo. Yo estoy tratando de recordar si ahora que los tuvimos con tú tía Esperanza estaban capeados.*
Meredith: *Sí, sí estaban.*
Duvi: *Esta bien que no vayan capeados, para comer menos grasa.*

56. Mi mamá ya que está muy próxima la fecha de que tenemos que hacer los chiles, [ella] siempre pone una fecha e invita a toda su familia, mis tíos. O sea, lo hace en grande mi mamá. . . . Es una ocasión especial. Que después dices, "¡hay tantos trastes!" Pero en ese momento es padre.

57. Había días que llovía y no se vendía nada, nada, nada. Y daba una tristeza como nó tienes idea. Yo desde chica trabajé en el campo, sembrando, arrancando frijol. En México. Yo realmente no tuve niñez, porque el tiempo que era para mí, para divertirme jugando con muñecas, yo no lo tuve. Yo no tuve ese tiempo. Porque yo desde chica andaba en friega [trabajando]. Por eso cuando mi hermano el más chico empieza como [a quejarse] digo, "mira hermanito no te burles porque tú veniste cuando el plato ya estaba servido." . . . En nuestra pobreza, cuando nó hay qué comer, ¿qué se come? Un taco de sal con chile. Cuando nó hay frijoles, una tortilla con chile y sal. Nostoros llegamos a comer eso. Porque llegó un tiempo donde nó había trabajo, nó había nada de campo. Estaba todo bien feo. El campo nó tenía nada de fruto.

58. Yo pues, sufrí pero aprendí. Porque quieras o no, yo sé de todo. Yo sé ordeñar vacas. Yo sé ordeñar chivas. Yo sé hacer queso. Yo sé de todo. A mí nadie me va a decir, "ésto no se hace así." Nó. Porque yo lo sé hacer. En el modo de hacer, en mí modo de pensar, a mí nadie me enseña porque yo lo sé hacer. Lo que no sé hacer, clarito digo, "no sé como se hace esto. ¿Dígame cómo?" Pero de hay enfuera.

59. ¿Qué quieren que les haga, pues? Yo les hago lo que sé. Lo que no sé no. [Los hijos contestan], "Haznos lasagna." Voy a preguntar cómo se hace la lasagna. Ya pregunté como se hacía la lasagna me dijeron, se las hice. ¡Ay nó! En eso duré horas, haciendo la mentada lasagna. Dije yá nó. Porque duré más haciéndola y sacándola del horno de la estufa [que ellos comiéndosela].

60. **Yaya:** *¡Ay veces que te salen algunos infelices [clientes], que hay Dios!*
Cliente: *Déme el vuelto.*
Yaya: *¿Cúal vuelto?*
Cliente: *Yo le dí un billete de a cien.*
Yaya: *¿Cúal billete de a cien? [Ese] día estuve a punto de cometer el error de llamar a la policía, porque el infelíz quería que le diera el vuelto de uno de a cien. A mi no me había dado ningúno de a cien. ¿Cómo le iba a dar el vuelto? Y el muchacho necio.*

Cliente: *Nó, yo le dí uno de a cien. Qué no sea abusiva, vaya a joder a otra gente, que a mi no. Si no me da el vuelto voy a llamar a la policía.*

Yaya: *Okay de dónde le voy a dar el vuelto si no tengo ningún billete. En eso venía el* manager *del parque y le hago la seña que se apurara que viniera rápido. Y llega el* manager *y me dice, "¿cuál es el problema?" Mire es que este señor dice que me dío un billete de a cien. Y yo no tengo ningún billete de a cien. Entonces yo le digo a él que llame a la policía o que la llamo yo. Y si yo tengo el billete de a cien que me lleven arrestada. Pero que si yo no tengo ningún de a cien que a él se lo lleven arrestado. Me page mi tiempo y mi insulto. Entonces el* manager *le dice al muchacho.*

Manager: *Mira si no le diste un billete de a cien, fíjate bien en lo que estás diciendo porque ella es mujer y tú eres hombre. Tú a ella la estas incriminando. Yo llamo a la policía . . . [y] si [a] ella no le encuentran ningún billete de a cien que tú le hayas dado, y si tú no traes ningún cinco en la bolsa, te llevan arrestado a tí y no a la señora.*

Cliente: *Nó, usted está de acuerdo con ella.*

Manager: *Nó, pero si quieres que llame, ahorita llamo.*

Yaya: *Entonces cuando él se puso a hablar, como el [cliente] no entendía inglés, echo a correr y se fué. Quería sacarme lo que era injusto. Quería sacarme el vuelto de uno de a cien, si yo no tenía ni vendidos veinte dolares. ¿De dónde iba a dar el cambio? Entonces, eso es algo que tienes que andar con cuidado porque la gente es canija.*

61. Ahora la policía anda brava. Antes no exigian que las sillas del niño [para los carros.]. No [exigían] que la aseguranza. Entonces la gente que tiene carro y no tiene aseguranza no van al parque. La gente que no tiene aseguranza prefiere no salir. La gente que tiene niños y no tiene aseguraza nó sale porque los paran y ahí los dejan bailando.

62. **Meredith:** *Oiga, ¿y por qué trajo comida? La invitamos a comer y viene con toda la comida.*

Yaya: *Y yo se, pero dije, "yo no se si Magui tendrá el arróz listo." Nó, nó. Yo mejor donde quiera que yo voy, yo llevo algo.*

Meredith: *Pero aquí trajo todo, carne, arróz, tortillas, sodas.*

Yaya: *Como a mi me ha tocado muchas veces, especialmente con la familia de mi esposo, que me invitaban a comer. Y cuando yo llegaba no había nada. Cuando mis hijos estaban chiquitos, para mi era una cosa terrible. Llegaba yo con los hijos chiquitos y pues yo no veía nada [de comida]. De ahí para acá, a mi se me quedo que donde quiera que yo vaya, llevo algo.*

Meredith: *Pero también aquí, en la casa de Scott and Magui, aquí siempre hay mucha comida.*

Yaya: Yo se, pero nosotros sabemos comer.
Meredith: Y, ¿aquí no sabemos comer?
Yaya: Nó, nó es eso. Pero mira, fíjate bien. Los americanos tienen su límite de comida. Okay, es como el tiempo. Fíjate bien en el tiempo. Los americanos tienen su hora exacta.
Meredith: ¿Hora exacta de qué?
Yaya: De todo, de comer, de todo. Los mexicanos, no. Los mexicanos no tenemos hora. Si tú traes Mexican time, dices a las tres y llegas a las cuatro o cuatro y media. That's Mexican time. American time is exact time. Lo mismo la comida. American people [ask], "how many people?" Si hacen un party, si invitan a alguien a comer, "how many people." Y ellos preparan la comida para esa cantidad de personas. Ellos núnca preparan comida de más. Okay, aquí [con Scott y Magui] es un poco diferente. Pero en la mayoría de americanos, yo he visto así que cuentan cinco o seis personas. Y exactamente hacen comida para esas personas. Mis hijos comen como lo que van a comer tres people. Nó. Olvídate. Yo mejor llevo comida.

63. O es deliciosa. Compro la carne ranchera que no este cortada a lo largo. La carne ranchera tiene que estar cortada y hecha bistec a lo a travesado para que esté blandita y esté sabrosa. Ya despúes para prepararla le pones cerveza. La de hoy no tenía cerveza porque los hijos [me dijeron] que no, porque Scott no toma cerveza. Entonces le exprimi una naranja, le puse un poco de mostaza y sal de ajo. Y fué todo. Y no se tiene que dejar muy asada. Se tiene que dejar como el *sirloin steak,* que quede jugosa para que esté sabrosa. Y si asas unas cebollitas mexicanas, acompañadas de frijoles, nopalitos. Las cebollas mexicanas son las cebollitas grandes. Son cebollitas blancas pero cabezonas. Y las americanas son las que estan flacas, paludas. Las que no tienen ni cabeza. Y no se envuelven las cebollas en aluminio. Nomás se ponen sobre el bracero y quedan jugozas.

Chapter 5

1. M. F. K. Fisher, *Gastrononical Me.*
2. Cervantes, "On Love and Hunger," 32.
3. Stowell and Foster, eds., *Appetite: Food as Metaphor,* 12.
4. Anna Shapiro, *Feast of Words,* 17.
5. Rebolledo, *Women Singing in the Snow,* 130.
6. Rebolledo and Rivero, *Infinite Divisions,* 158–59.
7. Ibid., 274.
8. Viramontes, "'Nopalitos': The Making of Fiction," 293 and 292.
9. André, "Culinary Fictions."

10. Batstone, "The Raw and The Cooked," 48.
11. André, "Culinary Fictions," 17.
12. Avakian, *Through the Kitchen Window*, 3.
13. Ibid., 6.
14. Morrison, *The Bluest Eye*, 128.
15. Quiñonez, "Spousal Rape," 101.
16. Stowe, *Uncle Tom's Cabin*.
17. Plante, *Women at Home in Victorian American*, 146.
18. The kitchens of this period became *separate zones* within the domestic space. Historian Ellen M. Plante in *Women at Home in Victorian America* (1997) suggests that location of the kitchen "not only diminished the threat of fire to the home, but prevented all trace of cooking odor from penetrating the best rooms," 55. I venture to wonder something slightly different. With the arrival of so many immigrants to the United States and their entrance, as well as slaves or ex-slaves, into the domestic sphere, could the early Victorian kitchen's design be a symbolic architectural manifestation of a national anxiety? Is the justification of the kitchen's location only to prevent the threats of fire and cooking odors from harming and entering the main house? A valid justification, but in my estimation a justification with a hidden agenda. Could the threat from the *separate* kitchen *zone* to the domestic sphere be a fear of new and different cultural practices entering into the fabric of the dominant cultural identity? Could the location of the early Victorian kitchen reveal an anxiety felt by those wanting to maintain a homogenous national cultural identity?
19. Gillian Brown, *Domestic Individualism*, 16.
20. Stowe, *Uncle Tom's Cabin*, 226 and 224.
21. Ibid., 225.
22. Gillian Brown, *Domestic Individualism*, 16.
23. Stowe, *Uncle Tom's Cabin*, 224.
24. Ibid., 227.
25. Ibid., 229.
26. Ibid., 227.
27. Ibid., 228.
28. Ibid., 227.
29. hooks, *Black Looks*, 115.
30. Ibid., 116.
31. Stowe, *Uncle Tom's Cabin*, 229.
32. Graciela Limón, *Day of the Moon*, 141.
33. Ibid., i.
34. Ibid., 9–10.
35. Bonfil Batalla, *México profundo*, xvi.
36. Ibid., 18.

37. Limón, *Day of the Moon,* 149.
38. De Valdés, *Shattered Mirror,* 193.
39. Limón, *Day of the Moon,* 142.
40. Ibid., 145.
41. Ibid., 146.
42. Ibid.
43. Limón, *Day of the Moon,* 141.
44. Garro's solution to the "painful heritage of mestizaje" is for Mexicans to accept their dual heritage. Cuban novelist Severo Sarduy recalls an episode when Elena Garro, then married to Octavio Paz, challenges Paz to accept his own dual heritage:

    Paz was working on the theory that the theme of incest, one of the ground themes in Mexican literature, was inherited from the Indians. He had been talking about this for several hours when at last Garro stopped him. "Instead of all this theory," she said, "why don't you try it out for once? I'll call your sister, and we'll all three head for the bedroom." With a hurt look on his face, Paz got up and left. "Now he'll never know if it's in his blood, will he?" said Elena. Quoted in Manguel, Other Fires, 159.

    Denial of a complicated history does not offer any favorable solutions.
45. Miller and González, "Elena Garro," 210.
46. Duncan, "La culpa es de los Tlaxcaltecas," 108.
47. Garro, "La culpa es de los Tlaxcaltecas," 133. ". . . con ojos interrogantes a la cocinera . . . confiada, se sentó junto a la estufa y miró su cocina como si no la hubiera visto nunca."
48. Duncan, "La culpa es de los Tlaxcaltecas," 113.
49. Gutiérrez, *Voces femeninas de Hispanoamérica,* 132. He represents "un hombre sin memoria, con un cuerpo deshabilitado. Es un hombre nuevo, o sea no evolucionado y al no tener memoria tampoco tiene recuerdo, o sea historia."
50. Garro, "La culpa es de los Tlaxcaltecas," 143. "Mamá, Laura le pidió al doctor la Historia. . . . de Bernal Díaz del Castillo. Dice que eso es lo único que le interesa." English translation in text is by Manguel, *Other Fires,* 174.
51. Garro, "La culpa es de los Tlaxcaltecas," 133.
52. Ibid., 146.
53. Lefebvre, *Production of Space.*
54. Douglas, *Active Voice,* 86.
55. Marin, *Food for Thought,* 121.
56. Batstone, "The Raw and The Cooked." 51.
57. Nicholson, "Food and Power."
58. Piercy, "What's That Smell in the Kitchen?," 1036.
59. Castellanos, "Lección de cocina."

60. This quote comes from Castellanos's poem, "Meditación en el umbral," in *Meditación en el umbral,* 316.
61. De Valdés, *Shattered Mirror,* 13.
62. Castellanos, "Lección de cocina," 7. "Mi lugar está aquí. Desde el principio de los tiempos ha estado aquí. En el proverbio alemán la mujer es sinónimo de Küche, Kinder, Kirche." English translation in the text is from *Another Way to Be,* Allgood, 104.
63. Castellanos, "Lección de cocina," 7. "... en aulas, en calles, en oficinas, en cafés; desperdiciada en destrezas que ahora he de olvidar para adquirir otras." English translation in text is from *Another Way to Be,* Allgood, 104.
64. Castellanos, "Lección de cocina," 14. "¿Pero quién soy yo? Tu esposa, claro. Y ese título básta para distinguirme de los recuerdos del pasado, de los proyectos para el porvenir." English translation in text is from *Another Way to Be,* Allgood, 107.
65. Castellanos, "Lección de cocina," 9. "Abro el compartimento del refrigerador que anuncia 'carnes' y extraigo un paquete irreconocible bajo su capa de hielo. La disuelvo en agua caliente y se me revela el título sin el cual no lo habría identificado jamás." English translation in text is from *Another Way to Be,* Allgood, 105.
66. Castellanos, "Lección de cocina," 105.
67. Quoted in Cynthia Duncan, "La culpa es de los Tlaxcaltecas," 105.
68. Castellanos, "Lección de cocina," 20. "Recapitulemos. Aparece, primero el trozo de carne con un color, una forma, un tamaño. Luego cambia y se pone más bonita y se siente una muy contenta. Luego vuelve a cambiar y ya no está tan bonita. Y sigue cambiando y cambiando y cambiando y lo que uno no atina es cuándo pararle el alto. Porque si yo dejo este trozo de carne indefinidamente expuesto al fuego, se consume hasta que no queden ni rastros de él. Y el trozo de carne que daba la impresión de ser algo tan sólido, tan real, ya no existe." English translation in text is from *Another Way to Be,* Allgood, 110–11.
69. Castellanos, "Lección de cocina," 21. "La carne no ha dejado de existir. Ha sufrido una serie de metamorfosis. Y el hecho de que deje de ser perceptible para los sentidos no significa que se haya concluido el ciclo sino que ha dado el salto cualitativo. Continuará operando en otros niveles. En el de mi conciencia, en el de mi memoria, en el de mi voluntad, modificándome, determinándome, estableciendo la dirección de mi futuro." English translation in text is from *Another Way to Be,* Allgood, 111.
70. Soja, *Thirdspace,* 81.
71. Classen, *Aroma,* 3.
72. Brinson Curiel, "Recipe: Chorizo con Huevo Made in the Microwave."
73. Rebolledo, *Women Singing in the Snow,* 137.

74. Brinson Curiel, "Recipe: Chorizo con Huevo Made in the Microwave," 273–75.

75. Ibid., 273.

76. Ibid., 274.

77. Rebolledo, *Women Singing in the Snow*, 137.

78. Brinson Curiel, "Recipe: Chorizo con Huevo Made in the Microwave," 274.

79. Ibid., 273.

80. Belasco and Scranton, *Food Nations*, 2 and 16.

81. Molina, *El amor que me juraste*, 76. "Me senté en un rincón, bajo un ventilador, y pedí una Corona helada. El olor de la comida que preparaban me recordó la cocina de mi madre, donde yo era felíz. Allí, mi familia se reunía la mayor parte del tiempo."

82. Ibid. "No era sólo la diferencia de olores y sabores lo que hacía la cocina de mi casa distinta: era ella, mi madre, la pasión con la que cocinaba para nosotros, porque no cumplía con un acto obligatorio ni monótono sino que realizaba una ceremonia de la que se sentía orgullosa, la que no le pesaba. Cocinar, tejer y tenerle miedo a mi papá fue lo único que supo hacer con naturalidad."

83. Ibid., 155.

    —*No todas las mujeres tienen la suerte de vivir lo que tú.*

    —*¿Le llamas suerte?*

    —*De versa.*

    —*¿De sufrir así?*

    —*Vendrá otro Eduardo, ya te dije . . .*

    —*¡Dios me guarde!*

    —*Acéptate.*

84. Ibid., 76. "a ella le debo el [gusto] de la cocina . . . Para mí es divertido escoger los ingredientes de los platillos, combinarlos, jugar en ese laboratorio donde uno inventa fórmulas, experimenta, ensaya, tantea."

85. Pacheco, *Sopita de fideo*, 115. "Josefina va triste. El tintineo del portaviandas vacío la sofoca. Mientras se decide a subir las escaleras para abordar el Metro de regreso, piensa en Lety [su hermana menor], en sus hermanos esperando la hora de comer, en la madre que tuvo que alejarlos para que no devoraran la ración de su padre. Temerosa de saber que un castigo severo la aguarda, lo que más le duele es pensar en que hoy no comerá su padre."

86. Escamill, "Pan Birote," 19.

87. Ibid., 22.

88. Ibid.

89. Ibid., 23.

90. Ibid., 22.

91. De Valdés, *Shattered Mirror*, 110–11.

92. Silva, "Sin ti no soy nada / Without You I Am Nothing," 359.
93. Rebolledo, *Women Singing in the Snow,* 142.
94. Evelina Fernandez, "How Else Am I Supposed to Know I'm Still Alive," 160.
95. Ibid., 162.
96. Ibid., 163.
97. Ibid., 164.
98. Ibid., 162.
99. Ibid., 165.
100. Ibid., 167.
101. Ibid., 164.
102. Ibid., 160.
103. Gaspar de Alba, "Making Tortillas," 355–56.
104. Pilcher, *¡Que vivan los tamales!,* 58.
105. Ibid.
106. Sensual sí. Sexual no. Porque depende de como tú lo pienses. Sexual dicen porque cuando uno está moliendo en el metate, mueves toda la colera.
107. Pero depende de como lo tomes. Porque si tú lo tomas como una cosa que vas a hacer pues está bien [es sólo un trabajo]. Pero si tú lo tomas como agarrar la mano del metate y estar moviendo.
108. Y estar moviendo el chilique y bailando, allí es otra cosa. Depende de como lo tomen, de como lo piensen. Depende de la mentalidad de la persona.
109. Vigil-Piñón, "Kitchen Talk," 163.

Conclusion

1. Latina Feminist Group, *Telling To Live,* 2.
2. Quoted in Padilla, "Recovering Mexican-American Autobiography," 168–69.
3. Latina Feminist Group, *Telling To Live,* 13.
4. Ibid.
5. Laslett, "Personal Narratives as Sociology," 392 b.
6. Considerando de la pobreza aquélla de donde vengo, de la ignorancia, yo siento que he llegado muy lejos, quizás no tan lejos como yo quisiera, pero si he llegado lejos.
7. De Valdés, *Shattered Mirror,* 114–15.
8. Montoya, "Máscaras, Trenzas y Greñas," 205.
9. *Licha: Estabamos muy niñas cuando nos conocimos las dos [la Flaca y yo]. Y luego fuimos creciendo en tiempo, no en estatura. [risas de todas] En tiempo, eh. . . . Ahora, debo decirte que yo tuve una mamá [que gracias a ella], que por lo menos yo en mi persona [así*

lo veo], no pasamos hambres en la infancia. Estuvimos privados de muchas cosas pero no [con] hambre. Porque mi mamá era muy luchona para hacernos de comer. A mi me tocó [ver] que había gente más adinerada, que mi mamá les ofrecía un taco a los niños [de esa familias] y se iban los niños con el taco. Y llegaban [con] mi mamá a ofrecerle: "hay Marianita yo le doy de mi comida, deme usted de la suya." Unos simples tacos, de esos que ahora llaman flautas, de requesón. Pero era [mi mamá] de las personas que una salsa hacía le quedaba sabrosisisísima. ¿Qué le ponía? Yo creo todo el amor del mundo pa' llenar tanta raza. Porque si éramos muchisisísimos. Mira, éramos ocho, yo soy la mayor de ocho. Pero mi mamá crió dos chamacas hijas de una hermana de ella. Entonces, mi mamá las crió. Obviamente, ya éramos diez. Más ellos los dos. Éramos doce.

Lupita: *Más la visita que llegaba.*

Licha: *Siempre hubo gente en la casa. Pero mi mamá tenía toda la fé de que cuando tú compartías los alimentos que Dios te daba con alguien, nunca te iba a faltar. Siempre ibas a tener con que no fueras miserable.*

Meredith: *Que compartir de una manera hace que tengas más. El dar hace que tengas para segir dando.*

Licha: *Ajá. Ella decía que mientras que a ella no le faltara una mazorca en la casa, nunca iba a faltar para compartir lo que Dios arrimaba a su mesa. Nuestra mesa, ahora he visto una madera toda carcomida que en aquella época a mi se me hacia fea, pero que ahora es carisisisísima.*

Meredith: *Ahora es el* fashion. *El* country look.

Licha: *Sí. Entonces, no teníamos sillas; usabamos unas bancas. Todo rústico que en aquella época, y no apreciabamos las cosas, ¿verdad? Pero que ahora yo ya las quisiera esas tablas. De veras, eh. Aquellos manteles, que te digo, ¡una cosa tan hermosa! Pero fíjate que mi mamá no fue a la escuela. Nació y murió analfabeta. Pero nunca dejó que algien se arrimara a la mesa encuerado a comer. Desnudo del dorso, ¿verdad? Siempre por los menos [con camisetas]. Decía que [la comida] eran los sagrados alimentos. Decía, "¿Qué es lo que le pides a Dios en el Padre Nuestro?" Dices, "Que nos des hoy nuestro pan de cada día." Y ella decía que tenemos que asercanos a la mesa con respeto. Entonces, la comida, nosotros gracias a Dios, hambres no pasamos porque mi mamá era muy luchona para hacernos de comer.*

Meredith: *Y, ¿qué tipo de cosas hacía de comer?*

Licha: *Bueno, en aquella época, almorzabamos quelites—*

Meredith: *¿Qué son quelites?*

Licha: *Unas yerbitas que se daban en el campo, que ahora, ya como dijó mi mamá, "Todo se acabo por el cemento." [También] ya empezaron a poner tantisísimo insecticida para otras cosas y todo eso acabó un poco con la vegetación de Apatzingán.*

Aurora: *Ella, [la mamá de Licha], era una señora, como dice Licha, no estudiada pero inteligente. Muy inteligente.*

Licha: *[En forma de broma] Un desperdicio, un desperdicio de cerebro, como dice mi'jo. Ja, Ja, Ja. Decía ella, mi mamá, que ella no conoció una escuela hasta que ya fue mamá mia. Ni sabía lo que era una escuela. Pero como quiera era de mente bien ágil. Pero fíjate que el no trabajar [en casa] es un decir. Porque, que bruta. ¡Cómo trabajaba! Mira mi mamá en aquella época, que lavadora ni que ojo de acha. Nada de lavadora. ¿Planchar? No teníamos electicidad. Teníamos que planchar con unas planchas que se ponen al comal. Teníamos que agararlas con un trapo. ¡Y era planchar! Porque se almidonada y había que hacer el almidón. Teníamos que acarrear el agua. ¡Tenía mi mamá un jardín! Y había que acarrear el agua para regar. Acarreabamos el agua para regar la calle. Pero mira, no nada más nosotras. La vecina de en ferente lavaba su mitad de calle. Se veía aquella calle que pensabas que había llovído porque estaba toda mojada. Y nadie se iba a quedar atrás.*

Nunca te puedes imaginar, viviendo por allá, que la vida te da tantos cambios. En aquella época, pece a que vivíamos pobres, no pensabamos así como ahora que se trauman de cualquier cosa. Nosotros no teníamos esa mentalidad. Nosotros lo que queríamos era hacer pronto el quehacer para salirnos a andar haciendo travesuras. Yo nunca me he sentido afectada emocionalmente. Yo en lo personal, yo tuve una infancia bonita. Yo no me pudeo quejar. Yo no tengo amarguras de mi infancia, así como otras personas le echan la culpa a los padres de que, "yo sufrí por esto o por otro." Nó, porque mi mamá hizo lo que humanamente pudo por nosotros. Si lo hizo o no lo hizo bien, era lo que podía hacer. Okay, mi mamá pensaba que nomás con darnos de tragar y enseñarnos a hacer quehacer, eso era suficiente. Y así lo aceptamos. No hizo más porque no pudo más. Pero es muy duro criar tanta familia en un medio en que no había los avances que tenemos hoy día. Entre lo que ibas creciendo en tiempo, no en estatura, mi mamá nos iba diciendo a cada quien lo que teníamos que hacer.

Meredith: *¿Tu mamá te enseñó a cocinar?*

Licha: *Sí. Primero ayudándole. Después a mí se me dió por salirme de la casa. Me fuí a México. Siempre aprendes. Algunas cosas las aprendes de la gente adulta que te rodea. Dicen que nosotros los* *padres les enseñamos a los hijos. Yo más bien creo que nosotros, los papás, aprendemos de los hijos. Casi, casi te puedo asegurar que nosotros, como padres, aprendemos más con los hijos, que los hijos con nosotros.*

••••••••••••••••

Licha: *Yo aquí [en Nuevo Laredo] llegué a cumplir los veinte y un año. Tengo cincuenta y tres. Que te está diciendo, que tengo más de la mitad de mi vida aquí. Obviamente me siento de acá, ¿verdad?*

Lupita: *Al principio, ¿te acuerdas que no encontramos trabajo aquí, mi'ja?*

Licha: *Nó, porque nos pedían "pickinglis" [speak English], y nosotros no sabíamos.*

Lupita: *Y que fueramos de la, ¿cómo era? S.O.—*

Licha: *S.M.O.P. O sea, del sindicato.*

Lupita: *Teníamos que pertenecer al sindicato para poder conseguir trabajo.*

Meredith: *Y, ¿eso era aquí en Nuevo Laredo o en Laredo?*

Lupita: *Aquí, aquí [en Nuevo Laredo].*

Licha: *Ya ahorita ya no priva eso. Ya ahorita Nuevo Laredo—mira, es que antes sólo la capital era México, lo demás era rancho.* Okay.

Meredith: *No, y especialmente el norte de México, todo el norte de México siempre se ha sentido muy aislado, muy alejado del centro.*

Licha: *Sí, como dijó Porfirio Díaz: "Pobre México, tan lejos de Dios y tan cerca de Estados Unidos." Entonces a nosotros [aquí en Nuevo Laredo] hasta la fecha, todavía anda el presidente de aquí peleando las participaciones de los puentes porque dejan tantisísimo dinero. Y este dinero que dejan los puentes se van a hacer beneficios a otras partes de la república.*

Meredith: *A las bolsas de los políticos.*

Licha: *Sí. Y nosotros ni para barrer las calles le dejan al pobre presidente, ¿verdad? Y entonces te digo, ya ahora no somos un rancho. Y digo somos porque yo tengo tantos años de vivir aquí y aquí formé mi familia que yo realmente yá me siento de aquí porque ya tengo muchos años, ¿verdad?*

••••••••••••••••

Licha: *Mi'ja, hacer enchiladas es un cuete, eh, porque te tienes que esmerar muchisísimo pa' que te queden verdaderamente bien. A mi me ha tocado ir con mucha gente que dice, "hay, las enchiladas." Y yo digo, las enchiladas muy famosas que yo conozco son las de Apatzingán. Y son bien diferentes a las otras enchiladas que he comido en todas partes. . . . Una tía de Fausto vendía cena allí en Apatzingán. Y iba Teresa, la hermana de Fausto a ayudarle, y yo allí vi como hacían las enchiladas. Pero es muy, muy diferente. Porque* *lleva hasta rábanos. Se hierve un tomate en consomé de pollo. Y se licúa, sin picante, sin cebolla, sin ajo. Sin nada. Y previamente ya desfemastes, eso es a tu gusto ya sea con limón o con vinagre, una cebolla desde temprano. Desde temprano para que se le quite lo picoso, lo que no te guste de la cebolla. Y le pones sal de ajo y tantito orégano a la cebolla. Y lo tapas. Lo estas volteando para que fermente todo, o se desfeme todo. Como quieras aplicar la palabra. Y este, luego tantito de ese vinagre con el orégano y ya con el sabor de las cebollas, lo puedes poner a este tomate hervido. Previamente ya herviste tantita zanahoria. Yo prefiero hervirla que freírla.*

Meredith: *Para que no lleve tanta grasa.*

Licha: *Hey. Hervir la zanahoria y picadito [se] lo pones a ese tomate con unos rabanitos. Ahora ya el chile. Tienes que dorar el chile en tantito aceite. Y acitronas también tantito el ajo y tantito el tomate. Y lo licúas todo junto y ya lo guisas. Lo tienes que hervir ya que lo colaste todo. Lo hierves, de tal manera que ya después que metes las tortillas allí al chile rojo y luego las metes al aceite. Que quede muy especito para que la tortilla no quede muy descoloridotota como la primera que me quedó a mi. Y ya envuelves la tortilla y le pones cebolla, que ya desfemaste previamente y queso.*

Itzel: *Y adentro, ¿no le pones nada?*

Licha: *Sí, cebolla y queso.*

Bibliography

Abarca, Meredith E. "Authentic or Not, It's Original." *Food and Foodways: A Routledge Journal* 12, no. 1 (January–March, 2004): 1–25.

———. "Los chilaquiles de mi 'amá: The Language of Everyday Cooking." In *Pilaf, Pozole, and Pad Thai: American Women and Ethnic Food,* edited by Sherrie A. Inness, 119–44. Amherst: University of Massachusetts Press, 2001.

Aboites, Jaime A. *Breve historia de un invento olvidado: Las máquinas tortilleras en México.* Mexico City: Universidad Autónoma Metropolitana, 1989.

Abrahams, Roger D. "Ordinary and Extraordinary Experiences." In *The Anthropology of Experience,* edited by Victor Turner and Edward Bruner. Urbana: University of Illinois Press, 1986.

Abu-Lughod, Lila. *Writing Women's Worlds.* Berkeley: University of California Press, 1993.

Agrest, Diana. *Architecture from Without: Theoretical Framing for a Critical Practice.* Cambridge, Mass.: MIT Press, 1991.

Agrest, Diana, Patricia Conway, and Leslie Kanes Weisman, eds. *The Sex of Architecture.* New York: Harry N. Abrams, 1996.

Ahrentzen, Sherry. "The Space between the Studs: Feminism and Architecture." *Signs: Journal of Women in Culture and Society* 29, no. 1 (Autumn, 2003): 179–206.

Ainley, Rosa, ed. *New Frontiers of Space, Bodies and Gender.* New York: Routledge, 1998.

Alarcón, Norma. "Anzaldúa's *Frontera:* Inscribing Gynetics." In *Decolonial Voices: Chicana and Chicano Cultural Studies in the Twenty-first Century,* edited by J. Arturo Aldama and Naomi H. Quiñonez, 113–26. Bloomington: Indiana University Press, 2002.

———. "The Theoretical Subject(s) of *This Bridge Called My Back* and Anglo-American Feminism." In *Making Face, Making Soul: Haciendo caras,* edited by Gloria Anzaldúa, 356–69. San Francisco: Aunt Lute Foundation Book, 1990.

———. "Traddutora, Traditora: A Paradigmatic Figure of Chicana Feminism." In *Scattered Hegemonies: Postmodernity and Transnational Feminist Practices,* edited by Inderpal Grewal and Caren Kaplan. Minneapolis: University of Minnesota Press, 1994.

Alcoff, Linda Marin. "Feminist Theory and Social Science: New Knowledge, New Epistemologies." In *BodySpace: Destabilizing Geographies of Gender and Sexuality,* edited by Nancy Duncan. New York: Routledge, 1996.

Aldama, Arturo J., and Naomi H. Quiñonez, eds. *Decolonial Voices: Chicana and Chicano Cultural Studies in the 21st Century.* Bloomington: Indiana University Press, 2002.

Allende, Isabel. *Afrodita: Cuentos, resetas y otros afrodisíacos.* New York: HarperLibros, 1997.

Allgood, Myralyne F. *Another Way to Be: Selected Works of Rosario Castellanos.* Athens: University of Georgia Press, 1990.

André, María Claudia, ed. "Culinary Fictions." In *Chicanas and Latin American Women Writers Exploring the Realm of the Kitchen as a Self-Empowerment Site.* Lewiston, N.Y.: Edwin Mellen Press, 2001.

Anzaldúa, Gloría. *Borderlands/La Frontera: The New Mestiza.* San Francisco: Spinsters/Aunt Lute, 1987.

Appadurai, Arjun. "How to Make a National Cuisine: Cookbooks in Contemporary India." *Comparative Studies in Society and History* 30, no. 1 (January, 1988): 3–24.

Ardener, Shirley, ed. *Women and Space: Ground Rules and Social Maps.* New York: Berg, 1997.

Arreola, Daniel D. *Tejano South Texas: A Mexican Cultural Province.* Austin: University of Texas Press, 2002.

Arrom, Silvia Marina. *The Women of Mexico City, 1790–1857.* Stanford, Calif.: Stanford University Press, 1985.

Avakian, Arlene Voski, ed. *Through the Kitchen Window: Women Explore the Intimate Meaning of Food and Cooking.* Boston: Beacon Press, 1997.

Bartra, Eli. *En busca de las diablas: Sobre arte popular y genero.* Mexico City: Tava Editorial, 1994.

Batstone, Kathleen. "The Raw and The Cooked: Cooking and the Transgression of Boundaries in *Like Water for Chocolate.*" In *Chicanas and Latin American Women Writers Exploring the Realm of the Kitchen as a Self-Empowerment Site,* edited by María Claudia André, 47–73. Lewiston, N.Y.: Edwin Mellen Press, 2001.

Bauer, Arnold J. "Millers and Grinders: Technology and Household Economy in Meso-America." *Agricultural History* 64, no. 1 (Winter, 1900): 1–17.

Bausinger, Hermann. *Folk Culture in a World of Technology,* translated by Elke Dettmer. Bloomington: Indiana University Press, 1990.

Becker, Howard S. *Art Worlds.* Berkeley: University of California Press, 1982.

Becker, Marion Rombauer, Irma S. Rombauer, and Ethan Becker. *The Joy of Cooking.* New York: Bobbs, 1963.

Behar, Ruth. "Sexual Witchcraft, Colonialism, and Women's Powers: Views from the Mexican Inquisition." In *Sexuality and Marriage in Colonial Latin America,* edited by Asunción Lavrín. Lincoln: University of Nebraska Press, 1980.

————. *Translated Woman: Crossing the Border with Esperanza's Story.* Boston: Beacon Press, 1993.

Behar, Ruth, and Deborah A. Gordon, eds. *Women Writing Culture.* Berkeley: University of California Press, 1995.

Belasco, Warren, and Philip Scranton, eds. *Food Nations: Selling Taste in Consumer Societies.* New York: Routledge, 2002.

Bell, David, and Gill Valentine, eds. *Consuming Geographies: We Are Where We Eat.* New York: Routledge, 1997.

Bentley, Amy. "From Culinary Other to Mainstream American: Meaning and Uses of Southwestern Cuisine." *Southern Folklore* 55, no. 3 (1998): 238–52.

Benjamin, Walter. "The Storyteller." In *Illuminations.* New York: Schocken Books, 1985.

Benzel, Kathryn N., and Lauren Pringle De La Vars, eds. *Images of the Self as Female: The Achievement of Women Artists in Re-Envisioning Feminine Identity.* Lewiston, N.Y.: Edwin Mellen Press, 1992.

Biasin, Gian-Paolo. *The Flavors of Modernity: Food and the Novel.* Princeton, N.J.: Princeton University Press, 1993.

Bloom, Harold. *The Western Canon: The Books and School of the Ages.* New York: Harcourt Brace, 1994.

Blunt, Alison, and Gillian Rose, eds. *Writing Women and Space.* New York: Guilford Press, 1994.

Bober, Phyllis Pray. *Art, Culture, and Cuisine: Ancient and Medieval Gastronomy.* Chicago: University of Chicago Press, 1999.

Bonfil Batalla, Guillermo. *México profundo: Reclaiming a Civilization,* translated by Philip A. Dennis. Austin: University of Texas Press, 1996.

Bordo, Susan. *Unbearable Weight: Feminism, Western Culture, and the Body,* 10th anniversary edition. Berkeley: University of California Press, 2003.

Bourdieu, Pierre. *Distinction: A Social Critique of the Judgement of Taste.* Cambridge Mass.: Harvard University Press, 1984.

Bourke, John G. "The Folk-Foods of the Rio Grande Valley and of Northern Mexico." *Journal of American Folk-Lore* (1895): 41–71.

Boydston, Jeanne. *Home and Work: Housework, Wages, and the Ideology of Labor in the Early Republic.* New York: Oxford University Press, 1990.

Boydston, Jeanne, Mary Kelly, and Anne Margolis. *Limits of Sisterhood.* Chapel Hill: University of North Carolina Press, 1988.

Braudel, Fernand. *The Structures of Everyday Life: The Limits of the Possible.* Vol. 1 of *Civilization and Capitalism, 15th–18th Century,* translated by Siân Reynolds. New York: Harper and Row, 1979.

Brenner, Leslie. *American Appetite: The Coming of Age of a Cuisine.* New York: Avon Books, 1999.

Brillat-Savarin, Jean Anthelme. *The Physiology of Taste, or Meditations on Transcendental Gastronomy.* New York: Dover, 1960.

Brinson Curiel, Bárbara. "Recipe: Chorizo con Huevo Made in the Microwave." In *Speak to Me from Dreams.* Berkeley: Third Woman Press, 1989.

———. "Recipe: Chorizo con Huevo Made in the Microwave." In *Literatura chicana, 1965–1995,* edited by Manuel de Jesús Hernández-Gutiérrez and David William Foster, 273–75. New York: Garland, 1997.

Broude, Norma, and Mary D. Garrard, eds. *The Power of Feminist Art: The American Movement of the 1970s.* New York: Harry N. Abrams, 1996.

Brito, Aristeo. *El diablo en Texas/The Devil in Texas.* Tempe, Ariz.: Bilingual Press/Editorial Bilingüe, 1990.

Brown, Gillian. *Domestic Individualism: Imagining Self in Nineteenth-Century America.* Berkeley: University of California Press, 1990.

Brown, Linda Keller, and Kay Mussell, eds. *Ethnic and Regional Foodways in the United States: The Performance of Group Identity.* Knoxville: University of Tennessee Press, 1984.

Brown, de la Peña M. H. "Una Tamalada: The Special Event." *Western Folklore* 40 (1981): 64–71.

Bueno, Carmen. *Preparación y venta de comida fuera del hogar: Un estudio cualitativo de la ciudad de México.* Mexico City: El Colegio de México/Centro de Estudios Sociológicos, 1988.

Bulnes, Francisco. *El provenir de las naciones Hispano-Americanas ante las conquistas recientes de Europa y los Estados Unidos.* Mexico City: Imprenta de Mariano Nava, 1899.

Burciaga, José Antonio. "I Remember Masa." In *Weedee Peepo: A Collection of Essays,* 96–101. Edinburg, Tex.: Pan American University Press, 1988.

Bynum, Caroline Walker. *Holy Feast and Holy Fast: The Religious Significance of Food to Medieval Women.* Berkeley: University of California Press, 1987.

Cabeza de Baca, Fabiola. *The Good Life: New Mexico Traditions and Food.* Santa Fe: Museum of New Mexico Press, 1982.

———. *Historic Cookery.* Las Vegas, N.M.: La Galería de los Artesanos, 1970. Originally published in 1949.

Calvo, Luz. "Decolonizing Methodologies: Research and Indigenous People by Linda Tuhiwai Smith." *Signs: Journal of Women in Culture and Society* (Autumn, 2003): 255–56.

Calvo Fajardo, Yadira. *A la mujer por la palabra.* Heredia, Costa Rica: Editorial de la Universidad Nacional, 1990.

Camporesi, Piero. *Exotic Brew: The Art of Living in the Age of Enlightenment,* translated by Christopher Woodall. Cambridge, Mass.: Polity Press. 1994.

Cantú, Norma E., and Olga Nájera-Ramírez, eds. *Chicana Traditions: Continuity and Change.* Urbana: University of Illinois Press, 2002.

Carrillo, Ana María. *La cociana del tomate, frijol, y calabaza.* Mexico City: Clío, 1998.

Castellanos, Rosario. "Lección de cocina." In *Álbum de familia.* Mexico City: Joaquín Mortiz, 1971.

———. *Meditación en el umbral: Antología poética,* edited by Julian Palley, prologue by Elena Poniatowska. Mexico City: Fondo de Cultura Económica, 1985.

Castillo, Ana. *Massacre of the Dreamers: Essays on Xicanisma.* Albuquerque: University of New Mexico Press, 1994.

Castillo, Debra. *Talking Back.* Ithaca, N.Y.: Cornell University Press, 1992.

Cervantes, Lorna Dee. "On Love and Hunger." In *From The Cables of Genocide: Poems on Love and Hunger.* Houston, Tex.: Arte Público Press, 1991.

Chabram Dernersesian, Angie. "And, Yes . . . The Earth Did Part: On the Splitting of Chicana/o Subjectivity." In *Building with Our Hands: New Directions in Chicana Studies,* edited by Adela de la Torre and Beatríz M. Pesquera, 34–56. Berkeley: University of California Press, 1993.

Chadwick, Whitney. *Women, Art, and Society.* New York: Thames and Hudson, 1990.

Chávez, Adolfo, and José Antonio Roldán. "Los alimintos de México: La alimentación de los señores y de los plebeyos." *Mexico Desconocido* 17, no. 191 (January, 1993): 60–65.

Cixous, Hélène. "The Laugh of the Medusa." *Signs: Journal of Women in Culture and Society* (Summer 1976): 875–93.

Classen, Constance, David Howes, and Anthony Synnott. *Aroma: The Cultural History of Smell.* New York: Routledge, 1994.

Clifford, James. "On Collecting Art and Culture." In *The Cultural Studies Reader,* edited by Simon During, 49–73. New York: Routledge, 1993.

Clifford, James, and George Marcus, eds. *Writing Culture: The Poetics and Politics of Ethnography.* Berkeley: University of California Press, 1986.

Coates, Jennifer. *Women, Men, and Language: A Sociolinguistic Account of Sex Differences in Language.* New York: Longman, 1986.

Coe, Sophie D. *America's First Cuisine.* Austin: University of Texas Press, 1994.

Coleman, Debra, Elizabeth Danze, and Carol Henderson, eds. *Architecture and Feminism.* New York: Princeton Architectural Press, 1996.

Collings, Glen. "The Americanization of Salsa." *New York Times,* January 9, 1997.

Colwin, Laurie. *Home Cooking: A Writer in the Kitchen.* New York: Alfred A. Knopf, 1988.

———. *More Home Cooking: A Writer Returns to the Kitchen.* New York: HarperPerennial, 1995.

Cook, Sherburne F., and Woodrow Borah. "Indian Food Production and Consumption in Central Mexico before and after the Conquest (1500–1650)." In *Essays in Population History: Mexico and California,* edited by Sherburne F. Cook and Woodrow Borah. Berkeley: University of California Press, 1979.

Cooper, Ann. *"A Woman's Place Is in the Kitchen": The Evolution of Women Chefs.* New York: Van Nostrand Reinhold, 1998.

Córdova, Teresa. "Power and Knowledge: Colonialism in the Academy." In *Living Chicana Theory,* edited by Carla Trujillo, 17–45. Berkeley: Third Woman Press, 1998.

Córdova, Teresa, ed. *Chicana Voices: Intersections of Class, Race, and Gender.* Albuquerque: University of New Mexico Press, 1993.

Cosman, Madeleine Pelner. *Fabulous Feasts: Medieval Cookery and Ceremony.* New York: George Braziller, 1976.

Counihan, Carole M. *The Anthropology of Food and Body.* New York: Routledge, 1999.

———. *Around the Tuscan Table: Food, Family, and Gender in Twentieth-Century Florence.* New York, Routledge, 2004.

———. *Food in the USA: A Reader.* New York: Routledge, 2002.

Counihan, Carole M., and Penny Van Esterik, eds. *Food and Culture, A Reader.* New York: Routledge Press, 1997.

Cowan, Ruth Schwartz. *More Work for Mother: The Ironies of Household Technology from the Open Hearth to the Microwave.* New York: Basic Books, 1983.

Curtin, Deane W. "Food/Body/Person." In *Cooking, Eating, Thinking: Transformative Philosophies of Food,* edited by Deane W. Curtin and Lisa M. Heldke, 3–22. Bloomington: Indiana University Press, 1992.

———. "Recipes for Values." In *Cooking, Eating, Thinking: Transformative Philosophies of Food,* edited by Deane W. Curtin and Lisa M. Heldke, 123–44. Bloomington: Indiana University Press, 1992.

Curtin, Deane W., and Lisa M. Heldke, eds. *Cooking, Eating, Thinking: Transformative Philosophies of Food.* Bloomington: Indiana University Press, 1992.

Dandekar, Hemalata C., ed. *Shelter Women and Development: First and Third World Perspectives.* Ann Arbor, Mich.: George Wahr Publishing Company, 1993.

Davalos, Karen Mary. *Exhibiting Mestizaje: Mexican (American) Museums in the Diaspora.* Albuquerque: University of New Mexico Press, 2001.

de Certeau, Michel. *The Practice of Everyday Life,* translated by Steven Rendall. Berkeley: University of California Press, 1984.

de Certeau, Michel, Luce Giard, and Pierre Mayol. *The Practice of Everyday Life: Volume Two: Living and Cooking,* translated by Timothy J. Tomasik. Minneapolis: University of Minnesota Press, 1998.

de la Cruz, Sor Juana Inés. *The Answer/La Respuesta.* Eds. and trans., Electra Arenal and Amanda Powell. New York: The Feminist Press, 1994.

de San Pelayo, Gerónimo. *Libro de cocina del hermano fray Gerónimo de San Pelayo.* Colección Recetarios Antiguos. México: Consejo nacional para la cultura y las artes, 2000.

de Silva, Cara., ed. *In Memory's Kitchen: A Legacy From the Women of Terezín.* Northvale, N.J.: Jason Aronson, 1996.

de Valdés, María Elena. *The Shattered Mirror: Representations of Women in Mexican Literature.* Austin: University of Texas Press, 1998.

———. "Verbal and Visual Representation of Women: *Como agua para chocolate/Like Water for Chocolate.*" *World Literature Today* (June, 1993): 78–82.

Dewhurst, Kurt, Betty MacDowell, and Marsha MacDowell, eds. *Artists in Aprons: Folk Art by American Women.* New York: E. P. Dowell, 1979.

Dinesen, Isak. "Babette's Feast." In *Babette's Feast and Other Anecdotes of Destiny.* New York: Vintage Books, 1988.

Domingo, Xavier. *De la olla al mole.* Madrid: Ediciones Cultura Hispánica, 1984.

Domosh, Mona, and Joni Seager, eds. *Putting Women in Place: Feminist Geographers Make Sense of the World.* New York: Guilford Press, 2001.

Douglas, Mary. *Active Voice.* Boston: Routledge and Kegan Paul, 1982.

———. "Deciphering a Meal." In *Implicit Meanings: Essays in Anthropology,* 249–75. London: Routledge and Kegan Paul, 1979.

———. *Food in Social Order.* New York: Russell Sage Foundation, 1984.

Duncan, Cynthia. "La culpa es de los Tlaxcaltecas: A Reevaluation of Mexico's Past through Myth." *Critica Hispanica* 7, no. 2 (1985): 105–20.

Duncan, Nancy. "Introduction (Re)placing." In *BodySpace: Destabilizing Geographies of Gender and Sexuality,* edited by Nancy Duncan. New York: Routledge, 1996.

Ehrlich, Elizabeth. *Miriam's Kitchen: A Memoir.* New York: Penguin Books, 1997.

El cocinero mexicano, vol. 1. Mexico 1831. Colección Recetarios Antiguos. Mexico City: Consejo nacional para la cultura y las artes, 2000.

El maíz, fundamento de la cultura popular mexicana. Mexico City: Museo Nacional de Culturas Populares, 1982.

Engels, Friedrich. *The Origin of the Family, Private Property, and the State.* New York: International Publishers, 1942.

Epstein, Barbara Leslie. *The Politics of Domesticity: Women, Evangelism, and Temperance in Nineteenth-Century America.* Middletown, Conn.: Wesleyan University Press, 1981.

Escamill, Edna. "The Pan Birote." In *Pieces of the Heart: New Chicano Fiction,* edited by Gary Soto, 18–23. San Francisco: Chronicle Books, 1993.

Esquivel, Laura. *Como agua para chocolate.* New York: Doubleday, 1993.

Farb, Peter, and George Armelagos. *Consuming Passions: The Anthropology of Eating.* Boston: Houghton Mifflin, 1982.

Fausch, Deborah. "The Knowledge of the Body and the Presence of History—Toward a Feminist Architecture." In *Architecture and Feminism,* edited by Debra Coleman, Elizabeth Danze, and Carol Henderson, 38–59. New York: Princeton Architectural Press, 1996.

Fernandez, Evelina. *How Else Am I Supposed to Know I'm Still Alive.* In *Contemporary Plays by Women of Color,* edited by Kathy A. Perkins and Roberta Uno, 158–67. New York: Routledge, 1996.

Fernandez, Ramona. *Imagining Literacy: Rhizomes of Knowledge in American Culture and Literature.* Austin: University of Texas Press, 2001.

Ferré, Rosario. "La cocina de la escritura," In *La sartén por el mango,* edited by Patricia González and Eliana Ortega, 137–54. Rio Piedras, Puerto Rico: Ediciones de Huracán, 1984.

Fisher, M. F. K. *The Gastronomical Me.* New York: North Point Press, 1997.

Fischer-West, Lucy. *Child of Many Rivers: Journeys to and from the Rio Grande.* Lubbock: Texas Tech University Press, 2005.

Flores y Escalante, Jesús. *Brevísima historia de la cocina mexicana.* Mexico City: Asociación Mexicana de Estudios Fonográficos, 1994.

Flusty, Steven. *De-Coca-Colonization: Making the Globe From the Inside Out.* New York: Routledge, 2004.

Fontento, Karen. "Consuming Culture: The Role of Food in Creating and Maintaining Cultural Identity." Conference paper. Fourth Annual Congress of the Americas. Puebla, Mexico. October, 1999.

Fussell, Betty. *My Kitchen Wars.* New York: North Point Press, 1999.

———. *The Story of Corn.* New York: North Point Press, 1992.

Gabaccia, Donna R. *We Are What We Eat: Ethnic Food and the Making of Americans.* Cambridge, Mass.: Harvard University Press, 1998.

Galindo, Letticia D. "Caló and Taboo Language Use among Chicanas." In *Speaking Chicana: Voice, Power, and Identity,* edited by Letticia D. Galindo and María Dolores Gonzales. Tucson: University of Arizona Press 1999.

García, Alma M. *Narrative of Mexican American Women: Emergent Identities of the Second Generation.* New York: Altamira Press, 2004.

Garrido Aranda, Antonio, ed. *Comer cultura: Estudios de cultura alimentaria.* Córdoba, Spain: Universidad de Córdoba, 2001.

Garro, Elena. "La culpa es de los Tlaxcaltecas." In *Voces femeninas de Hispanoamérica,* edited by Gloria Bautista Gutiérrez, 133–46. Pittsburgh: University of Pittsburgh Press, 1996.

Gaspar de Alba, Alicia. *Chicano Art: Cultural Politics and the CARA Exhibition.* Austin: University of Texas Press, 1998.

———. "Making Tortillas." In *Infinite Divisions: An Anthology of Chicana Literature,* edited by Tey Diana Rebolledo and Eliana Rivero, 355–56. Tucson: University of Arizona Press, 1993.

———. "The Philosophy of Frijoles." *Hanging Loose* 57, no. 2 (1990).

———, ed. *Velvet Barrios: Popular Culture and Chicana/o Sexualities.* New York: Palgrave Macmillan, 2003.

Geertz, Clifford. *Local Knowledge.* New York: Basic Books, 1983.

Goldman, Anne. "'I Yam What I Yam': Cooking, Culture, and Colonialism." In *De/Colonizing the Subject: The Politics of Gender in Women's Autobiography,* edited by Sidonie Smith and Julia Watson, 169–95. Minneapolis: University of Minnesota Press, 1992.

———. *Take My Word: Autobiographical Innovations of Ethnic American Women.* Berkeley: University of California Press, 1996.

Gonzales, María Dolores. "Crossing Social and Cultural Borders: The Road to Language Hybridity." In *Speaking Chicana: Voice, Power, and Identity,* edited by D. Letticia Galindo and María Dolores Gonzales. Tucson: University of Arizona Press, 1999.

Goody, Jack. *Cooking, Cuisine, and Class: A Study in Comparative Sociology.* Cambridge: Cambridge University Press, 1982.

Granta: Food the Vital Stuff, edited by Ian Jack. Number 52, Winter, 1995.

Grosz, Elizabeth. "Contemporary Theories of Power and Subjectivity." In *Contemporary Feminist Theories,* edited by Stevi Jackson and Jackie Jones. Edinburgh: Edinburgh University Press, 1998.

———. *Space, Time, and Perversion.* New York: Routledge, 1995.

Guerrero Guerrero, Raúl. *Toneucáyotl: El pan nuestro de cada día.* Mexico City: Instituto Nacional de Antropología e Historia, 1987.

Gullestad, Marianne. *Everyday Life Philosophers.* Oslo and Boston: Scandinavia University Press, 1996.

Gutiérrez, Gloria Bautista. *Voces femeninas de Hispanoamérica.* Pittsburgh: University of Pittsburgh Press, 1996.

Hall, Stuart. "Notes on Deconstructing the Popular." In *People's History
and Socialist Theory,* edited by Raphael Samuel. London: Routledge
and Kegan Paul, 1981.

Hall, Stuart, and Paddy Whannel. *The Popular Arts.* New York: Pantheon
Books, 1964.

Hammersley, Martyn. *Reading Ethnographic Research.* New York: Longman, 1998.

Haraway, Dona. "Situated Knowledge: The Science Question in Feminism
and the Privilege of Partial Perspective." *Feminist Studies* 14 (1988):
575–99.

Hardy-Fanta, Carol. *Latina Politics, Latino Politics: Gender, Culture, and
Political Participation in Boston.* Philadelphia: Temple University
Press, 1993.

Harris, Jessica B. *Iron Pots and Wooden Spoons: African's Gifts to New
World Cooking.* New York: Atheneum, 1989.

Harris, Marvin. *Good to Eat: Riddles of Food and Culture.* New York: Simon
and Schuster, 1985.

Hastrup, Kirsten. *A Passage to Anthropology: Between Experience and Theory.* New York: Routledge, 1995.

Hauck-Lawson, Annie. "Hearing the Food Voice: An Epiphany for a Researcher," *Digest: An Interdisciplinary Study of Food and Foodways*
12, nos. 1 and 2 (1992): 6–7.

Hayden, Dolores. *The Power of Place: Urban Landscape as Public History.*
Cambridge, Mass.: MIT Press, 1995.

Heldke, Lisa M. *Exotic Appetites: Ruminations of a Food Adventurer.* New
York: Routledge, 2003.

———. "Food, Politics, Political Food." In *Cooking, Eating, Thinking:
Transformative Philosophies of Food,* edited by Deane W. Curtin
and Lisa M. Heldke, 301–27. Bloomington: Indiana University Press,
1992.

———. "Foodmaking as a Thoughtful Practice." In *Cooking, Eating, Thinking: Transformative Philosophies of Food,* edited by Deane W. Curtin
and Lisa M. Heldke, 203–29. Bloomington: Indiana University Press,
1992.

Hermanuz, Ghislaine. "Housing for a Postmodern World: Reply to Alice F.
Friedman." In *The Sex of Architecture,* edited by Diana Agrest, Patri-
cia Conway, and Leslie Kanes Weisman, 233–40. New York: Harry N.
Abrams, 1996.

Heyd, Thomas. "Rock Art Aesthetics and Culture Appropriation." *Journal
of Aesthetics and Art Criticism* 61, no. 1 (Winter, 2003): 37–46.

Hobsbawm, Eric. "Introduction: Inventing Traditions." In *The Invention of*

Tradition, edited by Eric Hobsbawm and Terence Ranger. Cambridge: Cambridge University Press, 1983.

Hollis, Susan Tower, Linda Pershing, and M. Jane Young, editors. *Feminist Theory and the Study of Folklore.* Urbana: University of Illinois Press, 1993.

Homi, Bhabha. *The Location of Culture.* New York: Routledge, 1994.

———. "The Third Space: Interview with Homi Bhabha." In *Identity: Community, Culture, Difference,* edited by Jonathan Rutherford. London: Lawrence and Wisart, 1990.

hooks, bell. *Art on My Mind: Visual Politics.* New York: The New Press, 1995.

———. *Black Looks: Race and Representation.* Boston: South End Press, 1992.

———. *Feminist Theory from Margin to Center,* 2nd ed. Boston: South End Press, 2000.

———. *Sisters of the Yam: Black Women and Self-Recovery.* Boston: South Press, 1993.

———. *Talking Back: Thinking Feminist, Thinking Black.* Boston: South Press, 1989.

———. *Yearning: Race, Gender, and Cultural Politics.* Boston: South End Press, 1990.

Hough, Sheridan. "Phenomenology, Pomo Baskets, and the Work of Mabel McKay." *Hypatia: A Journal of Feminist Philosophy* 18, no. 2 (Spring, 2003): 103–13.

Howes, David. *Variety of Sensory Experience.* Toronto: University of Toronto Press, 1991.

Hurtado, Aída. "Relating to Privilege: Seduction and Rejection in the Subordination of White Women and Women of Color." In *Theorizing Feminism: Parallel Trends in the Humanities and Social Sciences,* edited by Anne C. Herrmann and Abigail J. Stewart. Boulder, Colo.: Westview Press, 1994.

———. "Sitio y lenguas: Chicanas Theorize Feminisms." In *Decentering the Center: Philosophy for a Multicultural, Postcultural, and Feminist World,* edited by Uma Narayan and Sandra Harding, 128–55. Bloomington: Indiana University Press, 2000.

Inness, Sherrie A., ed. *Kitchen Culture in America: Popular Representations of Food, Gender, and Race.* Philadelphia: University of Pennsylvania Press, 2001.

———. *Pilaf, Pozole, and Pad Thai: American Women and Ethnic Foods.* Amherst: University of Massachusetts Press, 2001.

Jaffe, Janice. "Hispanic American Women Writer's Novel Recipes and Laura Esquivel's *Como agua para chocolate.*" *Women's Studies* 22, no. 2 (1993): 217–28.

Jaramillo, Cleofas M. *The Genuine New Mexico Tasty Recipes.* Santa Fe: Ancient City Press, 1981. Originally published 1945.

———. *Romance of a Little Village Girl.* San Antonio, Tex.: Naylor, 1955.

Jean, Norma, and Carole Darden. *Spoonbread and Strawberry Wine: Recipes of a Family.* New York: Anchor Press/Doubleday, 1978.

Jones Owen, Michael. "A Feeling for Form, as Illustrated by People at Work." In *Folklore on Two Continents,* edited by Nikolai Burlakoff and Carl Lindahl. Bloomington, Ind.: Trickster Press, 1980.

Joseph, Suad. "Searching for Baba: Personal Notes on Rights and Post-Colonialites." Contested Polities. *Stanford Humanities Review* 5, no. 1 (1995).

Juárez, José Luis. "La lenta emergencia de la comida mexicana, ambigüedades criollas, 1750–1800." Licenciado tesis, Escuela Nacional de Antropología e Historia, 1993. *Mosaic* (Winnipeg) 24, nos. 3–4 (Summer–Fall, 1991).

Katrak, Ketu H. "Food and Belonging: At 'Home' and in 'Alien-Kitchens.'" In *Through the Kitchen Window: Women Explore the Intimate Meaning of Food and Cooking,* edited by Arlene Voski Avakian, 263–75. Boston: Beacon Press, 1997.

Keith Michael, and Steve Pile, eds. *Place and The Politics of Identity.* New York: Routledge, 1993.

Keller, Gary D., ed. *Contemporary Chicana and Chicano Art: Artists, Work, Culture, and Education,* Vol. II. Tempe, Ariz.: Bilingual Press, 2002.

Kennedy, Diana. *Recipes from the Regional Cooks of Mexico.* New York: Harper and Row, 1978.

Keremitsis, Dawn. "Del metate al molino: La mujer mexicana de 1910–1940." *Historia Mexicana* 33 (October–December, 1983): 285–302.

Korsmeyer, Carolyn. *Making Sense of Taste: Food and Philosophy.* Ithaca, N.Y.: Cornell University Press, 1999.

Krauss, de Gortari Yuri, and Edmundo Escamilla Solis, eds. *Gisos y golosos del barroco,* vol. 3. Mexico City: Clío, 2000.

Kreitlow, Bert. "The Culture of Maize: In Zacapoaxtla, Mexico, 1974–1982." Conference paper. Fourth International Congress of the Americas. Puebla, Mexico: Universidad de las Américas, October 1999.

Kriby, Andrew. *The Politics of Location.* New York: Methuen, 1982.

la Chrisx, "La Loca de la Raza Cósmica." In *Infinite Divisions: An Anthology of Chicana Literature,* edited by Tey Diana Rebolledo and Eliana Rivero, 84–87. Tucson: University of Arizona Press, 1993.

Lakoff, George, and Mark Johnson. *Philosophy in the Flesh: The Embodied Mind and Its Challenge to Western Thought.* New York: Basic Books, 1999.

Lambert Ortiz, Elisabeth. *The Encyclopedia of Herbs, Spices and Flavourings: A Cook's Compendium.* New York: Dorling Kindersley, 1992.

Lamphere, Louise, Helena Ragoné, and Patricia Zavella. *Situated Lives: Gender and Culture in Everyday Life.* New York: Routledge, 1997.

Laslett, Barbara. "Personal Narratives as Sociology." *Contemporary Sociology* 28, no. 4 (July, 1999): 391–400.

Latina Feminist Group. *Telling To Live: Latina Feminist Testimonios.* Durham, N.C.: Duke University Press, 2001.

Lavín, Mónica, and Ana Benítez Murro, eds. *Dulces hábitos, golosinas de convento: Cocina virreinal novahispana.* vol. 1. Mexico City: Clío, 2000.

Lawless, Cecilia. "Experimental Cooking in *Como agua para chocolate.*" *Monographic Review* 8 (1992): 261–72.

Lefebvre, Henri. *The Production of Space,* translated by Donald Nicholson-Smith. Cambridge, Mass.: Blackwell Publishers, 1991.

Leonardi, Susan J. "Recipes for Reading: Summer Pasta, Lobster à la Rischolme, and Key Lime Pie." *Publications of the Modern Language Association* 104, no. 3 (1989): 340–47.

Levíns Morales, Aurora. *Medicine Stories: History, Culture, and the Politics of Integrity.* Cambridge, Mass.: South End Press, 1998.

———. *Remedios: Stories of Earth and Iron from the History of Puertorriqueñas.* Boston: Beacon Press, 1998.

Lévi-Strauss, Claude. "The Culinary Triangle." In *Food and Culture: A Reader,* edited by Carole Counihan and Penny Van Esterik. New York: Routledge, 1997.

———. *The Raw and the Cooked,* translated by John Doreen. New York: Harper and Row, 1969.

Limón, Graciela. *The Day of the Moon.* Houston, Tex.: Arte Público Press, 1999.

Limón, José E. *Dancing with the Devil: Society and Cultural Poetics in Mexican-American South Texas.* Madison: University of Wisconsin Press, 1994.

Long, Janet, ed. *Conquista y comida: Consecuencias del encuentro de dos mundos.* Mexico City: Universidad Nacional Autónoma de México, 1997.

Long, Lucy M. "Culinary Tourism: A Folkloristic Perceptive on Eating Otherness." *Southern Folklore* 55, vol. 3 (1998): 182.

López González, Aralia. "Dos tendencias en la evolución de la narrativa contemporánea de escritoras mexicanas." In *Mujer y literatura mexicana y chicana: Culturas en contacto,* edited by Aralia López González, Amelia Matagamba, and Elena Urrutia. Mexico City: El Colegio de la Frontera Norte, 1994.

López, Rosalva Loreto, and Ana Benitez Muro, eds. *Un bocado para los angeles: La cocina de los conventos,* vol. 2. Mexico City: Clío, 2000.

Lorde, Audre. *Zami: A New Spelling of My Name.* New York: Crossing Press, 1982.

Lupton, Deborah. *Food, the Body, and the Self.* London: Sage Publications, 1996.

Lust, Teresa. *Pass the Polenta: And Other Writings from the Kitchen.* New York: Ballantine Books, 1998.

Lutz, Catherine A., and Lila Abu-Lughed, eds. *Language and the Politics of Emotions.* Cambridge: Cambridge University Press, 1990.

MacClancy, Jeremy. *Consuming Culture: Why We Eat What We Eat.* New York: Henry Holt, 1993.

Manguel, Alberto. *Other Fires: Short Fiction by Latin American Women.* New York: Clarkson Potter, 1986.

Marin, Louis. *Food for Thought,* translated by Mette Hjort. Baltimore, Md.: Johns Hopkins University Press, 1989.

Marshall, Paule. "The Making of a Writer: From the Poets in the Kitchen." In *Merle: A Novella and Other Stories.* New York: Virago Press, 1983.

Martin, Patricia Preciado. *Songs My Mother Sang to Me: An Oral History of Mexican American Women.* Tucson: University of Arizona Press, 1992.

Martinez, Theresa. "Tortilla Making as Feminist Action." *Network* (May, 1996): 11–14.

Massey, Doreen. *Space, Place, and Gender.* Minneapolis: University of Minnesota Press, 1994.

Mauss, Marcel. *The Gift.* New York: Norton, [1925] 1967.

McCracken, Ellen. *New Latina Narrative: The Feminine Space of Postmodern Ethnicity.* Tucson: University of Arizona Press, 1999.

McDowell, Linda. *Gender, Identity, and Place: Understanding Feminist Geographies.* Minneapolis: University of Minnesota Press, 1999.

———. "Spatializing Feminism: Geographic Perspective." In *BodySpace: Destabilizing Geographies of Gender and Sexuality,* edited by Nancy Duncan, 28–44. New York: Routledge, 1996.

McGee, Harold. *On Food and Cooking: The Science and Lore of the Kitchen.* New York: Charles Scribners, 1984.

McKie, Linda, Sophia Bowlby, and Susan Gregory, eds. *Gender, Power, and the Household.* New York: St. Martin's Press, 1999.

McRobbie, Angela. *Postmodernism and Popular Culture.* New York: Routledge, 1994.

Michie, Helena. *The Flesh Made Word: Female Figures and Women's Bodies.* New York: Oxford University Press, 1987.

Miller, Beth, and Alfonso González. "Elena Garro." In *26 Autoras del México actual,* 210. Mexico City: B. Costa-Amic, 1978.

Minh-ha, Trinh T. *Woman, Native, Other.* Bloomington: Indiana University Press, 1989.

Molina, Silvia. *El amor que me juraste*. Mexico City: Joaquín Mortiz, 1998.

Montes, Luz. "See How I Am Received: Nationalism, Race, and Gender in *Who Would Had Thought It?*" In *Decolonial Voices: Chicana and Chicano Cultural Studies in the 21st Century*, edited by J. Arturo Aldama and Naomi H. Quiñonez, 177–94. Bloomington: Indiana University Press, 2002.

Montoya, Margaret E. "Máscaras, Trenzas y Greñas: Un/Masking the Self While Un/Braiding Latina Stories and Legal Discourse." In *Speaking Chicana*, edited by D. Letticia Galinda and María Dolores Gonzales, 205. Tucson: University of Arizona Press, 1999.

Mora, Pat. *Nepantla: Essays from the Land in the Middle*. Albuquerque: University of New Mexico Press, 1993.

———. "Layers of Pleasure: Capirotada." In *Through the Kitchen Window: Women Explore the Intimate Meaning of Food and Cooking*, edited by Arlene Voski Avakian, 148–54. Boston: Beacon Press, 1997.

Morrison, Toni. *The Bluest Eye*. New York: Washington Square Press, 1970.

———. "The Site of the Truth." In *The Art and Craft of Memoir*, edited by W. Zinsner. Boston: Houghton Mifflin, 1987.

Moya, Paula M. L. "Postmodernism, 'Realism,' and the Politics of Identity: Cherríe Moraga and Chicana Feminism." In *Feminist Genealogies, Colonial Legacies, Democratic Futures*, edited by M. Jacqui Alexander and Chandra Talpade Mohanty, 125–50. New York: Routledge, 1997.

Mujica, María Elena. "Meals, Solidarity, and Empowerment: Communal Kitchens in Lima, Peru." Working Paper No. 246. University of Massachusetts, October, 1994.

Mullins, Maire. "Home, Community, and the Gift that Gives in Isak Dinesen's 'Babette's Feast.'" *Women's Studies* 23 (1994): 217–28.

Murphy, Mary A. "The Theory and Practice of Counting Stitches as Stories: Material Evidence of Autobiography in Needlework." *Women's Studies* 32, no. 5 (July–August, 2003): 641–56.

Nabhan, Gary Paul. *Coming Home to Eat: The Pleasures and Politics of Local Foods*. New York: Norton, 2002.

Narayan, Uma. *Dislocating Cultures: Identities, Traditions, and Third-World Feminism*. New York: Routledge, 1997.

———. "Eating Cultures: Incorporation, Identity, and Indian Food." *Social Identities* 1, no. 64 (1995).

Nava, Yolanda. *It's All in the Frijoles*. New York: Simon and Schuster, 2000.

Nestle, Marion. *Food Politics: How the Food Industry Influences Nutrition and Health*. Berkeley: University of California Press, 2003.

Nicholson, Mervyn. "Food and Power: Homer, Carroll, Atwood, and Others." *Mosaic* (1987).

Nochlin, Linda. "Why Have There Been No Great Women Artists?" In *Theorizing Feminism*, edited by Anne C. Herrmann and Abigail J. Stewart, 93–116. San Francisco: Westview Press, 1994.

Ockman, Joan, ed. *The Pragmatist Imagination.* New York: Princeton Architectural Press, 2000.

Ohunki-Tierney, Emiko. *Rice as Self: Japanese Identities through Time.* Princeton N.J.: Princeton University Press, 1993.

Ong, Aihwa. "Colonialism and Modernity: Feminist Re-Presentations of Women in Non-Western Societies." *Inscription* 3, no. 4 (1988): 79–93.

Ong, Walter. *Oralidad y escritura,* translated by Angélica Scherp. Mexico City: Fondo de Cultura Económica, 1987.

Ostriker, Alicia. *Stealing the Language: The Emergence of Women's Poetry in America.* Boston: Beacon Press, 1986.

Pacheco, Cristina. *Sopita de fideo.* Mexico City: Ediciones Océano, 1988.

Padilla, Genaro M. "Recovering Mexican-American Autobiography." *Recovering the U.S. Hispanic Literary Heritage,* edited by Ramón Gutiérrez and Genaro Padilla, 153–78. Houston, Tex.: Arte Público Press, 1993.

Patterson, Laura. "From Courtship to Kitchen: Reading Domesticity in Twentieth-Century Southern Women's Fiction." *Women's Studies* 32 no. 8 (December, 2003): 907–36.

Paz, Octavio. *The Labyrinth of Solitude.* New York: Grove, 1985.

Pérez, Emma. *The Decolonial Imaginary: Writing Chicanas into History.* Bloomington: Indiana University Press, 1999.

———. "Speaking from the Margin: Uninvited Discourse on Sexuality and Power." In *Building with Our Hands: New Directions in Chicana/o Studies,* edited by Adela de la Torre and Beatríz M. Pesquera, 57–71. Berkeley: University of California Press, 1993.

Pérez, Ramona L.. "Kitchen Table Ethnography and Feminist Anthropology." Conference Paper. The Association for the Study and Food and Society (ASFS) and the Agriculture, Food, and Human Value Society (AFHVS). June, 2004. The Culinary Institute of America. Hyde Park, New York.

Piercy, Marge. "What's That Smell in the Kitchen?" In *The Norton Introduction to Literature,* edited by Carl E. Bain, Jerome Beaty, and J. Paul Hunter, 1036. Sixth Edition. New York: W. W. Norton, 1995.

Pilcher, M. Jeffrey. *¡Que vivan los tamales!: Food and the Making of Mexican Identity.* Albuquerque: University of New Mexico Press, 1998.

Pinedo, Encarnación. *Encarnación's Kitchen: Mexican Recipes from Nineteenth-Century California.* Berkeley: University of California Press, 2003.

Plante, M. Ellen. *The American Kitchen 1700 to the Present: From Hearth to Highrise.* New York: Facts on File, 1995.

———. *Women at Home in Victorian American: A Social History.* New York: Facts on File, 1997.

Podles, Mary Elizabeth. "Babette's Feast: Feasting with Lutherans." *Antioch Review* 50, no. 3 (Summer, 1992): 551–65.

Pollock, Griselda. "Feminist Interventions in the Histories of Art." In *Art History and Its Methods: A Critical Anthology,* edited by Eric Fernie. London: Phaidon Press, 1995.

———. *Vision and Differences.* New York: Routledge, 1988.

Pratt, Scott L. *Native Pragmatism: Rethinking the Roots of American Philosophy.* Bloomington: Indiana University Press, 2002.

Probyn, Elpeth. *Carnal Appetites: Food, Sex, Identities.* New York: Routledge, 2000.

Quintana, Alvina E. "Beyond the Anti-Aesthetic: Reading Gloria Anzaldúa's *Borderlands* and Maxine Hong Kingston's *The Woman Warrior.*" In *Chicana (W)rites: On Word and Film,* edited by María Herrera-Sobek and Helena María Viramontes, 245–55. Berkeley: Third Woman Press, 1995.

Quiñones, Naomi. "Spousal Rape." In *Chicana Creativity and Criticism,* edited by María Herrera-Sobek and Helena María Viramontes. Albuquerque: University of New Mexico Press, 1996.

Ramírez, Orlando. "Soup." In *New Chicana/Chicano Writings,* vol. 1, edited by Charles M. Tatum. Tucson: University of Arizona Press, 1992.

Rebolledo, Tey Diana. *Women Singing in the Snow: A Cultural Analysis of Chicana Literature.* Tucson: University of Arizona Press, 1995.

Rebolledo, Tey Diana, and Eliana S. Rivero, eds. *Infinite Divisions: An Anthology of Chicana Literature.* Tucson: University of Arizona Press, 1993.

Reichl, Ruth. *Tender at the Bone: Growing Up at the Table.* New York: Broadway Books, 1998.

Revel, Jean-Francois. *Culture and Cuisine: A Journey through the History of Food,* translated by Helen R. Lane. Garden City, N.Y.: Doubleday, 1982.

Rich, Adrienne. "Notes Towards a Politics of Location." In *Blood, Bread, and Poetry: Selected Prose, 1979–1985.* New York: W. W. Norton, 1986.

Ríos, Alberto Álvaro. "Pig Cookies." In *Pig Cookies and Other Stories.* San Francisco: Chronicle Books, 1995.

Rosaldo, Renato. *Culture and Truth.* Boston: Beacon Press, 1989.

Rozin, Paul. "Human Food Selection." In *The Psychology of Human Food Selection,* edited by Lewis M. Barker. Westport, Conn.: Avi Publishing Company, 1982.

Ruiz, Vicki L. *From Out of the Shadows: Mexican Women in Twentieth-Century America.* New York: Oxford University Press, 1998.

Sandstorm, Alan R. *Corn Is Our Blood: Culture and Ethnic Identity in a Contemporary Indian Village.* Norman: University of Oklahoma Press, 1991.

Sandoval, Chela. *Methodology of the Oppressed.* Minneapolis: University of Minnesota Press, 2000.

Sen XV, Soshitsu. *Tea Life, Tea Mind.* New York: Weatherhill, 1979.

Seton, Nora. *The Kitchen Congregation: A Daughter's Story of Wives and Women Friends.* New York: Picador, 2000.

Shange, Ntozake. *If I Can Cook / You Know God Can.* Boston: Beacon Press, 1998.

Shapiro, Anna. *A Feast of Words: For Lovers of Food and Fiction.* New York: W. W. Norton, 1996.

Shapiro, Laura. *Perfection Salad: Women and Cooking at the Turn of the Century.* New York: Modern Library, 2001.

Sheraton, Mimi. *From My Mother's Kitchen: Recipes and Reminiscences.* New York: Harper and Row, 1979.

Shohat, Ella, and Robert Stam. *Unthinking Eurocentrism: Multiculturalism and the Media.* New York: Routledge, 1994.

Shortridge, Barbara G., and James R. Shortridge, eds. *The Taste of American Place: A Reader on Regional and Ethnic Foods.* New York: Rowman and Littlefield, 1998.

Silva, Beverly. "Sin ti no soy nada / Without You I Am Nothing." In *Infinite Divisions: An Anthology of Chicana Literature,* edited by Tey Diana Rebolledo and Eliana Rivero, 359. Tucson: University of Arizona Press, 1993.

Sklar, Kathryn Kish. *Catharine Beecher: A Study in American Domesticity.* New Haven, Conn.: Yale University Press, 1973.

Smith, Linda Tuhiwai. *Decolonizing Methodologies: Research and Indigenous Peoples.* New York: Zed Books Ltd., 1999.

Snow, Kimberly. *In Buddha's Kitchen: Cooking and Being Cooked at a Meditation Center.* Boston: Shambhala, 2003.

Soja, Edward. *Thirdspace: Journeys to Los Angeles and Other Real-and-Imagined Places.* Cambridge, Mass.: Blackwell, 1996.

Solís, Felipe. *La cultura del maíz.* Mexico City: Clío, 1998.

Soustelle, Jacques. *La vida cotidiana de los aztecas,* translated by Carlos Villegas. Mexico City: Fondo de Cultura Económica, 1970.

Spivak, Chakrovorty Gayatri. "Can the Subaltern Speak?" In *Colonial Discourse and Post-Colonial Theory: A Reader,* edited by Patrick Williams and Laura Chrisman. New York: Columbia University Press, 1994.

Start, Kathy. *The Soul of Southern Cooking.* Jackson: University of Mississippi Press, 1989.

Stoller, Paul. *The Taste of Ethnographic Things: The Senses in Anthropology.* Philadelphia: University of Pennsylvania Press. 1989.

———. *Embodying Colonial Memories.* New York: Routledge, 1995.

Stowe, Harriet Beecher. *Uncle Tom's Cabin.* New York: Signet Classic, 1966.

Stowell, Phyllis, and Jeanne Foster, eds. *Appetite: Food as Metaphor.* Rochester, N.Y.: BOA Editions, 2002.

Strehl, Dan, ed. and trans. *Encarnación's Kitchen: Mexican Recipes from Nineteenth-Century California.* Berkeley: University of California Press, 2003.

Sutton, E. David. *Remembrance of Repasts: An Anthropology of Food and Memory.* New York: Berg, 2001.

Swain, Sally. *Great Housewives of Art.* New York: Penguin, 1988.

Tannahill, Reay. *Food in History.* New York: Crown, 1988.

Tausend, Marilyn, and Miguel Ravago. *Cocina de la familia,* translated by Pilar Barnard Baca and Carmen Bernard Baca. New York: Simon and Schuster, 1997.

Tawadros, Gilane. "Beyond the Boundary: The Work of Three Black Women Artists in Britain." *Third Text* (Autumn/Winter, 1989): 121–50.

Taylor, Barbara Howland. *Mexico: Her Daily and Festive Breads.* Claremont, Calif: The Creative Press Box 89, 1969.

Theophano, Janet. *Eat My Words: Reading Women's Lives through the Cookbooks They Wrote.* New York: Palgrave, 2002.

Torres, E. Edén. *Chicana without Apology: The New Chicana Cultural Studies.* New York: Routledge, 2003.

Toussint-Samat, Maguelonne. *A History of Food,* translated by Anthea Bell. Cambridge, Mass.: Blackwell, 1992.

Townsend, Dabney. "Tomas Reid and the Theory of Taste." *Journal of Aesthetics and Art Criticism* 61, no. 4 (Fall 2003): 341–51.

Trujillo, Carla., ed. *Living Chicana Theory.* Berkeley: Third Woman Press, 1998.

Turner, Victor W., and Edward M. Bruner, eds. *The Anthropology of Experience.* Urbana: University of Illinois Press, 1986.

Valdés, Gina. "English con Salsa." In *Cool Salsa: Bilingual Poems on Growing Up Latino in the United States,* edited by Lori M. Carlson. New York: Henry Holt, 1994.

Valle, Victor M., and Mary Lau Valle. *Recipe of Memory: Five Generations of Mexican Cuisine.* New York: New Press, 1995.

Verhovck, Sam Howe. "Making Jalapeños for Tender Tongues." *New York Times,* May 15, 1996.

Vigil-Piñón, Evangelina. "kitchen talk." In *Infinite Divisions: An Anthology of Chicana Literature,* edited by Tey Diana Rebolledo and Eliana S. Rivero, 163. Tucson: University of Arizona Press, 1993.

Villaseñor Black, Charlene. "Sacred Cults, Subversive Icons: Chicana and the Pictorial Language of Catholicism." In *Speaking Chicana: Voice, Power, and Identity,* edited by D. Letticia Galindo and María Dolores Gonzales. Tucson: University of Arizona Press, 1999.

Viramontes, Helena María. "'Nopalitos': The Making of Fiction." In *Making Face, Making Soul: Haciendo Caras,* edited by Gloria Anzaldúa. San Francisco: Aunt Lute Foundation Book, 1990.

Visser, Margaret. *Much Depends on Dinner.* New York: Grove, 1986.

Walker, Alice. *In Search of Our Mothers' Gardens*. New York: Harcourt Brace Jovanovich, 1967.

Weiss, Allen S. *Feast and Folly: Cuisine, Intoxication, and the Poetics of the Sublime*. Albany: State University of New York Press, 2002.

Werner, Louis. "El laberinto genetico del maíz." *Américas* 52, no. 3 (Mayo/Junio 2000): 6–13.

Williams, Brett. "Why Migrant Women Feed Their Husbands Tamales: Foodways as a Basis for a Revisionist View of Tejano Family Life." In *Ethnic and Regional Foodways in the United States: The Performance of Group Identity*, edited by Linda Keller Brown and Kay Mussell. Knoxville: University of Tennessee Press, 1984.

Winchester, James J. *Aesthetics across The Color Line: Why Nietzsche (Sometimes) Can't Sing the Blues*. Lanham, Md.: Rowman and Littlefield, 2002.

Wolterstorff, Nicholas. "Why Philosophy of Art Cannot Handle Kissing, Touching, and Crying." *Journal of Aesthetics and Art Criticism* 61, no. 1 (Winter, 2003): 17–27.

Yarbo-Bejarano, Yvonne. "Chicana Literature from a Chicana Feminist Perspective." In *Chicana Creativity and Criticism*, edited by María Herrera-Sobek and Helena María Viramontes. Albuquerque: University of New Mexico Press, 1996.

Young, Iris Marion. "The Ideal Community and the Politics of Differences." In *Feminism/Postmodernism*, edited by Linda Nicholson. New York: Routledge, 1990.

Young, Jane M., and Kay Turner. "Challenging the Canon: Folklore Theory Reconsidered from a Feminist Perspective." In *Feminist Theory and the Study of Folkore*, edited by Susan Hollis Tower, Linda Pershing, and M. Jane Young, 9–28. Urbana: University of Illinois Press, 1993.

Index

Abarca, Félix, 22, 125, 172, 197
Abarca, Hugo Uriel, 125, 197
Abarca, Juan, 22, 112, 172, 193
Abarca, Juan Antonio (Paqui), 16, 48, 178
Abarca, Salvador (Chava), 23, 172
Abarca, Verónica: cooking as a way of establishing community, 128–29; life story, 16; preparing *chilaquiles*, 70–71; recipe as personal narrative, 127
Active Voice, 194, 205
aesthetics, 11, 78, 113, 192; aesthetic value, 32, 80–82; as affirmation of self, 81; of the moment, 100–108
Aesthetics across the Color Line, 171, 181
A Feast of Words: For Lovers of Food and Fiction, 136
"A Feeling for Form," 186
Agrest, Diana I., 33, 35, 174–75
Aguililla, Michoacán, 14–15, 45–46, 177
Ahrentzen, Sherry, 22, 172, 174, 175
Alarcón, Norma, 171, 190, 191–92
al gusto/a su gusto (to your liking), 68–71, 74–75, 119, 128, 138, 141, 170; as determinant of subjectivity, 111; as feminist culinary theoretical concept, 68

ama de casa (lover of the home), 44, 48–49, 178
American Kitchen 1700 to the Present, 173
André, María Claudia, 138, 201, 202
Angell, Katherine, 86
Another Way to Be, 204
Anthropology of Food and Body: Gender, Meaning, and Power, 181
Antigüedades de la Nueva España, 191
Anzaldúa, Gloria, 121, 176, 191, 196; "*Frontera*: Inscribing Gynetics," 212
Apatzingán, Michoacán, 14, 46, 167, 169, 177, 208–209
Appadurai, Arjun, 113, 194
Appetite: Food as Metaphor, 136, 201
Arau, Alfonso, 79
architecture: as cultural code, 13, 18–19, 33–36, 173
Architecture from Without: Theoretical Framing for a Critical Practice, 33, 174–75
Aristotle, 55, 57, 80
Aroma: The Cultural History of Smell, 58, 180, 204
Around the Tuscan Table, 194
Art, Culture, and Cuisine: Ancient and Medieval Gastronomy, 79
"Arte Chicano: Images of a Community," 82

art-in-process, 81–83, 90, 94, 98, 106–108, 188; as a challenge to social norms, 188, 192; as field of study, 96; merit of, 92; outside of the Western definition of aesthetics, 100–101; as theoretical challenge, 88; of tortilla-making, 190

artistic meals, 79

Artists in Aprons: Folk Art by American Women, 82

art of practice, 81–82

Art on My Mind: Visual Politics, 187

art vs. craft, 79–85

Art Worlds, 187

Atlisco, Puebla, 41, 96, 190

authenticity, 28, 120–22

authentic presence (of food), 105

Axel, Gabriel, 79

Babette's Feast, 79

Batman, 186

Batstone, Kathleen, 138, 202, 203

Bauer, Arnold J., 65–66, 182

Bay Window, California, 76, 185

Becker, Howard S., 187

"Beyond the Anti-Aesthetic," 193

biculturalism, 122

Billy, Susan, 105–106

Black Looks: Race and Representations, 142–43, 202

Bloom, Harold, 186

Bluest Eye, 135–36, 139, 202

Bocuse, Paul, 84

Bonfil Batalla, Guillermo, 31, 99, 144, 191, 202

Borderlands/La Frontera, 121, 196

borderless boundary zone, 24, 33, 36–38, 40, 45

Boydston, Jeanne, 30, 173, 174

Breedlove, Pecola (Toni Morrison), 139–40

Brinson Curiel, Bárbara, 153–54, 204, 205

broccoli salad, 126

Brown, Gillian, 140–41, 173, 202

Buchtenkirch, Lyde, 85

Building with Our Hands: New Directions of Chicana/o Studies, 187

Bulnes, Francisco, 96, 190

Burciaga, José Antonio, 122, 192, 196

California cuisine, 16

California Culinary Art Academy in South Pasadena, California, 16, 106

Californios, 113

Cantú, Norma E., 185

Cárdenas, María Luisa (Licha): chemical culinary understanding, 64; cooking as a form of self-giving, 167; cooking as a way of establishing community, 167; economic hardship, 167; formal education, 167; importance of healthy food, 170; language, 169; learning to cook, 168; life story, 166; religion, 167

carne ranchera, 133, 201

carrot salad, 124, 126

Castellanos, Rosario, 149–53, 203, 204

Castillo, Debra, 37, 175

Cervantes, Lorna Dee, 135, 201

Chabram-Dernersesian, Angie, 176

charla culinaria, 4–5, 8–10, 11, 78, 101, 164

charla matrimonial, 40, 178

Chava. *See* Salvador Abarca

chemical reactions, 64; cooking as a way of establishing community, 119; economics, 27; kitchen as a place of obligatory labor, 19; life story, 13; marriage as a catalyst for change, 19; methodological process of making *enchiladas*, 69–70, 111; non-written recipes, 74–75; preparing beans, 66–67; sexuality, 26–27; *sazón* as cognitive sensory-logic, 63–64; sociocultural etiquette, 121–22

Chicana Traditions: Continuity and Change, 115, 185

Chicana Voices, 187

chilaquiles, 3
*Child of Many Rivers: Journeys To and
From The Rio Gande,* 17
chiles en nogada, 75, 127–28, 198
Chiltepin (Edna Escamill), 157–58
chiste (twist): 11, 115, 126, 138, 180,
189, 195; as narrative; 116, 118,
120–122; as technical skill, 91,
123, 148, 154
Cixous, Hélène, 193
Classen, Constance, 58, 180, 204
classist, 95, 103
Clifford, James, 120, 196
"Colonialism and Modernity," 175
community politics, 92, 95
confianza (trust), 8, 26, 27, 47, 115, 147
*Conquista y Comida: Consecuencias del
encuentro de dos mundos,* 191
conscientización (consciousness): 8, 27,
44, 117, 150
Consuming Geographies, 175
Consuming Passions, 182, 194
*Contemporary Chicana and Chicano
Art,* 83
Contreras, Alma: assertion of agency
through creative expression, 109;
authorship, 119
Cooking, Eating, Thinking, 102, 181,
187, 191
cooks-as-artists, 79–80, 83, 90–94,
107–108; redefining aesthetics, 83,
103; redefining domestic tradition,
97
Cooper, Barbara, 22, 187, 188, 194
Cortés, Hernan, 32
Cortes, Hilaria (Yaya): appropriating
American foods, 67–68; as food
vendor, 15, 129; economic hardship, 129; frugality in cooking, 130;
holistic artistic creation, 106; inability to achieve perfect tortillas
by hand, 91; learning to cook, 90;
life story, 15, 129; marriage, 27;
sazón as cognitive sensory-logic,
62; self-assuredness and justice,
130–32; sensuality vs. sexuality,

163; sociocultural etiquette, 132–
33; tortilla-making process, 31–32;
vergüenza, 132
costumbre (habit), 61–62, 66, 179, 181
Counihan, Carole M., 116, 181
cross-cultural, 69, 181, 187
"Crossing Social and Cultural Borders,"
194
cuaresma (lent), 123, 196
"Culinary Fictions," 138, 201, 202
Culinary Institute of America (CIA),
85–86
culinary memoir, 11, 110, 164–165
cultural resistance, 99
culture-in-transition, 69
"Culture of Maize," 30–31, 174
Curiel, Brinson, 153–54, 204, 205
Curtin, Deane W., 56, 102–103, 105,
181, 187, 191, 192

Dōgen, 105
Dávalos, Karen Mary, 100, 191
Day of the Moon, 143–44, 147, 202, 203
de Beauvoir, Simone, 173
de Certeau, Michel, 60, 82, 117, 176,
181, 183, 184, 185, 187, 188, 195;
institutions of power, 176; popular
culture, 82
De-Coca-Colonization, 120, 195
Decolonial Methodologies, 87
decolonizing, 5, 37, 171, 188, 189
de-indianization, 99–100
De La Cruz, Sor Juana Inés, 54–55,
173
"Del Metate al Molino," 31
de Pizan, Christine, 173
de Sahagún, Bernardino, 191
de Valdés, María Elena, 150, 193, 203,
204, 205, 206; definition of narratives, 111; on language, 112; testimonial literature/testimonial biography, 165
Diaz, Porfirio, 169, 209
Dinah (Harriet Beecher Stowe): on
sazón, 141; on space, 140, 141–43,
145

Dislocating Cultures, 173, 190
Distinction: A Social Critique of the
    Judgement of Taste, 181
"doing" cooking, 71
Domosh, Mona, 29, 173, 174
Douglas, Mary, 112, 148, 194, 203
Duncan, Cynthia, 147, 203, 204
Duvi. *See* Liduvina Vélez

Eastern philosophy, 101
Eat My Words, 113, 187, 194
El amor que me juraste, 155, 205
el arte culinario casero (culinary home
    art), 11, 78, 97, 101, 107–108
"Elena Garro," 146, 203
El porvenir de las naciones Hispano-
    Americas (The Future of the
    Hispanic-American Nations), 96,
    190
Embodying Colonial Memories, 59, 180,
    185
Encarnación's Kitchen: Mexican Recipes
    from Nineteenth-Century Califor-
    nia, 113, 194
enchilada, 67–70, 109–113, 120–123,
    159, 169, 183, 193, 196, 209
Encyclopedia of Herbs, Spices & Fla-
    vorings, 191
entomatadas, 123, 196
erudite cuisine, 84
Escamill, Edna, 157–58, 205
eurocentric, 60
Exhibiting Mestizaje, 191
Exotic Appetites, 195, 196

Fausch, Deborah, 34, 175
Feast and Folly: Cuisine, Intoxication,
    and the Poetics of the Sublime, 79
Feast of Words: For Lovers of Food and
    Fiction, 136, 201
"Feminist Interventions in the Histo-
    ries of Art," 187
Fernandez, Evelina, 159, 161, 163, 206
Ferré, Rosario, 114–15, 194
Fisher, M.F.K., 135, 201
Fischer-West, Lucy: life story, 16–17;
    sharing a meal as means of com-
    munication, 102; Tibetan Bud-
    dhism, 101–102
flan, 121
flautas, 167, 207
Florentine Codex: General History of
    the Things of New Spain, 191
Flores, Guadalupe (Lupita): apprecia-
    tion, 21, 125–26; audience, 125–
    26; cooking without a recipe, 126;
    disinterest in cooking, 124; impor-
    tance of healthy food, 123–24; life
    story, 13–14; marriage, 123
Flores, Itzel, 166, 170, 210
Flusty, Steven, 120, 195
folklore, 10, 12, 87, 115, 187
"Food and Belonging," 171
"Food and Power," 203
food as voice, 4, 116, 135
"Food/Body/Person," 192
Food-centered life histories. *See*
    Carole M. Couniham
Food for Thought, 203
Food Nations, 205
Food, the Body, and the Self, 61, 181,
    183
foodways, 7, 55–56, 82
Foster, Hal, 107
Foster, Jeanne, 136, 201
Foucault, Michel, 10, 21
frijoles, 53, 137, 180, 182–83, 199, 201

Gabaccia, Donna, 66, 182
García Viuda de Melo, Susana: as food
    vendor, 16, 117–18; kitchen as a
    space of economic substance, 38–
    39; life story, 16; non-written reci-
    pes, 76
Garro, Elena, 146, 148, 203
Gaspar de Alba, Alicia, 161–63, 187,
    188, 206
gastronomy, 83, 85, 149
Gender, Identity and Place, 35, 172
geo-social culinary techniques, 69
Giard, Luce, 69, 71–72, 74, 183, 184,
    185, 187, 188
Gift, 73, 184
globalization, 86, 120, 154

Goldman, Anne, 113, 188, 194, 195
Gonzales, Gloria, 11, 194
Gonzales, María Dolores, 114
González de la Vera, Martín, 191
Good Life: New Mexican Traditions and Food, 79
gracia: as a technical skill, 71, 91, 126
grassroots theories, 9, 12, 61, 62, 68, 75, 77, 80–81, 136
Grosz, Elizabeth, 59, 68, 181, 183, 185
Gualpa, Mexico, 98
Gutiérrez, Gloria Bautista, 147, 203

Hakuli, Tata, 144
Hardy-Fanta, Carol, 45, 177
Hauck-Lawson, Annie, 4, 171
haute cuisine, 83–85, 97
Hegel, 56–57
Heldke, Lisa M., 102, 119–20, 180, 181, 187, 191, 195, 196; separation of mind and body, 56
Hernández, Francisco, 191
Herrera, Ángeles, 16, 98
her-stories, 113, 116
higher senses, 57–58, 138
Home and Work, 173, 174, 187
homeplace, 49
hooks, bell, 49, 81, 100, 142, 179, 187, 191, 192, 202
hospitalidad (hospitality), 97
hot dogs/*perros calientes*, 67–68, 182–83
Hough, Sheridan, 106, 193
housework, 30, 35, 80, 86, 92, 141
"Housing for a Postmodern World," 175
How Else Am I Supposed to Know I'm Still Alive, 159–61, 206
Howes, David, 58, 180
"How to Make a National Cuisine," 194
Hubbard, Ruth, 25–26, 28
humility, 7–10, 51

imperialism, 86, 119–20
In Buddha's Kitchen, 102, 191
Infinite Divisions, 137, 201

In Search of Our Mothers' Gardens, 105, 192
"I Yam What I Yam," 188, 194, 195

Jones, Michael Owen, 80, 186
Joseph, Suad, 28, 173

Kadi, Joanna, 120
Kant, Immanuel, 186
Katrak, Ketu H., 11, 171
Keremitsis, Dawn, 31
"Kitchen Table Ethnography and Feminist Anthropology," 194
kitchen table ethnography. *See* Ramona Lee Pérez
"Knowledge of the Body and the Presence of History—Toward a Feminist Architecture," 175
Korsmeyer, Carolyn, 56, 58, 138
Kreitlow, Bert, 30, 174

Labyrinth of Solitude, 174
"La Culpa es de los Tlaxcaltecas," 143, 203, 204
Laredo, Texas, 14, 125, 169, 209
La Respuesta, 55, 180
Latina Feminist Group, 164, 193, 194, 206
Latina Politics, Latino Politics, 177
"Laugh of the Medusa," 193
Laura and Nacha (Elena Garro), on space, 147
Lawless, Cecilia, 113, 194
"Lección de Cocina" ("Cooking Lesson"), 149–50, 153, 203, 204
Lefebvre, Henri, 34, 148, 175, 180, 184, 185, 203
lemon pie, 124
Leonardi, Susan, 118, 195
Levíns Morales, Aurora, 114, 165, 187, 194
Like Water for Chocolate, 128, 184, 189
Limón, Graciela, 143, 145, 147, 202, 203
Long, Lucy M., 7, 171, 182
Lorde, Audre, 184
Loreto López, Rosalva, 191

Los Angeles, California, 15, 68
lower senses, 57–58, 60–61, 64, 77,
    138, 149
Lupton, Deborah, 61, 181, 183

McDowell, Linda, 10, 19, 23, 35, 171,
    172, 175, 179
"Making of a Writer: From the Poets in
    the Kitchen," 193
"Making Tortillas," 161–62, 206
Malinche, 30, 32
Malintzín, 32
Manguel, Alberto, 148, 203
Marin, Louis, 148, 203
Marshall, Paule, 110, 193
"Máscaras, Trenzas y Greñas," 206
Mascualpakilstili, 105
mashed potatoes, 124
Massey, Doreen, 20, 48, 62, 138, 172,
    173, 178, 181
Mauss, Marcel, 73, 184
medieval, 181
Meditación en el umbral, 204
Menlo Park, California, 12
Mennell, Stephan, 85
Merlo, Raquel: sazón as experience,
    51
Mesoamerica, 65, 95, 99, 144
mestizaje, 100, 143–45, 191, 203
mestizo, 32, 105, 143–44
methodology: 6–8, 62; cooking as a de-
    colonizing methodology, 5, 12, 37,
    87; methodology of the charlas, 9
Mexican spaghetti, 122
México profundo, 31, 191, 202
Minh-ha, Trinh T., 122, 196
Modernism, 146
mole poblano, 97–100
Molina, Silvia, 155, 205
Montoya, Margaret E., 166, 206
Mora, Pat, 105, 192
Morales, Erika: chemical culinary un-
    derstanding, 65; learning to cook,
    89; life story, 15; sazón as knowl-
    edge, 51; special skill in making
    tortillas, 91; tortillas as connected
    to Catholic faith, 104

Morales, Cheryl, 119, 195
morisqueta, 45, 89, 177, 188
Morrison, Toni, 135–36, 139–40, 202
Mostly Martha, 79
multiculturalism, 66, 68

Nájera-Ramírez, Olga, 186
Narayan, Uma, 25, 60, 173, 181, 182,
    186, 190
Nellie and Angie (Evelina Fernandez):
    on space, 159–61
Nepantla, 105, 192
Nettelbeck, Sandra, 79
Nicholson, Mervyn, 149, 203
Nietzsche, 57, 61
nixtamal, 31, 44, 90, 96, 174, 181, 184,
    189, 191
Nochlin, Linda, 83, 87–90, 97, 108, 188
nonprogressive, 21, 25
nonspoken, 115–16
nontraditional, 6, 51, 103
nonwritten, 115
nopalitos, 121, 133, 201
"'Nopalitos': The Making of Fiction,"
    201
Nuevo Laredo, Tamaulipas, 13–14, 44,
    46, 125, 166, 169, 197, 209

Ockman, Joan, 37, 175
Ohnuki-Tierney, Emiko, 120
Oldenburg, Veena Talwar, 25
"On Collecting Art and Culture," 120,
    196
Ong, Aihwa, 6, 37
oppositional gaze, 142–43
oral narrative, 165
"Origen y Virtudes del Chocolate," 191
Origin of the Family, 173
Ortiz, Lambert, 191
Other Fires, 203

Pacheco, Cristina, 156–57, 205
Palacios, Nicholette, 97
"Pan Birote," 157–58
Paqui. See Juan Antonio Abarca
Paz, Octavio, 32, 159, 174, 203
pellagra, 65–66

Pérez, Emma, 5–6, 10, 51, 171, 175, 186
Pérez, Ramona Lee, 116, 194
Perkins Gilman, Charlotte, 173
perros calientes. See hot dogs
personal narrative. *See charla culinaria*
"Personal Narratives as Sociology," 206
"Phenomenology, Pomo Baskets, and the Work of Mabel McKay," 106, 193
Piercy, Marge, 135, 149, 153, 203
Pilcher, Jeffrey, 30, 174, 187, 190, 206
Pinedo, Encarnación, 113–14
pipián verde, 64–65, 75, 91, 182, 189
place: as theoretical concept, 19–20, 23, 33, 35, 37, 174
Plato, 80, 103
Poetics of Women's Autobiography, 164
Pollock, Griselda, 83, 187
popular cuisine, 84–85, 108
popular culture, 82, 186, 195. *See also* Michel de Certeau.
Porfiriato era (1877–91), 99–100
Postmodernism and Popular Culture, 195
Poststructuralism, 68–69
"Power and Knowledge," 193
Pozole, 45, 63, 67, 75, 118–19, 177, 195
Practice of Everyday Life: Volume Two: Living and Cooking, 183, 184, 185, 187, 188
pragmatism, 37, 171, 180
Pragmatist Imagination: Thinking about "Things in the Making," 37, 175
pre-colombian, 105
preinscribe, 33
private space/sphere, 24, 29–30, 35
Production of Space, 34, 175, 180, 184, 185, 203
Public space/sphere, 21, 24, 29–30, 35
Puebla, Puebla, Mexico, 13, 16, 78, 96, 103, 127, 129, 190, 198; Puebla cuisine, 15, 78, 98, 108
pumpkin pie, 124, 126

punto: as technical skill, 91, 181
Putting Women in Place: Feminist Geographers Make Sense of the World, 29, 173, 174

quelites, 167, 207–208
Que vivan los tamales! Food and the Making of Mexican Identity, 30, 174, 187, 190, 206
Quiñonez, Naomi, 140, 202

rasquachismo, 82
"Raw and the Cooked," 202, 203
Rebolledo, Tey Diana, 159, 171, 193, 201, 204, 205, 206; Chicana writers as writers-as-cooks, 110; definition of writers-as-cooks, 136–37
recipe: as embedded narrative, 113, 115, 118
"Recipe: Chorizo con Huevo Made in the Microwave," 153, 204, 205
Recipe of Memory, 190
"Recipes for Reading," 195
"Recovering Mexican-American Autobiography," 206
Redwood City, California, 14, 89
Reik, Theodor, 152
Remedios, 114, 194
Revel, Jean-François, 83–85, 107, 151
Rice as Self: Japanese Identities through Time, 120
Rivera, Eliana S., 137
rol-pa,102
Romero Soto, Don Luis, 30
Roth, Frances, 86
Ruvalcaba, Ana María, 118
Ruiz, Vicki, 176

saber/conocer (to understand/to know), 54, 108
Sacramento, California, 15, 16
"Sacred Cults, Subversive Icons," 194
Saint Augustine, 127, 198
Salazar, Norma, Chef: aesthetics of the moment, 107; learning to cook, 16; life story, 16
Saldívar-Hall, Sonia, 6

Sandoval, Chela, 10, 175, 190
San Miguel del Zapote, Jalisco, 31–32, 106
Santa Rosa Convent, Puebla, Mexico, 98
Santiago, Úrsula (Graciela Limón): on religious mestizaje, 143; on space, 145
sazón: corporeal knowledge, 34, 49, 60, 74–75; sensory logic, 38, 61–66
science of singularity, 60
scientific knowledge,62–65, 66, 96, 148
Seager, Joni, 29, 173, 174
"Searching for Baba," 173
"See How I Am Received," 191
Shapiro, Anna, 136, 201
Shattered Mirror, 193, 203, 204, 205, 206
Silva, Enrique, 92, 189
Silva, Imelda: cooking as a way of establishing community, 92–93; learning to cook, 89–90; life story, 14; *sazón* as ability, 51
Silvia, Beverly, 159
"Sin Tí No Soy Nada / Without You I Am Nothing," 159, 206
Smith, Linda Tuhiwai, 5, 8, 87, 92, 95, 175
Smith, Sidonie, 164–65
Snow, Kimberley, 102, 191
socio-ideological, 190
sociolinguist, 115
sociopolitical, 26
Soja, Edward, 147, 175, 204
Soltner, Andre, 188
Songhay, 56
Sopita de fideo, 156–57, 205
sopitos, 67, 122, 126, 196
South Pasadena, California, 15, 16, 106
space: as rhetorical, 55
space and place: as challenged concepts, 27, 36
"Space between the Studs," 174, 174, 175
Space, Time, and Perversion, 181, 183, 185

"Spatializing Feminism," 171
Speaking Chicana: Voice, Power, and Identity, 114–15
spinach salad, 98, 126
Spivak, Gayatti, 9–10
"Spousal Rape," 140, 202
Stoller, Paul, 56–57, 59–60, 77, 180, 181, 183, 185
Stowe, Harriet Beecher, 135–36, 140, 141, 145, 201, 202
Stowell, Phyllis, 136, 201
subaltern, 9–10
survival politics, 45
Synnott, Anthony, 58, 180

tacos, 129, 166–67, 199, 207
Talking Back, 175
tamal: 124, 137, 145, 159, 183, 188–89, 196–97; *amarillos,* 14; *corundas,* 90; *uchepos,* 122, 196
Taste of Ethnographic Things, 56, 180
Telling to Live, 116, 187, 193, 194, 206
temporarity, 103–105
testimonial: autobiography, 11, 164; biography, 165; literature, 156, 165
Theophano, Janet, 113, 194
"Theoretical Subject(s) of This Bridge Called My Back and Anglo-American Feminism," 171
theory from the ground up, 5–6, 9–10, 17, 190
thirdspace, 5, 33, 37–38, 147–48, 204
third-world, 25, 62, 86, 111, 122
"Thomas Reid and the Theory of Taste," 192
Through the Kitchen Window, 25–26, 138–39, 173, 202
Tia Celia, 41, 176, 188
Tia Dora, 41, 96–97, 106, 190–91
Tibetan Buddhism, 101
Tijuana, Baja California, Mexico, 95
Tio Mayolo, 41, 176
Tlaxcaltecas, 146
Toneucáyotl, 192
tortas de papa, 124, 196

tortilla discourse, 98–100, 162, 190
tostadas, 45, 64, 119, 121, 177, 195
Townsend, Dabney, 192
tradition: as a challenged concept; 84–87; as conceptualization, 86–87
transcendental, 80, 103
Turner, Kay, 87, 188

Unbearable Weight, 183
University of California, Santa Barbara, 102
Uruapan, Michoacán, Mexico, 90

Valle, Mary Lau, 95, 190
Valle, Victor, 95, 190
Vásquez, Irma: learning to cook, 88–89; life story, 14; *metate* as essential to *sazón,* 73–74; sense-driven knowledge, 57–58; sexuality, 162
Vásquez, Luis, 112, 194
Veale, Abraham, 114
Vélez, Esperanza: chemical culinary understanding, 64–65; cooking as a form of self-giving, 24; culinary authority, 53; life story, 13–14; non-written recipes, 75; preparing beans, 53–54; religion, 52–53; tortillas as connected to Catholic faith, 104–105
Vélez, Federico, 40–41
Vélez, Liduvina (Duvi): aesthetics in tortilla making, 80–81, 82; appropriation of the kitchen space, 18–19, 23; being *ama de casa,* 44, 48–49; class prejudice, 96–97; cooking as a way of establishing community, 44; critique of food additives, 117; first kitchen, 42–43; as food vendor, 45–47; formal education, 43; holistic artistic creation, 106; importance of sensory knowledge, 62–63; individual experimentation as means of learning to cook, 90; kitchen as a place of freedom and empowerment, 18, 20, 22–23; life story, 13, 40–41; marriage, 18,

41–42, 47; non-written recipes, 76; preparing *chilaquiles,* 71; *sazón* as gift, 51–52; self-esteem, 46–47, 91, 95; spoken language as indicator of reality, 112; tortillas as affirmation of self, 108
Veracruz cuisine, 15, 65
Vigil-Piñón, Evangelina, 163, 206
Villanueva, Alicia (Licha): life story, 14–15; *metate* as part of familial history, 72–73
Villaseñor Black, Charlene, 114–15, 194
Villicaña, María Luisa: artistic significance of food, 94; culinary hospitality, 97–98; importance of audience, 94; learning to cook, 88–89; life story, 14; mole as affirmation of self, 108
Viramontes, Helena María, 137, 201
Virgin of Guadalupe, 144
von Herder, Johann Gottfried, 87
Voski Avakian, Arlene, 25–26, 28, 138–39

Walker, Alice, 105, 192
We Are What We Eat: Ethnic Food and the Making of Americans, 182
Welty, Alma, 78–79, 102, 108; learning to cook, 89–90; life story, 15–16
Western aesthetics, 80
Western Canon: The Books and School of the Ages, 186
"Western Enlightenment Project," 87
Western philosophy and thought, 20, 56–58, 80, 103, 138
Western values, 96
Whalen, Margie (Magui), 132–33, 200–201
"What's That Smell in the Kitchen?" 135, 149, 203
"Why Have There Been No Great Women Artists?" 87, 188
"Why Philosophy of Art Cannot Handle Kissing, Touching, and Crying," 191

William, Raymond, 81
Winchester, James J., 171, 181
Wollstonecraft, Mary, 173
Woman, Native, Other, 196
Women at Home in Victorian America,
    173, 202
"Women Owning the Knife: Women in
    the Professional Kitchen," 86
Women Singing in the Snow, 136, 171,
    187, 193, 201, 204, 205, 206
writers-as-cooks: mentioned, 12, 110,

135, 153, 158, 163, 193. *See* Re-
    bolledo

Xipe Totec, 145

Yaya. *See* Hilaria Cortez
Ybarra-Frausto, Tomás, 82
Yearning, 179, 187, 191, 192
Young, M. Jane, 87, 188

Zami, 184

CPSIA information can be obtained
at www.ICGtesting.com
Printed in the USA
LVOW07s0400011217

558215LV00002B/14/P